An outstanding collection of papers on one of the most central and controversial themes of Christian doctrine. The contributors have demonstrated their masterly grasp of both the theological issues at stake and the scholarly tools needed to assess those issues for the present day. A first-class symposium.

Dr Gerald Bray
Beeson Divinity School,
Birmingham, Alabama

The most important question in history remains, 'What do you think of Christ?' In this diverse and extremely competent symposium scholars from the fields of New Testament studies, systematic and historical theology contribute to the answer. Each writes about a specific and significant issue in their discipline and the resulting mosaic gives a fascinating, if not complete, perspective on Christ. The papers remind me of a Scandinavian smorgasbord. Here is a rich variety of wonderfully produced food. The laden table invites all to eat. And there is something that everyone can enjoy. In days of historical scepticism and philosophical barrenness, this book demonstrates something of the positive contribution evangelicals have to make to the debate about Jesus Christ.

Revd Dr Derek J Tidball,
Principal,
London Bible College

Here we have evangelical scholarship at its best. It is orthodox, yet probing; erudite, yet useful; apologetic, yet non-contentious. Not surprisingly, then, the present volume succeeds in upholding the Christology of the ancient church while also contributing to the ongoing theological task. Throughout, the various authors emanate an infectious confidence in Christ, which is so essential to a bold Christian testimony in the church, the academy and society during these early years of the third millennium. Only an informed and Spirit-filled confidence can once again turn the world upside down!

Revd Dr Tim J. R. Trumper
Westminster Theological Seminary,
Philadelphia, Pennsylvania

Christian Focus Publications publishes biblically-accurate books for adults and children. The books in the adult range are published in three imprints.

Christian Heritage contains classic writings from the past.

Christian Focus contains popular works including biographies, commentaries, doctrine, and Christian living.

Mentor focuses on books written at a level suitable for Bible College and seminary students, pastors, and others; the imprint includes commentaries, doctrinal studies, examination of current issues, and church history.

For a free catalogue of all our titles, please write to
Christian Focus Publications,
Geanies House, Fearn,
Ross-shire, IV20 1TW, Great Britain

For details of our titles visit us on our web site
http://www.christianfocus.com

THE ONLY HOPE

JESUS
YESTERDAY • TODAY • FOREVER

EDITED BY MARK ELLIOTT + JOHN L. MCPAKE

MENTOR
RUTHERFORD HOUSE

ISBN 1-85792-717-6

Published in 2001
by Christian Focus Publications, Geanies House,
Fearn, Ross-shire, IV20 1TW, Great Britain
and
Rutherford House, 17 Claremont Park,
Edinburgh, EH6 7PJ

www.christianfocus.com

Cover design by Alister MacInnes

Printed and bound by Bell & Bain, Glasgow

Contents

Preface

Essays 1, 3, 4, 8, 9 and 11 were first delivered at the 1998 conference of the Scottish Evangelical Theological Society, gathered at Rutherford House, Edinburgh. Richard Bauckham's contribution was given there as the Finlayson Memorial Lecture and previously was published in the *Scottish Bulletin of Evangelical Theology*.

Essays 2, 5, 6, 7 and 10 were presented to the 1998 Christian Doctrine Study Group of the Tyndale Fellowship, which met in Tyndale House, Cambridge.

It seemed at least somewhat serendipitous, if not completely providential, that both groups should have been led to choose Christology for consideration in the same year. Perhaps it was a shared awareness, as matters millennial stole the headlines of religious publishing catalogues, of the confession that Jesus Christ is the same yesterday, today and forever. At a time when so much theology has been about the millennium and eschatology of various hues, or about whether late modernity and postmodernism were one and the same thing, it seemed timely to look closely at the subject of the Only Hope through the lenses of theologians of the present as well as yesteryear. It was also useful that a balance is preserved between ancient and modern in the offerings, though the very title of the first essay, by Howard Marshall, illustrates just how the subject matter resists, nay, leaps across any such lines of classification. The method of collecting essays from two conferences inevitably means some obvious gaps: later New Testament Christology, Calvin's teaching on the matter, Christological ethics, are ones obvious to the editors.

Nevertheless, these papers, published as the new millennium gets down to serious business, breathe with a sense of confidence that the only worthwhile account of the Mystery of Salvation is one which steers close to the historical orthodox and whole-scriptural vision of Jesus Christ. His being is the foundation of all we are and might be. May our thinking about his being be the foundation of all we think, feel and do.

Mark Elliott and John McPake
August, 2001

Contributors

1. I. Howard Marshall taught New Testament at the University of Aberdeen from 1964, becoming Professor in 1979, and retiring to a position as Honorary Research Professor of New Testament in 1999. He has served as President of the British New Testament Society and is currently Chair of the Tyndale Fellowship.

2. Anthony N. S. Lane teaches Christian doctrine at London Bible College; he is Professor of Historical Theology and Director of Research. He is also the Chair of the Tyndale Fellowship Doctrine Group.

3. Geoffrey Grogan is former Principal of Glasgow Bible College.

4. Donald Macleod is Professor of Systematic Theology at the Free Church College, Edinburgh, and visiting professor of theology at the University of Glasgow.

5. Mark W. Elliott is Lecturer in Christian Studies, Liverpool Hope University College. He is Secretary of the Tyndale Fellowship Christian Doctrine Group, and is editor of the Journal of European Theology.

6. David F. Wright is Professor of Patristic and Reformation History at the University of Edinburgh, New College and until recently was Chair of the Tyndale Fellowship.

7. Graham Macfarlane is lecturer in Systematic Theology and Assistant Director of Research at London Bible College, theological advisor to the Christian Medical Fellowship, and Course Tutor for the Institute of Counselling (Glasgow).

8. John L. McPake is convenor of Panel of Doctrine, and minister at Mossneuk Church of Scotland.

9. Moonjang Lee is lecturer at the Centre for Christianity in the Non-Western World, University of Edinburgh.

10. Timothy Bradshaw is lecturer in Christian Theology at Regent's Park College, Oxford, and is an ordained Anglican minister (St. Luke's, Oxford) who has devoted attention to both evangelical ethics (editing the St. Andrew's Day Statement on homosexuality) and ecumenical theology.

11. Richard Bauckham is Professor of New Testament at St. Andrews University (St. Mary's College) and is a Fellow of the British Academy.

1

Jesus at AD 2000

I. Howard Marshall

1. The Smorgasbord

On Saturday, 16th November, 1996, the *Daily Mail* began a serialised article based on a book called *The Holy Grail* by Laurence Gardner, which was introduced as follows:

> A new book claims that Jesus, far from being a meek religious martyr, was a revolutionary politician who faked his own death, married Mary Magdalene and fathered three children by her, starting a bloodline which carries down to the present day. This book, provocative as it may be, is not a work of fiction, but the product of years of painstaking academic research by the British genealogist Laurence Gardner who has devoted his life to researching this subject...

The introduction surprisingly went on to say 'Committed Christians will justifiably reject its conclusions'! However, you don't need to be a Christian, but simply a historical scholar committed to the impartial weighing of evidence, to see that much of what is said here about Jesus is a tissue of unsubstantiated conjecture. A book which has Jesus not dying but swooning and being resuscitated in the tomb by the aid of powerful drugs, and then marries him off to Mary to be the father of sundry children whose names and dates of birth are actually provided beggars belief. There is no evidence whatever for this kind of material; it is sheer fantasy, more characteristic of New Age speculations than historical study. Yet this author is not alone in producing what most intelligent people would regard as works of imagination.[1]

---

1. Such books are certainly not signs of the approach of AD 2000! They have been appearing for many years.

When we turn to the work of biblical scholars who have a right to be taken much more seriously than the sensation-mongers, we are faced not so much by the totally implausible and fictitious pictures of which *The Holy Grail* is an example as by the sheer variety of clashing portraits. They cannot all be true, and they leave the reader wondering where, if anywhere, the truth is to be found. Indeed, is it possible to find an agreed interpretation of evidence which has been adduced to support so many different theories?

We may begin our task with a quick survey of some of the portraits currently on offer, grouping them in broad categories.[2]

We have two extremes. At one end there is what I can only call *the Lunatic Fringe*. It is not surprising to find Laurence Gardner here. The strange thing is the way in which people who were once reputable scholars can turn to dabble in it, such as Barbara Thiering; unfortunately the sound reputation of such people as able scholars in the earlier part of their careers is no guarantee that they may not begin to pour out nonsense of a kind that reputable scholars find they must repudiate.[3] Sometimes these people have a particular axe to grind. It is impossible to debate rationally with them any more than it was with the opponents attacked in the Pastoral Epistles who engaged in nonsensical speculations. Clearly, there is no christology possible on this basis, since the result is that Jesus is degraded to a very ordinary type of human being.

At the other extreme we have the *Conservative Right*. Here the very genuine problems raised by differences between the Gospel accounts or clashes with other sources are brushed aside or given the minimum of attention, and there is the danger of letting people think that there are no problems or that people who perceive them are hostile rationalists. Efforts are still made to harmonise the

---

2. The task of categorising the various interpretations has been splendidly done by Ben Witherington III, *Jesus Quest* (books listed in the bibliography at the end of this chapter are referred to by the author's name and, where necessary, a short title), and my simplified list draws heavily on his classification.

3. For a survey see N. T. Wright, *Who was Jesus?*, G. N. Stanton, *Gospel Truth? New Light on Jesus and the Gospels* (London: Harper Collins, 1995), mentions Thiering but gives no bibliographical information about her book and says that it 'merits no further attention'.

different accounts on the assumption that the truth will be reached by adding everything together regardless of the fact that (for example) the Evangelists inevitably paraphrased what Jesus said in summarising it. *Christ on Earth* by Jakob van Bruggen, very able in its way and with some degree of originality in its hypotheses, stands towards this end of the spectrum. Even Robert Stein's *Jesus the Messiah* doesn't really recognise that its readership should be made aware of the problems, although the author himself has written helpfully about them elsewhere.

In between these two extremes there is a wide range of views. At the far left comes the *Minimalist Historical Jesus*. Here must be placed the activities of the *Jesus Seminar*. This is a well-publicised group of North American scholars who met to discuss the sayings attributed to Jesus in the Gospels and voted for and against their authenticity using coloured balls; they then produced an edition of the Gospels in which the sayings are coloured accordingly to indicate degrees of probable authenticity or inauthenticity. Broadly speaking, they and those who share a similar point of view operate on a minimalist historical view; they are trying to see what can be established positively as going back to Jesus or as being reasonably probable. But their scale of discrimination also includes indicating which texts are unlikely or highly improbable to go back to Jesus. The result is that their multi-coloured version of the Gospels doesn't simply indicate the degree of probability of texts going back in whole or part to Jesus but also expresses a definite negative verdict on texts which are said to be later accretions.

Now in principle there is something to be said for this procedure. The coming together of a group of scholars to pool their opinions and discuss matters as objectively as possible is only to be welcomed. However, it is to be feared that a secularist agenda controls the discussion; the chairperson of the group and some of the other players do appear to have a preconceived picture of Jesus which they are promoting, and they evidently have a vested interest in publicising the results of their discussions to as wide a public as possible. This may be partly in justified reaction to the more extreme forms of fundamentalist North American Protestantism.

Nevertheless, there has been much criticism of the Seminar from the mainstream of scholarship. W. R. Stegner argues that the mainstream of biblical scholarship is unconvinced by the seminar, and refers particularly to R. E. Brown's mainstream Roman Catholic treatment of the passion narrative over against the scepticism of the seminar.[4]

The second picture is of Jesus as an *Itinerant Cynic Philosopher*, which is promoted particularly by J. D. Crossan, *The Historical Jesus: The Life of a Mediterranean Jewish Peasant*. He makes out Jesus to be a rather ordinary person on the basis of a very complex and quite unconvincing analysis of the sources (including the apocryphal works – the Gospel of Peter and the Gospel of Thomas). Stegner, for example, questions the picture of Jesus as an illiterate Galilean artisan, showing that there is evidence for his being literate and educated, and disputing the possibility of Cynic influence in Galilee.[5] That Jesus' teachings were similar to those of the Cynics has been argued rather more soberly in this country by F. G. Downing.

Third, we have Jesus, *Man Of The Spirit*. Here there is a rather miscellaneous collection of scholars, of whom two deserve mention. G. Vermes, *Jesus the Jew*, was responsible for the picture of Jesus as being like a Jewish holy man (*hasid*) who had a close intimacy with God and was credited with working miracles. But it is very dubious whether this category actually existed. More recently, M. Borg has played down the eschatological teaching of Jesus and sees him as a charismatic figure who was concerned with politics and replaced the Pharisaic stress on purity with compassion. Here the problem is not so much what Borg affirms as what he denies and the consequent lack of a proper context for what he affirms about Jesus.

Fourth, there is the picture of Jesus as an *Eschatological Prophet* offered by E. P. Sanders and M. Casey. Sanders is a considerable figure in this area because of his detailed study of

---

4. W. R. Stegner, 'Some Personal Reflections on the Jesus Seminar', *Asbury Theological Journal* 52:2 (1997), 71-80.
5. See also the dialogue between N. T. Wright, 'Doing Justice to Jesus' and J. D. Crossan, 'What Victory?'.

Judaism, and his work sees Jesus as an apocalyptic teacher who is concerned with the restoration of Israel. This is a much more traditional picture than many of those on offer. A somewhat similar view is taken by M. Casey who is concerned to assert that the story in the Gospel of John is not true and reflects the later divinising of Jesus; Casey is also very important for his work in tracing the Aramaic wording of the teaching of Jesus.

Fifth, Jesus appears as a *Prophet Of Social Change* for G. Theissen and R. Horsley. For Theissen Jesus was a wandering charismatic prophet who proclaimed a radical ethic.[6] This point is developed by R. Horsley who sees Jesus as a prophet of social change rather than as a proclaimer of what God is going to do in the future.

Sixth, Jesus is a *Sage*, the wisdom of God, for E. S. Fiorenza and Ben Witherington includes himself as a proponent of this view.[7] There is not a lot of practical difference between this view and that which sees Jesus as a prophet, since in both he is the messenger of God. It is more a case of where you place the accent, whether you see Jesus more as a commentator on the current scene or more as a conveyor of eternal truths.

How can we hope to get at the truth when the scholars appear to be so hopelessly divided among themselves?

2. The importance of history for Christian doctrine
Faced by this plethora of understandings of Jesus which are held by reputable scholars, the ordinary Christian may well despair of finding the truth. Undoubtedly some of the scholars are influenced consciously or unconsciously by their own beliefs and cannot avoid the tendency to remake Jesus in an image that they find congenial. E. P. Sanders recognises this fact, and invites his readers to consider whether 'his' Jesus fits his theological heritage: 'I can explain simply: I am a liberal, modern, secularized Protestant, brought up in a church dominated by low christology and the social gospel. I

---

6. This, at least, is how Theissen initially saw Jesus in *Shadow*. His more recent work, *Historical Jesus*, is much more nuanced; see below.

7. But although he puts himself in this category there is a very considerable difference between Fiorenza and Witherington.

am proud of the things that that religious tradition stands for. I am not bold enough, however, to suppose that Jesus came to establish it, or that he died for the sake of its principles.'[8] If we cannot avoid being influenced to some extent by our subjectivity, how can we reach Jesus as he really was? It then becomes tempting to take R. Bultmann's quick-escape route, which was to say that we can know nothing about the historical Jesus (apart from a few sayings), but we don't need to know and we ought not to try. The gospel depends on the sheer fact of the Christian message and faith in it ceases to be faith when it assembles historical props to support itself.

I take the view that history does matter for Christian belief and doctrine. The point was put clearly by James Denney exactly 90 years ago when he asked, 'Can the Christian religion, as the New Testament exhibits it, justify itself by appeal to Jesus?... Is the mind of Christians about Christ supported by the mind of Christ about Himself?'[9] To pose this question is to accept that in some way the Christian estimate of the person and work of Jesus is justified by what Jesus himself taught and did during his earthly life. It would, for example, be impossible to justify the Christian doctrine of the sacrificial death of Jesus as a willing, but innocent victim, if he had been dragged struggling to his death after a life in which he had committed some crime. Nor would it make sense to regard him as the Son of God if he had repudiated belief in God. To be sure, people do not have to believe that they themselves are saints before other people can see saintliness in them, but one would have to be able to recognise saintly qualities in them. I take the view, then, that New Testament christology must in some way be the unfolding of what was present and latent in Jesus himself, because the question that is being asked is not simply 'Who is Jesus now, in the period after his death?' but also 'Who was Jesus?', and there must be some continuity between the answers to these two questions.

The point may be illustrated by the work of Maurice Casey, *From Jewish Prophet to Gentile God*. The essence of his position

---

8. *Jesus and Judaism*, 334.
9. J. Denney, *Jesus and the Gospel*, 2f.

is that christology is a matter of evolution rather than development. 'Development' for Casey is the unfolding of what is already there, so that the seeds of the later plant already contain the genes from which the development springs; 'evolution' refers to the changes brought about by response to stimuli from outside and thus is capable of discontinuities.[10] For Casey the major change was brought about by the move from the Jewish church to the Gentile church within which there could develop ideas of divinity that were simply not possible within a Jewish environment. Casey's thesis can be faulted at various points, not least for his insistence on the impossibility of christological developments towards divinity within the Jewish setting. However, the significant feature for our purpose is that he begins by constructing his view of the historical Jesus, and his Jesus is one who is strictly a prophet unconscious of divinity. Thus the foundation of his theory of christological evolution lies in a particular evaluation of the character of Jesus.[11] But in any case it is manifest that Casey could not develop his particular theory without asking the question about the historical Jesus.

History, then, in the sense of discovering, as far as we can, what actually happened, cannot be dispensed with.

3. The problem of history

We are thrown back, then, on the historical question of who Jesus was and what he was trying to do. The problems in dealing with it are well known. Let me list three of them, the first of which applies to history in general and the other two specifically to the question of the historical Jesus.

First, can we establish any of the crucial facts that would support the Christian, New Testament view of Jesus by some kind of historical proof, or, alternatively, can any of these alleged facts

---

10. For this contrast see J. D. G. Dunn, *The Making of Christology*, 437f., where he characterises Casey's view as 'evolution' (although Casey himself tends to refer simply to 'development', the publisher's note on the dustcover uses 'evolution').

11. To be sure, there is probably a dialectic between his reading of the evidence in the Gospels and the constraints imposed by his understanding of the framework of thought.

be historically disproved? In both cases what we are looking for is a combination of evidence and facts such as would convince a group of historians who are striving to be as objective as possible. Since it is of the nature of history that it can only establish probabilities rather than absolute certainties, we are looking for what we may call near-certainties.

One of the major problems with the study of the ancient world in particular is *the sheer lack of evidence* compared with the flood of it for many modern events. So it is not just the nature of historical methodology but also the comparative lack of attested material that contributes to our uncertainty. We cannot bring forward corroboration from outside sources for most of what the New Testament records. There are, to be sure, some points which are as certain as matters. In teaching my first-year New Testament class, when we come to discuss the chronology of the life of Jesus, I mention the fixed point afforded by the death of the Emperor Augustus on 19th August, AD 14, and I tell them that this is probably the one assured fact that they will learn in the class. Unfortunately, history is to a small extent the establishment of precise data of that kind, such as dates or a person's actual words (often referred to by the Latin phrase *ipsissima verba*); to a much greater extent it is the *interpretation* of the data and the relating of them to one another, and here there is vast scope for nuances of judgment by historians.

If, then, we cannot prove that certain things actually happened or that our interpretation of the evidence is the right one, we have to be content with statements of probability, and this always leave room for differences of opinion. So we are concerned with establishing judgments that would command reasonably broad assent. And this phrase 'broad assent' is critical. If we have a group of historians from different backgrounds, with different beliefs, there is a reasonable expectation that when they agree we have solid ground under our feet.

Second, in the case of the story of Jesus, we have to reckon with a considerable amount of material which assumes that *so-called supernatural events* took place, the chief of which is that Jesus, having been in effect certified dead by a competent authority, came to life again in a form which involved more than the resuscitation of a dead body. He is also credited with various actions which were understood at the time to be beyond normal human powers. There will inevitably be historians who query whether such things could in principle have happened. They will therefore be sceptical of these accounts and give explanations of how people could have come to create or develop such fictitious material. Note, however, that the historian has to allow that the followers of Jesus did believe that he could and did do mighty works and that they did believe in his resurrection from the dead, so that early christology did in fact develop on the basis of these beliefs. This can sometimes produce tensions in that you find sceptical historians assigning the origin of certain beliefs about Jesus to the effect of historical events such as the resurrection which they don't really believe happened, and not giving satisfactory explanations of how what really happened on their understanding of it could lead to the beliefs. If the resurrection did not happen, what alternative account of events is going to be adequate to explain the rise of faith in Jesus?

Third, and closely associated with the preceding point, is the fact that, whatever kind of person Jesus actually was, *after his death his followers came to hold exalted views about him*, and therefore it is often held that they told the story of his life as if he were the kind of person whom they now considered him to be; thus, if they believed that he was now the Lord of the universe, it would not be surprising if they told stories about how he had authority over the forces of nature such as the wind and the sea during his lifetime. Such stories may have been nothing more than mythical embellishments which people knew were not true literally, or they may have been understood as sober, matter-of-fact accounts. Either way, Jesus was being portrayed differently from what the actual facts of his life warranted.

These last two points create considerable obstacles for the historical investigator. The former is a matter of the historian's presuppositions: are the powers ascribed to Jesus indeed possibilities in this world? The latter is more a matter of the historian's estimate, based on analogous phenomena with other famous people in the ancient world and elsewhere, where people have been idealised after their death. This issue is particularly important for us, because the aim of our investigation is precisely to find out whether the actual facts of the life of Jesus justify the later estimate of him; here we have the possibility that we cannot get at the actual facts because the process of idealisation has already obscured them.

4. The relation of historical study to faith

These three considerations raise two general questions for us. The first concerns the place of history in relation to doctrine. The second concerns the problem of establishing the history.

So far as the first question is concerned, we face the difficulty that if the facts can be established only to a certain level of probability, then it follows for some people that they cannot be the basis for faith. If we could prove for certain that Jesus really came to life after his crucifixion, then this could be a basis for faith that God can raise people from the dead. The majority of Christian scholars would probably agree that the most we can have is a high probability that Jesus rose from the dead, and some would settle for much less. In that case the act of faith includes believing that Jesus rose from the dead as being the best explanation of the evidence and hence believing in the possibility of divinely-wrought resurrection. In this sense we have to say that faith is not based on history but faith is related to history.

It would, of course, still be possible to believe even if the evidence was rather contrary to the fact of Jesus' resurrection. A person might persist in believing that a friend was innocent of some crime despite apparently overwhelming testimony to the contrary. Such a belief might be subsequently vindicated by fresh evidence turning up which shattered the previous consensus. But there are situations in which such persistence may seem to be totally unfounded. In this hypothetical scenario it could be important that the person accused of the crime is somebody that I described as a friend; in other words, there could be a whole collection of pieces of evidence that the accused was a reliable, upright person who is most unlikely to have committed such a crime. Similarly, the question of belief in the resurrection of Jesus does not depend only on the actual evidence for that happening; it also depends on a whole collection of pieces of evidence for the character of Jesus and for the truth of a religion which is tied to the fact of his resurrection.

Consequently, although belief that Jesus rose from the dead may be in the end a matter of faith, it is still important that the historical evidence be assessed by the usual methods of historical study. Christian belief is not totally irrational but represents an attitude to the evidence that is reasonable, even if there are factors that other people may weigh differently and so come to a different set of beliefs or even to disbelief. In fact, most Christians would want to go much further than this with reference to Jesus and to hold that there is a rather strong connection between the facts about Jesus and their faith. For us, our faith is not just one possible attitude that people might have to Jesus out of a whole range of competing interpretations; it is the one that makes the best sense of the evidence. In other words, despite the ambiguity of the evidence and the difficulties of interpreting it, we believe that historical study confirms our interpretation of Jesus, renders other interpretations much less plausible and rules some of them out altogether.

5. The problems of establishing historicity
This leads us directly into the second question we raised at the beginning of the previous section, the problem of establishing what actually happened: how can we find out what Jesus said and did?

1. The nature of the Gospels
Clearly the first thing to be done is to enumerate the sources and to discuss their character. The evidence from outside the New Testament is small in extent and very limited in what it states. The evidence from the New Testament outside the Gospels is also limited, but we now have the important study by David Wenham, *Paul: Follower of Jesus,* which offers a maximalist view of the evidence, arguing for a good deal of detail about Jesus in the letters of Paul.

The vital evidence is contained in the Gospels. Here various questions arise. What were the Evangelists trying to do? Were they trying to tell a historical story or were they free to invent and create? The crucial evidence is that of Luke, who makes a very firm claim to be giving a historical record which will confirm what Theophilus has already heard. Whether Luke was competent at his job or not, the fact remains that this is what he was trying to do; he must, therefore, be taken at face value as a historian rather than as, say, a novelist or propagandist. It must also be observed that the Gospel of John claims to be based on reliable testimony, and this fact must be weighed against the apparent theological reconstruction that is going on. Here again David Wenham has made a valuable contribution in a simple but scholarly booklet on *John's Gospel*, prepared in connection with the Big Idea campaign.

After much discussion of their genre, the view appears to be gaining in strength that the Gospels are best understood against the background of their time as biographies. This case has been well argued by R. Burridge in both a technical book (*What are the Gospels?*) and also a popular presentation (*Four Gospels*). To be sure, this identification of the genre does not fully settle the matter of historicity. Ancient biography is not necessarily the same as modern and settling the question of the genre does not in itself settle the question of historicity: some historians may be more accurate, some less accurate. Nevertheless, the genre of the Gospels does suggest that the likelihood is that we are dealing with history rather than with fiction.

The fact that Matthew and Mark are broadly similar in character to Luke suggests that they were doing much the same as he was, namely writing biography; and if Luke made use of Mark as a source, this would show that he regarded Mark as a reliable source. Some people make much of the differences between the three Gospels when it comes to the details of the text. However, these differences are not so great as to suggest that the author of one Gospel using another (such as Luke in his use of Mark) thought that his source was very faulty and needed extensive correction.

2. The Evangelists and their sources

Next, we have to ask whether the Evangelists were competent historians. They could have misinterpreted the evidence available to them or they may have had misleading sources. We have to ask whether we can get behind them to their sources. Here we begin to move into areas of speculation.

There is first the question of the Synoptic Problem. There is certainly less unanimity on this now than there was forty years ago. Nevertheless, I think that the most plausible view is still the two-document theory, namely the use of Mark and the lost source 'Q' by Matthew and Luke; to put the point otherwise, I see no reasons to prefer any of the rival theories that are offered to us, specifically any theories which make Mark dependent on Matthew and/or Luke.[12] I am less clear about the existence and extent of Q as a document, but that there was a common source or collection of sources of sayings of Jesus used by Matthew and Luke seems fairly certain to me. If we do not accept the two-source hypothesis, we have even less historical certainty, since we are then in effect saying that we do not know what the processes of transmission were that led to the present form of Matthew and Luke.

Recently, a claim has been made that behind some of the material peculiar to Luke there can be detected a coherent, homogenous source, known as L, which may be of equal antiquity to Mark and Q but independent of both.[13] If this claim is justified, it adds a further source to the discussion.

As for the Gospel of John, even if it be granted that the author knew of the Gospel of Mark, as seems to be increasingly held by scholars, I am persuaded that there is still considerable evidence for the view that the author was able to draw upon independent streams of tradition for both factual and teaching material.[14]

Unfortunately, all of this does not take us very far back. If

---

12. Out of much discussion I single out P. M. Head, *Christology*, for a nuanced treatment.

13. K. Paffenroth, *The Story of Jesus according to L* (Sheffield: Sheffield Academic Press, 1997).

14. In addition to C. H. Dodd, *Historical Tradition*, see P. Ensor, *Jesus and His Works, The Johannine Sayings in Historical Perspective* (Tübingen: Mohr, 1996).

Mark is the earliest Gospel, source criticism has not taken us any further back and thus we are still where we started. As for Q, the present state of play is one of extreme scepticism about its historical value. We are invited to believe in a rather small core of sayings which was enlarged and edited in a number of stages, during which the picture of Jesus was considerably altered. I have not studied this matter in any detail, but I suspect that the hypothesis will collapse much like the efforts to do detailed reconstruction of the stages of some of the hypothetical sources of the pentateuch. A strongly conservative line is taken by E. P. Meadors,[15] but his book has not made the impact which I think it deserves to have done on the mainstream of writers on Q.

The waters are muddied by bringing in other putative sources. Crossan's reconstruction of the life of Jesus depends to a considerable extent upon the Gospel of Peter and the Gospel of Thomas and also upon the so-called Secret Gospel of Mark. None of these three sources can stand comparison with the canonical Gospels, and therefore Crossan's enterprise is questionable from the very start.

3. The handing down of the Tradition
One area in which we should expect to see a change of opinion is the assumption that the traditions about Jesus were handed down in the form of isolated units and that the chronological framework in which they have been placed in the Gospels is secondary and largely historically worthless. This theory was defended by K. L. Schmidt in 1919 and it has been accepted uncritically by scholars ever since. It has now been subjected to what I regard as a devastating attack by D. R. Hall (*The Gospel Framework*) who shows just how much it is based on arbitrary assumptions.

The next question is how the actual material was handed down and whether it was handed down reliably. Here there are two main contrasting positions.

On the one hand, we have the position of the dominant school in study of the Q document; it argues for a series of separable stages in which the material was radically developed, giving rather

---

15. *Jesus the Messianic Herald of Salvation* (Tübingen: Mohr, 1995).

different impressions of Jesus at each stage. This suggests very active creativity that was linked to the situation and needs of a specific community.

On the other hand, we have the sort of view espoused by R. Riesner[16] (and earlier by H. Riesenfeld and B. Gerhardsson[17]) which emphasises the role of Jesus as a teacher and the faithful handing down of his teaching by responsible people. This picture has received strong backing from K. E. Bailey with his theory of controlled tradition. Bailey distinguishes between what he calls informal uncontrolled oral tradition, formal controlled oral tradition and informal controlled oral tradition. The first of these categories is what Bultmann envisaged: oral transmission that was in no way controlled by the community and so was allowed to run riot. Over against this view was that of Riesenfeld and Gerhardsson which stressed the place of special persons, the apostles and others, in the preservation and memorisation of the 'holy word' concerning Jesus. Bailey advocates a third model, where traditions can be handed down flexibly (the wording is not sacrosanct) but nevertheless there is control exercised by the audience who know whether the stories they are hearing are faithful in substance to what they have heard previously. Thus in village communities the tradition is preserved in an authentic form. Bailey argues that this mechanism, which he has personally observed in the Middle East, gives us the clue to what went on in the early church. I find it very plausible.

4. Tests for the Tradition
Against this background of controlled tradition we can now rehearse some standard points concerning the analysis of the actual traditions.

a. Material which reflects Semitic ways of expression and especially that which is most plausibly explained as a literal translation from Aramaic clearly goes back at least to the earliest

---

16. His work is unfortunately untranslated: *Jesus als Lehrer* (Tübingen: Mohr, 1981).

17. H. Riesenfeld, *The Gospel Tradition and its Beginnings* (London: Mowbray, 1957); B. Gerhardsson, *Memory and Manuscript* (Uppsala: Gleerup, 1961).

days of the church when it was still an Aramaic-speaking or bilingual group in Jerusalem. But this principle cannot be used to rule out material which is more Greek or Hellenistic in character, since we know that Judaea and especially Galilee were subject to Hellenistic influences, and since people can have translated what Jesus said with greater or less literalism.

b. We can depend upon material which has been preserved against the interests of those who recorded it. For example, the accusations made by opponents against Jesus can be taken seriously; the early church is unlikely to have invented them (unless there was an aim of blackening the opponents by attributing extreme opinions about Jesus to them). This does not mean that the content of the accusations is true, but that the accusations have been reliably preserved.

c. We can also depend upon material where Jesus says things that are not in agreement with what his followers thought. His fairly absolute teaching on divorce and remarriage is a good example. But we cannot use this principle in an excluding manner to say that if something attributed to Jesus does agree with the thinking of his followers then it must have been original to them rather than to Jesus. The fact that early Christians taught an ethic of love does not imply that they put it inappropriately into the mouth of Jesus. As D. A. Carson tartly observes: 'In what other field of historical research would the most influential sayings of an extraordinarily influential individual be denied authenticity on the ground that because they were believed and repeated by the individual's followers they could not have been authentic?'[18]

d. We can also depend upon material where Jesus says things that are appropriate within the framework of contemporary Jewish thinking but which are not commonplace Jewish teachings. His teaching that the Kingdom of God had come, and indeed his whole emphasis on the Kingdom of God, is an important example. Equally, as with the previous point, we cannot use this argument to rigidly exclude material in which Jesus agrees with what other Jews of the time were saying.

---

18. 'New Testament Theology', in R. P. Martin and P. H. Davids, *Dictionary of the later New Testament and its Developments* (Downers Grove: IVP, 1997), 800f.

Both this point and the previous one figured in the principle of dissimilarity which dominated the 'new quest' of E. Käsemann and other former followers of Bultmann who reacted against his historical agnosticism. But it was based on dubious reasoning, and more recent scholars have replaced it with a criterion of 'plausibility' which asks: 'what is plausible in the Jewish context and makes the rise of Christianity understandable'?[19]

e. Material which is not overtly about the person of Jesus and the significance of his death is less open to critical suspicion than material which is. If suspicion attaches to prophecies of his death described fairly explicitly, it is difficult to reject statements about his facing a 'baptism' that use the term in a way that is not typical of his followers' manner of speech.[20]

f. There is the well-known principle that material which is attested in more than one source or form has strong claims to have been reliably remembered. The difficulty with applying the principle is that there is great uncertainty about what the sources are and to what extent they were independent of one another. It is not absolutely certain that Mark and Q are independent of one another. Although Mark does not appear to have used Q directly in the way that Matthew and Luke did on the two-source hypothesis, there are a significant number of so-called doublets (sayings found in both Mark and 'Q' material); here the possibility exists that the Marcan form of a saying of Jesus is dependent at some stage upon Q rather than being traceable back to Jesus by some independent line.

One particular development of this argument deserves mention. C. H. Dodd was able to list various facts about Jesus which are attested not only in independent sources (as he understood them) but also in different forms of material according to the classification made by form-criticism.[21]

---

19. G. Theissen and A. Merz, *The Historical Jesus*, 116-8.

20. H. F. Bayer, *Jesus' Predictions of Vindication and Resurrection* (Tübingen: Mohr, 1986).

21. In *History and the Gospel* Dodd's list of points is: 'Jesus as an historical personality distinguished from other religious personalities of His time by His friendly attitude to the outcasts of society' (94); 'Jesus was, with His followers, an exile from home and family' (96); Jesus brought salvation 'as well for the

g. This leads to the point made by various scholars including B. D. Chilton (*Pure Kingdom*): we have to ask the question: what generated the traditions that we have?[22] What was the creative impulse that led to the formulation of material that may have been developed by the early church but which can hardly be explained as a *creatio ex nihilo*? The question of an adequate starting point for the tradition is a crucial one. We do not want to finish up with a theory of creativity by a community which had nothing to stimulate its creativity, a theory which is more incredible than the theory that there was a creative individual called Jesus. And there is considerable plausibility in the view that creative individuals are thicker on the ground than creative communities.

h. All this leads me finally to what I call the crossword-clue factor. If you think that a crossword clue contains an anagram of the required word, whereas it is simply a cryptic definition, then you will be wasting your time on a totally misguided exercise if you try to work out an anagram from some words in the clue. The symposium edited by R. Bauckham (*Gospels*) is in effect saying that reading the Gospels as clues to the nature of the local communities for which they were written is wrong-headed because the Gospels were written for the church at large and not for specific local communities and their particular needs. Similarly, we need to ask the question whether the kind of analysis to discover successive stages of composition practised by, for example, the current school of Q investigators is wrong-headed because the document was not created in this kind of way. Some scholars are over-ready to find theological significance and clues to different communities to which their authors belonged in the differences between the Synoptic Gospels when nothing more than literary variation may be involved. I suspect that the same is true of the investigations of Q.[23]

---

body as for the soul' (97); there is a powerful contrast between the old and the new (99); 'the hopes of past generations are fulfilled in the experience of the disciples' (100); 'the rejection of Jesus by the Jews is a sign of divine judgment' (101).

22. Chilton applies this method particularly to the teaching of Jesus about the Kingdom of God in *God in Strength: Jesus' Announcement of the Kingdom* (Sheffield: Sheffield Academic Press, 1987).

To sum up this section: we should be asking whether the material that has been incorporated into the Gospels gives us a picture of Jesus (i) which is historically probable in that, by all the tests I have mentioned, specific pieces of evidence are best explained as being genuine; (ii) which is coherent in that, allowing for the gaps in the evidence, the picture that emerges is a consistent and unified one; and (iii) which is an apt basis for the picture of Jesus that subsequently emerged among his followers, i.e. which is necessary in order for the generation of the church's image of him.

6. The historical Jesus: a comprehensive guide

Against the background of these methodological considerations the next task should be to look at some of the reconstructions of Jesus which have been recently put forward and to evaluate them accordingly. Our task is made the easier by the existence of two excellent recent critical surveys by B. Witherington and M. A. Powell.[24] We can, therefore, pass over to the various scholars and their books which were listed earlier and concentrate our attention on two of the most recent works.

The first of these, *The Historical Jesus: A Comprehensive Guide*, is intended as a students' workbook and comes from Germany. The two authors, G. Theissen and A. Merz, believe that the question of the historical Jesus is theologically important, and they distinguish between the Californian Jesus of Crossan and other scholars and the Galilean Jesus of Sanders, with which

---

23. We may perhaps compare the elaborate attempts to trace different edition of the alleged documents behind the Pentateuch with J1, J2, and so on; I understand that this process is no longer attempted because it is based on a false understanding of how the Pentateuch came into being.

24. Witherington, *Jesus Quest*, surveys the work of the scholars listed earlier, drawing out the valuable and convincing points made by them as well as submitting implausible points to rigorous criticism. Powell, *Jesus Debate*, is more recent and covers much of the same ground. Both examine the work of J. P. Meier, the author of the (as yet unfinished) major North American contribution to our subject (*A Marginal Jew*). This book is meticulously   detailed in its discussion of the subject and offers a conservatively critical   major work on Jesus. In the light of their treatment I do not propose to discuss it here.

25. W. Pannenberg, *Jesus – God and Man* (London: SCM Press, 1968); G.

they find more sympathy. In the first part of their book they offer a detailed evaluation of the historical sources, listing and responding to thirteen objections to the historicity of the Jesus-tradition. They reject the traditional criteria for evaluating the tradition and argue for the principle of historical plausibility. The second part is concerned with background and chronology. In the third part they look at the activity and preaching of Jesus. They see Jesus as a 'charismatic' in the sociological sense of that term, thus joining forces with G. Bornkamm, M. Hengel, G. Vermes and M. Borg who in their various ways have emphasised the sheer authority of Jesus. Jesus is not unknown, as Bultmann claimed, but is known in his relationships with other people, about which we have a reasonable amount of information.

His message was about the kingdom of God. Both present and future statements are accepted as part of the message, but Jesus erroneously expected an imminent end to the world. As for his miracles, they reject those which have no analogies in experience (walking on the water, multiplying loaves) but accept those which do, namely the healings, which are attributed to paranormal gifts such as are found in the modern world. The Lord's Supper is seen as a replacement for the temple ritual, but the interpretation in terms of Jesus' death as a sacrifice took place only after the event. With respect to the Passion the authors largely agree with R. E. Brown. Jesus is depicted as an innocent, suffering, righteous man. Finally, there is a discussion of the resurrection. They contrast the objective theories of W. Pannenberg and the subjective theories of G. Lüdemann.[25] They firmly accept the historicity of the appearance of Jesus to the disciples as a group. They also believe that he appeared to Mary Magdalene. They do not think that the story of the empty tomb can be proved or falsified, but seem to lean towards acceptance.

I have been more than surprised by the sheer conservatism of this survey conducted by a leading German scholar and his colleague. It is extraordinarily traditional in its conclusions,

---

Lüdemann, *What Really Happened to Jesus? A Historical Approach to the Resurrection* (Louisville: Westminster John Knox, 1996).

26. See, for example, the dialogue between Wright and Crossan in

although it is based on a very careful analysis of the evidence. It demonstrates that one can defend an essentially orthodox picture of Jesus without resorting to any unusual hypotheses to do so.

But the book is not yet concluded, and the story so far is followed by a section on the beginnings of christology. A distinction is made between five ways in which christology may have a basis in the historical Jesus: (a) explicit christology, where Jesus expressed his authority with a title; (b) evoked christology, in which Jesus raised expectations among other people in his lifetime; (c) implicit christology, in which Jesus fulfilled the 'conditions' of being Messiah without using the title; (d) a heightened use of titles, in which the church gave titles used by Jesus a more transcendent claim; (e) an exclusivist use of titles, in which the early church restricted to Jesus titles under which he included others, such as a collective use of 'Son of man' or 'messiah'. Only categories (a)–(c) give a real basis for christology in the historical Jesus. Implicit christology is seen in the 'Amen' formula, the 'I' sayings and the 'I have come' sayings; the metaphor of God as Father, the granting of forgiveness, the causal attribution of the miracles and the assessment of John the Baptist. Evoked christology is seen in the assessment of Jesus as Messiah, a title which Jesus himself did not use although he had a messianic consciousness. Explicit christology is to be seen in the use of Son of man. 'An everyday expression which simply meant the human being or a human being was evaluated in "messianic" terms by Jesus. Only because of that could it become the characteristic way in which he described himself' (p. 553). The cross and Easter transformed this expectation, and the titles of 'Son of God' and 'Lord' developed as a result.

7. Jesus and the Victory of God

The second major work comes from this country, from Tom Wright who is engaged in a massive study of the origins of Christianity, scheduled to run to five volumes, of which *Jesus and the Victory of God* is the second. The first, *The New Testament and the People of God*, was to some extent a prolegomenon to this volume, and some of its material is helpfully repeated. The aim is to give a full-length reconstruction of the mission of the historical Jesus that will stand comparison with the other major studies that have come from contemporary scholars who stand generally well to the left of Wright. This book is thus the major conservative study of Jesus to appear in the twentieth century. What makes it distinctive, however, is that, though it may be conservative in the sense that it powerfully defends the reliability of the traditions recorded in the Gospels, it is fresh and creative in its interpretation of the evidence and there are many points where it offers a new picture of Jesus and his teaching.

In the preliminary Part I, Wright summarises earlier twentieth-century scholarship in terms of a polarity between the two scholars who dominated the discussion c. 1900, A. Schweitzer and W. Wrede, representing thoroughgoing eschatology and thorough-going scepticism respectively. The latter school, the dominant one at present, is so sceptical about the contents of the Gospels that it is able to reconstruct the historical Jesus pretty much as it pleases. Its reconstructions are so speculative as to arouse fairly thorough-going scepticism towards them, and Wright gives a powerful criticism of some of the writers I have briefly mentioned. He himself believes that Schweitzer points the way forward rather than Wrede, but he achieves this by a fairly radical reinterpretation of eschatology.

Wright's own contribution begins with an interpretation of the parable of the Prodigal Son, seen as a picture of Israel still in exile and being restored. 'Jesus is reconstituting Israel around himself' – this is the key thought. It depends upon the crucial thesis that Israel regarded itself as still in exile, for which Wright argued in his prior volume, and thus it begins with a controversial statement that needs to be defended.

In Part II, Jesus is then presented as a prophet, not as yet 'the' prophet, but a 'leadership' prophet who itinerated and no doubt kept on repeating the same teaching. Much of his teaching was done through parables. The key role is played by stories about the kingdom of God, in which he depicts the return of God to Zion.

This leads into the second feature of Wright's reconstruction. He disputes that the eschatological language refers to the end of the world; it is metaphorical, which means that it certainly still has a meaning, but this meaning turns out to be concerned with what is happening here and now. We have a firm belief that the kingdom is present. This is seen in the parable of the sower which is again about the return from exile which is now at hand bringing God's judgment on those who refuse his rule. People are called to repent and believe. There must be a renunciation of nationalist violence, but there is also the offer of forgiveness of sins and people can take their place in the restored people of Israel. Only in this sense does Jesus 'found' the church; he did not need to *found* one because there already was one, and what was needed was to *reform* it.

But what was going to happen? Here the question of eschatological language becomes acute. Where was it all going to end? Jesus foresaw the judgment to come upon Israel and specifically upon Jerusalem and the Temple, but his own followers would be vindicated in that they would constitute the new Temple. The prediction of the coming of the Son of man in Mark 13 is to be understood not literally of the end of the world but metaphorically of the vindication of Jesus through this judgment. The 'coming of the Son of man' is metaphorical language for the defeat of God's enemies and the vindication of his true people.

Such a message provoked opposition and controversy. It led to what Wright calls a clash of symbols. But whereas it is customary to see Jesus as primarily preaching a religion of inward observance rather than of outward observance of legal codes and criticising the Pharisees for their (hypocritical) affirmation of the latter, Wright wants to argue that the real controversy was about eschatology and politics. Jesus attacked the symbols characteristic of the nationalistic, anti-pagan attitude found in the teaching of the Pharisees. The Sabbath, food laws, the (physically defined) nation and family, the land, and the Temple were the specific objects of conflict. Jesus in effect redefined them all. He thus appeared as a deceiver of the people, a dangerous misguided prophet, against whom the authorities felt that they had to take action. Thus the question of his own role in God's plan became significant.

Jesus has now been seen in the different aspects of his prophetic role. In Part III of the book, Wright explains how Jesus applied to himself the three main aspects of his announcement of the kingdom: the return from exile, the defeat of evil and the return of YHWH to Zion. Jesus saw himself as the king through whose work YHWH was restoring his people. Here, therefore, we have a lengthy discussion of messiahship which shows that Jesus did not fulfil the expectations of Judaism; when his disciples recognised him as Messiah, it cannot have been simply because they believed that he had risen from the dead; there must have been something to guide their thoughts into that particular explanation of the implications of the resurrection. This leads Wright back again to consider the action of Jesus in the Temple and the authority which he displayed in it, coupled with other indicators that point in the same direction, what Wright calls 'royal riddles'. He boldly links together the material in Daniel 7 and 9 to show that Jesus spoke of his own vindication as messiah. It is this which is the key to the trial of Jesus. If Jesus had been speaking and acting as he did in regard to the temple, it implied that he thought that he was the Messiah; hence Caiaphas' question to him makes sense in the context. Equally the trial leads to the conclusion that Jesus is guilty of blasphemy through his attitude to the Temple, his claim to royal status (above all his enthronement to share the throne of YHWH), his prophecy of exaltation, and his role as a false prophet. But messiahship can now be seen to have been present earlier in his career.

Why, then, did Jesus die? Here Wright explores the relationship of the Roman and Jewish trials, repeating material already discussed to some extent, but moving on to the question of Jesus' own mindset. He follows Schweitzer in claiming that Jesus went to Jerusalem to die rather than to 'work'. His intention became clear at the Last Supper, understood as a quasi-Passover meal deliberately held a day earlier than the official date. At it there was a powerful retelling of Israel's story in which Jesus' own death became a focal point, a death in which he would follow his own teaching by taking up the cross and defeating evil by letting it do its worst to him. In this light several earlier riddling sayings take on meaning. But then the question of a background to this intention of Jesus arises, and Wright explores again the theme of Jesus incorporating in himself the sufferings of Israel through which the exile would be brought to an end. 'We can credibly reconstruct a mindset in which a first-century Jew could come to believe that YHWH would act through the suffering of a particular individual in whom Israel's sufferings were focused; that this suffering would carry redemptive significance; *and that this individual would be himself* (p. 593). Jesus saw his death as replacing the Temple and its sacrifices, and he renounced the battle against Israel's enemies, fighting instead against the forces of darkness.

Finally, what did Jesus believe about the return of YHWH to Zion? Jesus believed that he was to re-enact that event. The kingdom of God is God's own coming in power. Jesus as Son of man is the one in whom YHWH comes symbolically to Jerusalem as judge, and this is the context of the parables of the pounds and talents (which do not refer to the 'second coming').

This summary can in no way do justice to the richness of the argument and the wealth of detail in this book. What emerges is a traditional picture of Jesus with many differences that turn it into a new picture. The important thing about Wright's book is that it shows how an essentially traditionalist picture of Jesus can be developed and defended by a scholar who is prepared to offer fresh insights and to develop daring hypotheses. The sheer skill reflected in the book means that it will be taken seriously by critics.[26]

But of course it raises questions. Can the daring hypotheses be sustained, and to what extent does the total picture depend upon the validity of the hypotheses which are perhaps as yet untested? Specifically, did the Jewish people think of itself as still in exile, and did Jesus see himself as the leading figure in its restoration and return, and is Wright justified in seeing the eschatological/ apocalyptic language as referring to historical events in this world concerned with judgment upon the Jews rather than as referring to the end of the world and the final coming of the Son of man? These are questions that must be debated.

Nevertheless, the overwhelming impression which I gain from this book together with Theissen/Merz (and others could be added) is that there are scholars at work who are able to treat the traditions about Jesus in a positive and creative manner and yet are able to do justice to the problems that arise concerning his relationship both to Judaism and to the early Christians. Despite the initial appearance of total confusion in the scholarly arena, there are good grounds for affirming that reliable historical knowledge of Jesus is possible. We then have to go on to ask for ourselves Pilate's question, 'What shall I do, then, with the one you call the king of the Jews?' (Mark 15:12).

8. Conclusion

A number of conclusions sum up what I have been trying to say in this paper:

1. History is important for faith and for doctrine.

2. We have good grounds for affirming the possibility of researching the Jesus-tradition and establishing many historical facts about his life and teaching.

3. Despite the variety of pictures of Jesus currently available, it is possible to exercise a sensible historical judgment in order to discriminate between them and show up the shortcomings of those which are fantastic or which depend on dubious premises.

4. The major works of Wright and Theissen/Merz demonstrate that a picture of the earthly Jesus which can form a credible basis for the development of the early church's christology can be substantiated by historical criticism. Theissen/Merz offer the more 'traditional' critical picture, while Wright offers exciting new hypotheses. But between them they show that the 'new quest' for the historical Jesus is alive and well, and that Christians can go into the new millennium with considerable optimism. Certainly I would not want to lull you into a false sense of security by saying that we can now go on peacefully with our lives as Christians, preachers and teachers, and scholars, with the quest of the historical Jesus laid to rest, but we can say that the existence of a historical

basis for christology has been shown to be the probable alternative, even if lots of work remains to be done both on the details and on continuing to defend it against the assaults upon it which will assuredly continue.

Bibliography of some (mainly recent) works

K. E. Bailey, 'Informal controlled oral tradition and the Synoptic Gospels', *Themelios* 20:2 (Jan. 1995), 4-11.

— 'Middle Eastern Oral Tradition and the Synoptic Gospels', *Expository Times* 106:12 (Sept. 1995), 363-7.

R. Bauckham (ed.), *The Gospels for All Christians: Rethinking the Gospel Audiences* (Grand Rapids: Eerdmans, 1998).

C. L. Blomberg, *Jesus and the Gospels* (Leicester: Apollos, 1997).

M. Borg, *Conflict, Holiness and Politics in the Teachings of Jesus* (Lewiston: Mellen, 1984).

— *Jesus: A New Vision* (San Francisco: Harper, 1987).

R. E. Brown, *The Death of the Messiah: From Gethsemane to the Grave. A Commentary on the Passion Narratives in the Four Gospels* (London: Geoffrey Chapman, 1994).

R. A. Burridge, *What are the Gospels? A Comparison with Graeco-Roman Biography* (Cambridge: Cambridge University Press, 1992).

— *Four Gospels, One Jesus? A Symbolic Reading* (London: SPCK, 1994).

M. Casey, *From Jewish Prophet to Gentile God: The Origins and Development of New Testament Christology* (Cambridge: James Clarke, 1991).

— *Is John's Gospel True?* (London: Routledge, 1996).

B. D. Chilton, *Pure Kingdom: Jesus' Vision of God* (London: SPCK, 1996).

J. D. Crossan, *The Historical Jesus: The Life of a Mediterranean Jewish Peasant* (Edinburgh: T. and T. Clark, 1991).

— 'What Victory? What God? A Review Debate with N. T. Wright on *Jesus and the Victory of God*', *Scottish Journal of Theology* 50:3 (1997), 345-58.

J. Denney, *Jesus and the Gospel: Christianity Justified in the Mind of Christ* (London: Hodder and Stoughton, 1909).

C. H. Dodd, *History and the Gospel* (London: Nisbet, 1938).

— *Historical Tradition in the Fourth Gospel* (Cambridge: Cambridge University Press, 1963).

J. D. G. Dunn, 'The Making of Christology – Evolution or Unfolding', in J. B. Green and M. Turner (eds.), *Jesus of Nazareth: Lord and Christ* (Carlisle: Paternoster, 1994), 437-52.

F. G. Downing, *Christ and the Cynics: Jesus and Other Radical Preachers in First-Century Tradition* (Sheffield: Sheffield Academic Press, 1988).

E. S. Fiorenza, *In Memory of Her: A Feminist Theological Reconstruction of Christian Origins* (London: SCM Press, 1984).

D. R. Hall, *The Gospel Framework Fiction or Fact? A critical evaluation of* Der Rahmen der Geschichte Jesu *by Karl Ludwig Schmidt* (Carlisle: Paternoster, 1998).

A. E. Harvey, *Jesus and the Constraints of History* (London: Duckworth, 1982).

P. M. Head, *Christology and the synoptic problem. An argument for Markan priority* (Cambridge: CUP, 1997).

R. A. Horsley, *Jesus and the Spiral of Violence* (San Francisco: Harper, 1987).

J. P. Meier, *A Marginal Jew* (New York: Doubleday), Vol. 1, 1991; Vol. 2, 1994.

B. F. Meyer, *The Aims of Jesus* (London: SCM Press, 1979).

M. A. Powell, *The Jesus Debate. Modern Historians Investigate the Life of Christ* (Oxford: Lion, 1999).

E. P. Sanders, *Jesus and Judaism* (London: SCM Press, 1985).

G. N. Stanton, *The Gospels and Jesus* (Oxford: Oxford University Press, 1989).

R. Stein, *Jesus the Messiah* (Downers Grove: IVP, 1996).

G. Theissen, *The Shadow of the Galilean* (London: SCM Press, 1987) .

G. Theissen and A. Merz, *The Historical Jesus: A Comprehensive Guide* (London: SCM Press, 1998).

J. van Bruggen, *Christ on Earth: The Life of Jesus according to His Disciples and Contemporaries* (Grand Rapids: Baker, 1998).

G. Vermes, *Jesus the Jew* (New York: Macmillan, 19832).

— *The Religion of Jesus the Jew* (Minneapolis: Augsburg-Fortress, 1990).

D. Wenham, *Paul: Follower of Jesus or Founder of Christianity?* (Grand Rapids: Eerdmans, 1995).

— *John's Gospel: Good News for Today* (Leicester: RTSF, 1997).

B. Witherington III, *The Christology of Jesus* (Minneapolis: Fortress, 1990).

— *The Jesus Quest: The Third Search for the Jew of Nazareth* (Downers Grove: IVP, 1995).

N. T. Wright, *The New Testament and the People of God* (London: SPCK, 1992).

— *Who was Jesus?* (London: SPCK, 1992).

— *Jesus and the Victory of God* (London: SPCK, 1996).

— 'Doing Justice to Jesus: A Response to J. D. Crossan', *Scottish Journal of Theology* 50 (1997), 359-79.

2

Cyril's *Twelve Anathemas*: An Exercise in Theological Moderation[1]

Anthony N. S. Lane

1. Background

a) The Characters

Perhaps the best-known episode in the early christological controversies is the clash between Cyril and Nestorius around the year 430. One of the fruits of this controversy is Cyril's notorious *Twelve Anathemas* (also known as the *Twelve Chapters*). But before considering the anathemas, we will review their background for the benefit of those who are unfamiliar with it or who have forgotten it. Orthodox Christology, as defined at the Council of Chalcedon in 451, makes four positive assertions in opposition to four heresies. The first two of the heretics lived in the fourth century. *Arius* denied the true deity of Christ. This teaching was condemned at the Council of Nicea in 325 and the condemnation was reaffirmed at the Council of Constantinople in 381.

One of Arius's most persistent opponents was *Apollinaris* of Laodicea, who himself had the misfortune to be branded a heretic at the end of his life. Apollinaris was clear on the deity of Christ, but portrayed Christ as less than fully human. He held that in Christ the eternal Word took the place of a rational human soul or spirit, whichever was perceived to be the highest human faculty. He held to the incarnation of the divine Word, but in such a manner that the incarnate one was less than fully human. Apollinaris was condemned at the Council of Constantinople in 381.

1. I am grateful to those who have commented on earlier versions of this paper, especially Drs Graham Gould and Norman Russell. They are not to be held responsible for any remaining aberrations.

By this stage the full deity and full humanity of Jesus Christ were clearly defined. In many ways this was the easy part. There now remained the daunting task of showing how deity and humanity could be combined in the one Christ. The remaining two heretics, Nestorius and Eutyches, erred in their attempts to do this.

Nestorius was an Antiochene theologian with a considerable reputation as a preacher. In 428 he was appointed patriarch of Constantinople. But while he may have been a gifted preacher, his actions as patriarch demonstrated a lack both of diplomacy and of political prudence. He preached against the doctrine, by now well-established amongst the Alexandrians, that the Virgin Mary was *theotokos*, the one who gave birth to God. He soon found himself in trouble with Cyril, the patriarch of Alexandria.

Cyril had been patriarch since 412, in succession to his uncle Theophilus. There had been rivalry between the sees of Alexandria and Constantinople since the third canon of the Council of Constantinople in 381 had declared that 'the bishop of Constantinople is to be honoured next after the bishop of Rome, because Constantinople is the new Rome.' Through this canon Constantinople supplanted Alexandria as the leading eastern see. But the new patriarchs of Constantinople had little practical power, while the patriarchs of Alexandria retained immense power, being described as the 'new pharaohs'. Cyril's predecessor Theophilus engineered the exile of the saintly John Chrysostom, Cyril had Nestorius branded a heretic and Cyril's successor Dioscorus did the same for Flavian of Constantinople. But while this ecclesiastical political dimension should not be forgotten, it would be mistaken to suppose that Cyril was simply out to humiliate his rival. The controversy with Nestorius involved serious christological issues about which both parties were deeply concerned.

b) Nestorius's Christology

Nestorius stood within the Antiochene, Word-Man tradition, though with his own distinctives. As with all of the Antiochenes, he was concerned to stress the transcendence, immutability and impassibility of the eternal Logos, in order to safeguard his deity.

Again in line with the Antiochene tradition, he sought to do this by making a sharp contrast between God the Word and Jesus the human being. It was the latter and not the former who was born of Mary, suffered and died for us. The Word experienced the sufferings of Jesus just as the emperor is dishonoured if someone throws rotten apples at his statue. This sharp contrast between Jesus and the Word is maintained because of Nestorius's concern to protect the transcendence and impassibility of the divine Word. Unfortunately the price for this protection is to all intents and purposes an abandonment of the doctrine of the incarnation. This was not a price that Cyril was prepared to pay.

Nestorius stressed the distinction between the deity and humanity of Christ. In Christ, he stated, there are two natures and two substances (deity and humanity). There are two beings or hypostases and Christ can even be described as two persons. It is not surprising that Nestorius, having ascribed to Christ two of each of the four entities discussed in the christological debates (nature, substance, hypostasis and person), found it hard to express the unity of Christ. His prime concern was the typical Antiochene one of protecting both the full deity and the true humanity of Christ. This he effectively does with his talk of two natures, two substances, two hypostases and two persons. But what of the unity of Christ? Nestorius wished to affirm this and attempted to do so. He did not wish to end with an Adoptionist view of Christ and sought to defend himself against the charge. The point that is at issue is not his desire to avoid Adoptionism nor his sincerity in claiming to have done so, but rather the effectiveness of his defence against Adoptionism.

Nestorius's Christology began with the human Jesus and the divine Word. He affirmed in Christ not just two natures (human and divine) but two persons (Jesus and the Word). These are two agents in the sense that some of the things recorded in the gospels are done by Jesus (e.g. sleeping) while others are done by the Word (e.g. miracles). For Nestorius these two persons or two agents are united in one Christ, but it is questionable whether any real unity can be achieved this way. Cyril certainly did not feel that Nestorius had safeguarded the unity of Christ.

c) Cyril's Christology

For Cyril the only way to arrive at one Christ is to recognise that it is God the Word who is the sole agent or subject in Christ. But what does it mean to say that the Word is the sole subject? Take the incident when Christ raised Lazarus. As a human being he wept over Lazarus, as God he raised him from the dead. But it was the same 'he' each time. Both were actions of the Word – acting in his own nature as God and acting in the flesh as human. Christ is one not because (as Nestorius suggested) the two persons Jesus and the Word are closely conjoined and united in purpose and will. Instead, he is one because Jesus *is* the Word, made flesh.

It is not that the Word inspires, indwells or cooperates with a human being (as the Antiochenes at times suggested) but rather that the Word becomes a human being (without ceasing to be God). Unless the Word is the one subject of Christ, there is no true incarnation. As Cyril argues, the Creed of Nicea says of the 'one Lord Jesus Christ' both that he is 'the Son of God, begotten from the Father' and that he (the same 'he') 'for us and for our salvation came down, was made flesh and became human'.

It follows simply that Mary is *theotokos*. Who was born of Mary? Jesus. Who is Jesus? The Word made flesh. As the creed states, he was begotten from the Father before all ages. He (the same he) was also born of Mary, who therefore bore the Word. He has a double birth: in eternity as God, in time as human. *Theotokos* affirms the fact that Jesus, who was born of Mary, is the incarnate Word not just a human being who was indwelt by the Word. Again, it was the Word who suffered, died and rose again. He did these things not (as Nestorius professed to believe Cyril to be saying) as God, in his divine nature, but as human. Of these two points, the issue of *theotokos* was resolved through the Nestorian controversy, while the issue of the suffering of the Word came to the fore in the 'Theopaschite' controversy of the sixth century.

Christ is not a conjunction (nor even a union) of Jesus and the Word. Instead, the divine Word unites to himself flesh animated by a living rational soul. He takes complete humanity (Cyril has learned from the condemnation of Apollinaris) but not an already existing human being. The Word and his humanity are united to form a single reality, a single hypostasis. Thus Cyril talks of the 'hypostatic union' of the Word with his flesh.

The Word unites with his humanity to form a single hypostasis and also a single nature. Cyril takes over the Apollinarian formula of 'the one incarnate nature of the Word'. After his condemnation Apollinaris' works were banned, but a number of them continued to circulate under the name of Athanasius. Thus Cyril adopted the formula, being unaware of its true origin. But while Cyril used an Apollinarian formula, it does not follow that he was guilty of Apollinarianism. On the point for which Apollinaris was condemned (denying the full humanity of Christ) Cyril is carefully orthodox. However, while Cyril took great care over his formal orthodoxy, maintaining that Christ had a human soul, he has been criticised (as has much of orthodox theology) for failing to give sufficient weight to the humanity of Christ in practice.

What of the suffering of Christ? Cyril believed, with all of the early church, that the Word as God is impassible, incapable of suffering. But his doctrine of the incarnation, his belief that the Word is the one subject in Christ, means that the same Word suffered in the flesh, as a human being. This was a paradox which Cyril captures nicely in a phrase: 'he suffered impassibly'. To be more precise, he impassibly made his own the sufferings of his own flesh.

For Cyril, the Word becomes flesh/a human being. But this does not involve any change in or diminution of the divine nature. It is not incarnation by mutation – the Word does not exchange a human for a divine nature, like a prince turning into a frog. Nor is it incarnation by diminution or subtraction – the Word's divine nature does not shrink to the size of human nature, like a balloon being deflated. Instead it is incarnation by addition – the Word takes human nature in addition to his divine nature, as an apple branch might be grafted onto a pear tree. (These three analogies are mine, not Cyril's.) Thus the incarnation involves no interruption of the divine life of the Word. While he was a baby in his mother's arms he was still filling the universe as God.

For Cyril, as for all of the early fathers, the doctrine of the person of Christ is important for the doctrine of salvation. Like Apollinaris, he stresses that we receive life from the lifegiving flesh of Christ (John 6). This is possible because the flesh of Christ is not just that of a human being closely united to the Word but is itself the flesh of the Word incarnate.

d) The Controversy

It should by now be clear why Cyril was concerned about Nestorius's teaching. In the late summer of 429 he wrote his *First Letter to Nestorius*, urging him to accept that Mary was *theotokos*. Nestorius sent an evasive reply. Cyril responded with his *Second Letter to Nestorius*, one of the texts that was officially approved at the Council of Chalcedon. At that stage Cyril had yet to win the support of Rome. This letter is carefully written. Nestorius had accused Cyril of teaching that it was the divine nature of the Word that was born of Mary, suffered and died. Cyril devotes as much space to refuting this charge as he does to attacking Nestorius. He takes care to adopt a reasonable and courteous tone towards Nestorius. On June 15th 430 Nestorius responded. He did not seem to have grasped Cyril's point, still accusing him of teaching that the divine *nature* of the Word is passible and had its beginning with the Virgin Mary.

In the summer of 430 Cyril wrote to Rome against Nestorius. On August 11th a synod met there and decided against Nestorius. He was required to recant within ten days of being informed, Cyril being entrusted with the execution of this. Early in November Cyril wrote his *Third Letter to Nestorius*. The tone of this letter is very different from the previous one. Now that Cyril has the support of Rome he need no longer tread softly. Nestorius is simply required to recant. *Twelve Anathemas* are appended to the letter for Nestorius to sign. These are drafted in such a way as to guarantee that Nestorius would not sign them.

Essentially the message of both the letter and the anathemas is very simple. Cyril is repeating one basic point, which he expresses in many different ways: Jesus Christ is not a human being who was in a unique relationship with God the Word but he is himself the divine Word, made flesh. In other words, rather than speak of

Jesus *and* the Word we must confess that Jesus *is* the Word. It is this point that comes up in all of the issues that Cyril tackles. Nestorius is guilty not of twelve different errors but of one error that has implications in twelve different areas. Cyril responds not with twelve different doctrines but with one doctrine which has implications in twelve different areas.

At this stage it will be helpful to examine the text of the *Twelve Anathemas*:[2]

1. If anyone does not acknowledge that Emmanuel is truly God and therefore that the holy Virgin is *theotokos* (for she gave fleshly birth to the Word of God made flesh): let him be anathema.

2. If anyone does not acknowledge that the Word of God the Father has been hypostatically united with flesh and that he is one Christ with one flesh, so that the same one [Christ] is at once both God and human, let him be anathema.

3. If anyone [when talking of] the one Christ divides the hypostases after the [hypostatic] union, joining them together merely in a conjunction on the basis of dignity, authority or power, instead of combining them into a natural union, let him be anathema.

4. If anyone divides between two persons or hypostases the terms contained in the Gospels and apostolic writings or applied to Christ by the saints or by himself, and applies some to the man considered separately from the Word of God and others to the Word of God the Father alone (on the grounds that they are divine), let him be anathema.

5. If anyone has the nerve to state that Christ is a God-bearing man [i.e. indwelt by God] instead of saying that he is truly God, being [God's] one Son by nature because 'the Word became flesh' and 'shared in flesh and blood like us' [Heb. 2:14], let him be anathema.

---

2. The translation is my own.

6. If anyone says that the Word of God the Father is Christ's God or Lord instead of acknowledging the same [Christ] as at once God and human, on the scriptural ground that 'the Word became flesh', let him be anathema.

7. If anyone says that the human Jesus is merely energised by God the Word and that the glory of the Only-begotten is attributed to Jesus [not as his own but] as given to him by someone else [i.e. the Word], let him be anathema.

8. If anyone has the nerve to state that we should worship the 'assumed man' [Jesus] along with God the Word, and that the one [Jesus] should be praised and called God along with the other [the Word] (for to add 'along with' will always imply this), instead of worshipping Emmanuel with a single worship and ascribing to him a single act of praise because 'the Word became flesh', let him be anathema.

9. If anyone says that the one Lord Jesus Christ has been glorified by the Spirit in such a way that (1) the power which Jesus exercised was someone's else received through the Spirit and (2) his power over unclean spirits and his power to perform miracles on people came from the Spirit, instead of saying that the Spirit by which he performed these miracles was his own Spirit, let him be anathema.

10. The divine Scripture states that Christ has been made 'the high priest and apostle of our confession' [Heb. 3:1] and that he 'gave himself up for us as a fragrant sacrifice to God the Father' [Eph. 5:2]. So if anyone says that it was not the Word of God himself who was made our high priest and apostle when he became flesh and a human being like us but another distinct from him, a man born of a woman yet separate from him, or if anyone says that [Jesus] offered his sacrifice not just for us alone but for himself as well (for he who knew no sin needed no sacrifice), let him be anathema.

11. If anyone does not acknowledge that the Lord's flesh is life-giving and that it belongs to the very Word of God the Father, but instead says that it belongs to someone different joined to him [the Word] by dignity or merely indwelt by God, rather than being (as we said) life-giving because it has become the flesh of the Word who is able to give life to all, let him be anathema.

12. If anyone does not acknowledge that the Word of God suffered in the flesh, was crucified in the flesh, tasted death in the flesh and became first-born from the dead because as God he is life and life-giving, let him be anathema.

Cyril's letter and anathemas brought the controversy to a head. Nestorius circulated the anathemas to a number of leading Antiochene theologians, who attacked them. Cyril responded. At Nestorius's request, the emperor called a council to meet at Ephesus. This was due to open on June 7th 431 but the Antiochenes were late arriving. On the 22nd Cyril proceeded without them and held a council which condemned Nestorius. Four days later the Antiochenes arrived and held a minority council which condemned Cyril and his anathemas. On July 10th the Roman delegates arrived and endorsed Cyril's council. For nearly two years there was a serious split between the Alexandrian and Antiochene parties in the East. This was brought to a conclusion by the Antiochenes accepting the condemnation of Nestorius and Cyril accepting an Antiochene declaration of faith called the *Formula of Reunion*. This is relevant to our present topic as it has been suggested that Cyril contradicted his *Twelve Anathemas* by accepting the *Formula*.

2. The Anathemas

a) Separate Issues

It is the contention of this paper that Cyril's *Twelve Anathemas* have been unfairly criticised and that they exemplify his theological moderation. We should clarify what is and is not being claimed. *First*, it is not being suggested that the anathemas are *diplomatically* moderate. Cyril's aim at this stage was not to negotiate with Nestorius but to face him with the choice of recantation or condemnation. It can freely be admitted that the anathemas are aggressive and provocative in their tone. Kelly's comment is fair: 'deliberately provocative, these anathemas summarize the Cyrilline Christology in uncompromising terms'.[3] Wickham refers to 'the peremptory, not to say insulting, nature' of Cyril's demand of Nestorius.[4]

Secondly, it is not being claimed that the errors condemned are all exact representations of Nestorius's teaching. Strictly speaking, Cyril does not say that they are, only that Nestorius should disown them. Of course, it was in Cyril's own interests to get near to his target. If the errors condemned were as far removed as some claim from what Nestorius taught, he would have had no problem in disowning them. As it is, the anathemas ruthlessly expose the weakness in Nestorius's christology. The Antiochenes attacked the anathemas not on the grounds that they misrepresent Nestorius but because they objected to the positive teaching contained in them, at least as they understood that teaching. This point will be examined carefully below.

Thirdly, Cyril is sometimes criticised for the one-sided character of the anathemas, for the fact that they repeatedly reject adoptionism without also rejecting Apollinarianism or the confusion of the deity and humanity of Christ. It is true that the anathemas are monotonously one-sided. The same basic point is repeatedly hammered home – you may not refer to Jesus *and* the Word as if they are two beings, but you must acknowledge that Jesus *is* the Word, made flesh. But the anathemas fail to condemn Apollinarianism for the same reason that they fail to condemn Donatism and atheism – these are not the heresies of which Nestorius was suspected. Sellers is not altogether fair to Cyril on this point: 'In his Anathematisms [Cyril] had not explicitly denied

---

3. J. N. D. Kelly, *Early Christian Doctrines* (London: A. & C. Black, 1977, 5th edition) 324.

4. L. R. Wickham, 'Cyril of Alexandria and the apple of discord,' *Studia Patristica* 15:I, 380.

the notion of the "confusion" of the natures of Jesus Christ, or the teaching of Apollinarius of Laodicea that the Logos had taken the place of the human rational soul in him.'[5] True, but that was not the purpose of the anathemas. Sellers does however proceed to note that Cyril's orthodoxy on both of these points is clear from his second and third letters to Nestorius. Others, following Cyril's Antiochene critics, do not merely charge the anathemas with failure to condemn Apollinarianism but claim that they actually fall into the error themselves. This charge will be considered later.

Finally, there is the question of Cyril's *linguistic* moderation. This is not strictly our present topic, but it should be noticed in passing that Cyril is cautious in this respect. He rejects talk of two hypostases or persons in Christ. Positively he calls upon Nestorius to accept the (new) term 'hypostatic union'. Christological terminology was still fluid at this stage[6] and Cyril seeks to justify his new formula. In response to Theodoret he states that it means 'nothing else than only that the nature of the Logos – that is, the hypostasis, which is the Logos himself was truly united to human nature, without any change or confusion'.[7] Cyril does not call upon Nestorius to renounce the traditional Antiochene talk of the two natures of Christ, though anathema 3 does refer to a 'natural union' (*henôsis physikê*).[8] This phrase offended the Antiochenes who took it to imply that the union was inevitable to the Word and not a voluntary expression of his love. In his reply to Theodoret, Cyril explains that *physikê* implies a 'real' union as opposed to a merely 'moral' or 'acquired' union, such as Nestorius taught.[9] Thus Cyril's terminology is not such as would altogether

5. R. V. Sellers, *The Council of Chalcedon* (London: S.P.C.K., 1961) 9.

6. Cf. Wickham, 'Cyril of Alexandria and the apple of discord,' 388; N. Russell, *Cyril of Alexandria* (London & New York: Routledge, 2000) 40f.

7. *Contra Theodoretum* 20 [on anathema 2] (*ACO* 1.1.6, 115), cited by R. A. Norris, 'Christological Models in Cyril of Alexandria,' *Studia Patristica* 13:II, 263.

8. J. Meyendorff, *Christ in Eastern Christian Thought* (New York: St Vladimir's Seminary Press, 1975) 21, is over-charitable to Cyril in stating that 'the "single nature" appears neither in the *Anathematisms* against Nestorius nor in the [*Formula of Reunion*]'.

9. *Contra Theodoretum* 27f., 30 (*ACO* 1.1.6, 118-20).

please an Antiochene, but it is not to be seen as precise, technical language. By affirming one hypostasis and person, hypostatic union, natural union, Cyril is simply expressing in different terms his basic conviction that there is a union between the Word and his flesh/manhood such that the Word is the sole subject of all the experiences of Jesus Christ.

b) Relation between the Anathemas and the Third Letter
Crucial to the interpretation of the anathemas is the question of their relation to the third letter to Nestorius. Two things are certain: that the anathemas were sent together with the letter and that they reached Theodoret and Andrew on their own, separated from the letter. This is very important for the Antiochene interpretation of the anathemas. It accounts for some of the vehemence of their reactions and has helped to gain for the anathemas the reputation of being extreme. But were the anathemas originally separate from the letter? R. Y. Ebied and L. R. Wickham have published a previously unknown letter apparently by Cyril. In it Cyril denies rumours that 'after he had changed his views he wrote the letter and put it at the head of the chapters'.[10] He claims that the anathemas were added after the letter was complete. The editors note that 'there is perhaps a certain difference in tone between the polemics of the [anathemas] and the (relatively) sober exposition of the [letter] which might give ground for the suspicion that the difference followed a change of mind'.[11] Either way, the fact remains that the anathemas as sent were appended to the letter and they must be interpreted in the context of and against the background of the letter. This point is fundamental for the interpretation of the anathemas. Frances Young calls the anathemas 'bald hostile statements asserted without the necessary niceties and safeguards which Cyril had taken the trouble to include in his more discursive explanations'.[12] This charge is plausible – but only so long as the anathemas are read in isolation from the letter which precedes them.

10. R. Y. Ebied & L. R. Wickham, 'An Unknown Letter of Cyril of Alexandria in Syriac,' *JTS* 23 (1971), 434.
11. Ibid., 425.
12. F. Young, *From Nicaea to Chalcedon* (London: SCM, 1983), 220.

What is the relationship between the letter and the anathemas? As is often noted, the subject matter is not totally identical and the order of the anathemas does not altogether correspond to the order of topics in the letter. Wickham offers a convincing explanation.[13] Pope Celestine charged Cyril to lay two distinct but related requirements before Nestorius: to affirm the catholic faith and to condemn his own errors. The letter, with its exposition of the Nicene Creed, presents him with the catholic faith; the anathemas present him with his errors.

c) Theological Moderation
Having dispensed with these preliminaries we come to our central point, the theological moderation of the anathemas. It is the contention of this paper that the anathemas express traditional Alexandrian christology clearly and succinctly, but not in an extreme form. The basic thrust of the anathemas is that Jesus of Nazareth is none other than the Word incarnate. The sole subject of the human life of Jesus is the Word. In a real sense the anathemas do no more than state this fact and draw out some of its implications. If such a belief is extreme, then so are the anathemas. Otherwise they are not. Frances Young concludes her discussion of the debate over the anathemas with an apposite comment: 'The essential difference remains: the Antiochenes could not make the Logos directly the subject of incarnation, passion and death, whereas that was precisely what Cyril was trying to do'.[14]

How can we demonstrate Cyril's theological moderation? The fairest way seems to be to consider the objections made by the Antiochenes at the time. We will consider the reactions of Theodoret and Andrew of Samosata.[15] In considering the justice

---

13. Wickham, 'Cyril of Alexandria and the apple of discord,' 390.
14. Young, *Nicaea to Chalcedon*, 228.
15. These works, together with Cyril's response to each and his *Explanation* of the anathemas are found in *PG* 76 and *ACO* 1.1.5-7. A useful summary for each anathema is found in H. T. Bindley/F. W. Green, *The Oecumenical Documents of the Faith* (London: Methuen, 1950, 4th edition), 124-37. Translations of Cyril's *Explanation* are found in J. A. McGuckin, *St. Cyril of Alexandria: The Christological Controversy* (Leiden, etc.: E. J. Brill, 1994) 282-93; Russell, *Cyril of Alexandria*, 175-89. Young, *Nicaea to Chalcedon*,

of their charges reference will be made especially to Cyril's third letter and also to his second letter and to his responses to the Antiochenes. The last will be used very sparingly as it could be claimed that Cyril was backing down in the face of criticism. The aim throughout is not to evaluate Cyril's christology as a whole but the specific statement of it found in the anathemas, understood in their context in the third letter.

d) The Charges

The Antiochenes make many accusations against Cyril, but these reduce to three basic charges. *First*, that the Word is not truly God, either because he changes or suffers or because he is divided from the Father – i.e. Arianism. *Secondly*, that Christ's humanity is incomplete, either because it is changed into deity or because some element of human nature is missing – i.e. Apollinarianism. *Thirdly*, that Christ's deity and humanity are confused together, i.e. what later came to be called Eutychianism. In other words, the Antiochenes are accusing Cyril of three out of the four heresies condemned at Chalcedon – the fourth being Nestorianism, of which he is not accused!

The specific charges will now be itemised, under these three headings. A sober consideration of the charges will lead us to the conclusion that compared with the anathemas, which point with painful precision and clarity to the central weakness of Nestorius's christology, the Antiochenes' criticisms are mostly wide of the mark and implausible.[16] However, it must be repeated in their

---

220-29 also surveys the debate, anathema by anathema. Further charges are found in some Nestorian texts published by L. Abramowski & A. E. Goodman: *A Nestorian Collection of Christological Texts* vol. 2 (Cambridge: C.U.P., 1972) 31-36, 75-88, 125-30 and there are twelve counter-anathemas by 'Nestorius' (found in the same section of Bindley/Green). These have been considered but add nothing of substance to the present discussion.

16. '[The Orientals], their minds warped through prejudice, went out of their way to misinterpret doctrinal statements drawn up solely in the anti-Nestorian interest' (Sellers, *Council of Chalcedon*, 9f.). Cyril was of course not the most honourable of opponents, as Sellers also observes. J. Mahé notes: 'Il me semble que Nestorius envoya à Antioche les Anathématismes *sans la lettre* qui les développait et les justifiait. On ne s'expliquerait guère autrement les objections, qui étaient presque toutes résolues à l'avance dans la lettre en

defence that they were considering the anathemas out of their setting at the end of Cyril's third letter.

First, the charge of *Arianism*. The most commonly repeated charge of the Antiochenes, found in response to no less than seven of the anathemas, is that the Word is *changed into* flesh, according to Cyril [1, 5, 6, 8, 9, 10, 11].[17] Apart from the fact that the anathemas never state this, the charge is clearly denied in the third letter:

> We declare that the flesh was not changed into the nature of Godhead and that neither was the inexpressible nature of God the Word converted into the nature of flesh. He is, indeed, utterly unchangeable and immutable ever remaining, as the Bible says, the same.[18]

It can safely be said that Cyril rejected no less vehemently than the Antiochenes any suggestion that Christ's deity was changed into humanity. More plausible is the next charge, that the Word *suffered* and is *passible* [4, 10, 12], the implication being that Cyril is either an Arian or a Patripassian[19] [12]. The twelfth anathema clearly states that the Word suffered. But here Cyril is often unfairly treated. Frances Young, for instance, states that '*without qualification*, suffering and death were predicated of the Logos'.[20] This is simply not true. There is the thrice-repeated qualification 'in the flesh' (*sarki*). If we read this in the light of the second and third letters to Nestorius, it is clear that Cyril held to the impassibility of the Word in his own divine nature. In the third letter he refers to the Word 'claiming the sufferings of his flesh as his own impassibly'[21] and the affirmation of impassibility is more explicit in the previous letter.

---

question' ('Les Anathématismes de Saint Cyrille d'Alexandrie,' *Revue d'Histoire Ecclésiastique* 7 (1906) 506 (his emphasis)).

17. The relevant anathemas are, here and hereafter, listed in the text within [ ].

18. Cyril of Alexandria, *Select Letters* (ed/tr L. R. Wickham) (Oxford: O.U.P., 1983) 17.

19. One would have expected the charge that Cyril was a Theopaschite rather than a Patripassian, but this is what the Orientals claimed: If the Word suffered *kata physin* and was *homoousios* with the Father, the Father also is passible (*ACO* 1.1.7, 61, lines 25-28).

20. Young, *Nicaea to Chalcedon*, 227 (my emphasis).

These two charges, that the Word is changed and that he is passible, are the most plausible ones under the general heading of Arianism. We need not detain ourselves with the less plausible charges that the Word is a creature [1, 4, 10], that the Son is divided from the Father [4] or even that Cyril denied the virgin birth [1].

The charge of Arianism is in fact the most common charge made by the Antiochenes, which in terms of frequency easily outweighs all the other charges put together. It is found in response to no less than nine of the *Twelve Anathemas*, while the combined charges of Apollinarianism and confusion of the natures ('Eutychianism') are found in response to only five of the anathemas. This is paradoxical since even Cyril's enemies today, who rush to accuse him of Apollinarianism and 'Eutychianism', would not consider the charge of Arianism to be plausible. No doubt the Antiochenes felt that Arianism was the most damning charge which they could try to bring against Cyril. But the fact that they prosecuted the charge so vehemently must be taken as evidence of the extent to which they simply failed to grasp the true nature of Cyril's christology.

The *second* charge is that of *Apollinarianism*. Theodoret denies that Christ's humanity was transmuted into the nature of God, which he thought Cyril to be teaching [8]. The Antiochenes feared that Cyril's talk of the Word and the flesh implied an incomplete humanity, devoid of a rational soul, which is Apollinarianism [11]. Here it must be admitted that there is nothing in the anathemas themselves to refute this. However, in the third letter Cyril qualifies 'he has become flesh' with the addition of 'that is to say a human being endowed with a rational soul' (*anthrôpos empsychômenos psychê logikê*).[22] Cyril retained the traditional Word-flesh terminology of Alexandria, while qualifying it in a suitably anti-Apollinarian way. The qualification is explicit in the third letter (as elsewhere) but not in the anathemas, hence the Antiochene misunderstanding. In his reply to Theodoret, Cyril states that he, like John in 1:14, was using flesh to mean the whole of humanity.[23]

---

21. Cyril, *Select Letters*, 21.
22. Ibid., 24, where the *m* is missing from *empsychômenos*. The translation is my own.

Von Campenhausen's claim that the anathemas 'were *rightly* interpreted as Apollinarian by the Antiochenes'[24] is without foundation when one sees them in their context at the end of the third letter.

The *third* and final charge is that of *confusing the natures* ('Eutychianism'). The Antiochenes repeatedly accuse Cyril of mixing or confusing Christ's humanity and deity by his teaching of hypostatic or natural union [2, 3, 4, 11]. As has already been seen, Cyril was adamant that the incarnation involves no change at all in the nature of Godhead or the divine nature of the Word.[25] In his reply to these accusations Cyril again emphasises that the incarnation does not involve any confusion or mixture of deity and humanity in Christ.[26] In his letter to John of Antioch accepting the *Formula of Reunion* Cyril protests against the charge:

As for those who say there was a mixture or confusion or blending of God the Word with the flesh, let thy Holiness deem it well to stop their mouths; for it is likely that some are commonly reporting this also about me, as though I had either thought or said so. But I am so far from thinking such a thing that I deem those to be actually out of their mind who can for a moment suppose it possible for a shadow of turning to take place in respect of the Divine Nature of the Word.[27]

e) The Fourth Anathema and the Formula of Reunion
One of the anathemas which provoked this charge is the infamous fourth anathema, in which Cyril prohibits the distribution of statements about Christ between two persons or hypostases, the Word and the man. It is so often stated that Cyril was forced to go against this in signing the *Formula of Reunion* that it has become something of a truism.[28] But on what grounds is Cyril's

---

23. *Contra Theodoretum* 87 [on anathema 11] (*ACO* 1.1.6, 143).

24. H. von Campenhausen, *The Fathers of the Greek Church* (London: A. & C. Black, 1963) 166 (my emphasis). W. H. C. Frend, *Saints and Sinners in the Early Church* (Wilmington (DE): Michael Glazier, 1985) 153 considers some of the anathemas 'obviously Apollinarian in inspiration'.

25. See at n. 18, above.

26. *Contra Theodoretum* 35f. [on anathema 4] (*ACO* 1.1.6, 123).

27. Bindley/Green, *Oecumenical Documents of the Faith*, 222.

28. H. Chadwick, 'Eucharist and Christology in the Nestorian Controversy,'

inconsistency repeatedly affirmed? Surprising though it may appear, most of those making the claim do so explicitly on the ground that the anathema prohibits the distribution of the sayings between two natures,[29] despite the fact that it does nothing of the sort. The anathema prohibits talk of two persons or hypostases, of a man Jesus separate from the Word. The *Formula* merely refers some sayings about Christ to one or other of his two *natures*. This was not new to Cyril, both in the sense that he had always distinguished between the 'divine' and 'human' sayings of Christ and that he had always recognised that some could not be referred to the divine nature. In the second letter to Nestorius, for example, he calls it sheer madness to refer Christ's death to his divine nature and attributes it instead to his flesh.[30]

Paul Galtier presents a detailed case against the fourth anathema.[31] He begins by claiming that in the fourth anathema 'saint Cyrille n'interdisait pas seulement de distribuer les paroles du Christ ou celles qui le concernaient entre deux *prosôpa*; même étant admis un seul *prosôpon*, il interdisait la répartition entre ses deux natures'.[32] But this is not true of the anathema itself. Galtier bases his claim on Cyril's three defences of his anathemas: his explanation of them at Ephesus and his replies to Theodoret and Andrew. On the basis of a general reference to these three works, he states:

> Il ne niait pas la diversité des paroles ni celle des natures suivant lesquelles le Fils de Dieu incarné les prononçait; les unes étaient *theoprepeis* et les autres *anthrôpoprepeis* ; mais il interdisait de les distribuer entre les deux natures comme entre deux êtres pris à part

---

JTS 2 (1951) 147; idem, *The Early Church* (Harmondsworth: Penguin, 1967) 199f.; E. Gebremedhin, *Life-Giving Blessing* (Uppsala: Uppsala University, 1977) 38 & n. 61; Meyendorff, *Christ in Eastern Christian Thought*, 218, n. 22; M. F. Wiles, *The Spiritual Gospel* (Cambridge: C.U.P., 1960) 130f.; Young, *Nicaea to Chalcedon*, 224.

29. Chadwick, *Early Church*, 199; Gebremedhin, *Life-Giving Blessing*, 38; Young, *Nicaea to Chalcedon*, 224. Cf. at nn. 32f., below.

30. Cyril, *Select Letters*, 9.

31. P. Galtier, 'Saint Cyrille d'Alexandrie et Saint Léon le Grand à Chalcédoine' in A. Grillmeier & H. Bacht (eds.), *Das Konzil von Chalkedon* vol. 1 (Würzburg: Echter-Verlag, 1979) 372-77.

32. Ibid., 372.

l'un de l'autre. Faire autrement lui paraissait imiter Nestorius et répartir ces paroles entre le Dieu et l'homme distingués dans le Christ.[33]

Now it is certainly true that Cyril rejects the distribution of the sayings to two persons and affirms that all can be attributed to the one subject. But the three works cited do not support the claim that Cyril widened his opposition to ban all distribution of the sayings between two natures, as Galtier states but neglects to substantiate from any specific passage. What Galtier does show is that while Cyril always recognised two sets of sayings about Christ (human and divine) he was reluctant to attribute the human sayings to a human nature, preferring to talk of 'the conditions of humanity'.[34] But the most that this would prove is that Cyril was himself reluctant to speak of two natures in Christ and (maybe) that his own christology is therefore weak at this point. While Cyril might reject a view of the two natures which divides them into two persons, he does not in the anathema or in the three resulting works ever reject two nature language as such. This is further evidence of the anathemas' moderation in that Cyril permits here (by his silence) that which he himself did not like (two natures language). What he does reject, repeatedly, is all talk of two persons or two hypostases or two sons. Equally he consistently recognises that some of the sayings are 'divine' and others 'human'.

It is clear from the passage as a whole that Galtier's real objection to Cyril is his insistence that all the sayings can be referred to one subject and the consequent conflict with Leo's *Tome*. Thus, 'Cyril avait beau protester qu'il tenait compte de l'incarnation et qu'il savait distinguer les paroles convenant à l'une ou à l'autre des deux natures, il n'en maintenait pas moins que toutes devaient être attribuées à l'unique hypostase, ou nature incarnée du Verbe'.[35] After this admission that Cyril was not totally opposed to two natures talk, it is not surprising that Galtier ends by

---

33. Ibid., 373.
34. Ibid., 373-77.
35. Ibid., 376. Cf. pp. 372, 375. Galtier bases the statement about two natures on a citation of *ACO* and *PG*, but is clearly working from *PG* since the reference to *physis* appears in *ACO* only as a variant reading.

concluding that while the *Formula of Reunion* expressed Andrew of Samosata's position on the sayings, 'ce n'était pas la contradiction formelle de son anathématisme'.[36] Cyril is utterly consistent in rejecting all attempts to apportion the sayings to two persons, hypostases, sons or subjects; he is less dogmatic about the use of the word nature, which is why he could accept the *Formula of Reunion*.

The compatibility of the *Formula of Reunion* with Cyril's christology is a complex issue. Graham Gould, in a recent article, examines this wider question.[37] He shows the tension that exists between Cyril's view that *all* of the sayings relate to the one person and the position of the *Formula* that *some* relate to the one person while others relate to the two natures. While this points to a possible inconsistency of Cyril's in accepting the *Formula*, Gould acknowledges[38] that this does not involve any explicit contradiction between the *Formula* and anathema 4, which is our present concern.

f) Conclusion
'The chapters will always shock timid minds. The delicate veil of nuanced provisos is torn away, and we are presented with the logical consequences of what we have been saying all along, if, that is, we have been speaking of Incarnation'.[39] This is one of the reasons why the anathemas have been seen as extreme – the brutal clarity with which they expose the weak point of Nestorius's christology. The other reason is the habit, begun in all innocence by Theodoret and Andrew, of interpreting them out of their context at the end of the third letter. In the light of that letter, it can be seen that Cyril's anathemas do no more than state traditional Alexandrian christology in a forthright manner. The charge of theological extremism is unfounded.

---

36. Ibid., 377.

37. G. Gould, 'Cyril of Alexandria and the Formula of Reunion,' *Downside Review* 106 (1988) 235-52, which examines Cyril's comments on the relevant passage after the event (especially *Letters* 41:13-20 (to Acacius) and 44 (to Eulogius)).

38. Ibid., 249. McGuckin, *St. Cyril of Alexandria*, 112, rejects Theodoret's charge that Cyril abandoned the Fourth Anathema.

39. Wickham in Cyril, *Select Letters*, xlii.

3

Christology From Below and From Above

Geoffrey Grogan

I want you to imagine that you know little of the Christian faith and that you are on a Mediterranean cruise. During this holiday, you visit two famous churches and you understand from your guide that they are both Christian places of worship. You enter both with the same question in your mind, 'Who is this Jesus of whom the Christians make so much?'

In the first church, a Roman Catholic one, you see a crucifix. On it is a Man evidently in his death agonies. Around this crucifix are a number of visitors, some of them obviously Roman Catholics themselves, treating the crucifix with great reverence and clearly much moved by it. Here then, you say, is the Jesus Christians love. You think much about this during your cruise and you reckon you are beginning to understand what Christianity is and why Jesus means so much to Christians.

Then you enter a second church, an Eastern Orthodox one. As soon as you enter, your senses are almost overwhelmed at the sight of a giant painting of the head and shoulders of a glorious Person, the Powerful Ruler of all, the Pantocrator, which occupies the whole of the east wall. At this church too a little crowd gathers to adore this picture. You enquire who it is and you are told that it is Jesus.

You are somewhat bewildered as you try to reconcile the two experiences. Perhaps, you say to yourself, there are two totally different conceptions of Jesus held by two different groups of Christians, possibly even two quite different religions both calling themselves Christian. But then you discover that you have a Roman Catholic and an Eastern Orthodox Christian among your fellow-passengers. In talking to them you find that the Orthodox one was very moved by the crucifix and the Catholic by the Pantocrator. Your perplexity increases, but you at least realise that these are not regarded by either of them as totally irreconcilable conceptions of Jesus, but rather that they reveal some difference of emphasis, the first on his humanity and all the trials and sufferings that involved, and the second on his deity and his great power and authority.

Is it really possible for the same person to be at once God and Man and to fulfil the very different roles of crucified Saviour and almighty Ruler? You decide to give the matter more thought. But where are you to begin? That is the big question. In your own attempted understanding of him, do you start with that tragic human figure or with the glorious Ruler of all?

It is not easy to answer this question simply by an appeal to the New Testament. Should we view Jesus as the first disciples did, seeing him first of all as the Man they encountered on the shore of the Sea of Galilee, a man of a particular age and appearance and occupation – or in the full blaze of Divine glory, as Paul saw him on the Damascus Road, especially as initially he apparently did not even identify him as Jesus, when he asked the question, 'Who are you, Lord?'

1. Some Basic Questions

(a) Is the issue one of method or of substance?

We should treat it as a matter of method. Questions of method are logically prior to processes of research and therefore to any conclusions on matters of substance which may be reached as a result of research. What then is our method to be? We may perhaps start with the facts concerning the life of Jesus and from those particular facts arrive at a conclusion as to who he is. On the other hand, we may begin with one of the great Christological statements of the New Testament, such as John 1:14, and construct our Christology on the basis of it. There is a parallel in the doctrine of Scripture, where we may begin either with the Biblical phenomena or with some great theological statement or statements of Scripture about itself.

Colin Gunton has said, 'In Christology, matters of method and content are closely related.... A Christology from below is hard put to avoid being a Christology of a divinized man.'[1] Perhaps, but this is not inevitable. We have some formidable historical examples, including Martin Luther, of a Christology that he at least thought of as from below – whether in fact this was really the case is arguable – which reaches the highest ontological conclusions about Jesus. He said, for instance, 'The Scriptures begin very gently, and lead us on to Christ as to a man, and then to one who is Lord over all creatures, and after that to one who is God. But the philosophers and doctors have insisted on beginning from above; and so they have become fools. We must begin from below and after that come upwards.'[2]

Brian Hebblethwaite writes of the dispute and he says, 'These are very confusing slogans; for clearly all Christology is from below in that it is a branch of theology undertaken by human beings. God does not write Christology books. But of course the slogans "from above" and "from below" are designed to mark the contrast between those who base their Christology on the man Jesus of Nazareth and those who base it on God's own being and acts in revelation and incarnation. But even here the distinction is not clear-cut. For it may be thought wise (or indeed essential) to begin from below, that is with the Man Jesus of Nazareth, and yet the enquiry may still lead us in the end to an understanding of Jesus as coming to us from the side of God, i.e. "from above". Only if one begins and ends with Jesus the man does one's Christology remain thoroughly earth-bound – "from below" – throughout.'[3]

---

1. C. Gunton, *Yesterday and Today: A Study of Continuities in Christology*, (London: Darton, Longman and Todd, 1983), p. 53.

2. English translation from M. Luther, *Werke: Kritische Gesamtamtausgabe* (Weimar: Herman Bohlau und Nachfolger, 1883ff), xii, p. 412, quoted in H.R. Mackintosh, *The Doctrine of the Person of Jesus Christ*, (Edinburgh: T. and T. Clark, 1912), p.232.

3. B. Hebblethwaite, *The Incarnation: Collected Essays in Christology*, (Cambridge, CUP, 1987), p. 80.

(b) Are these alternative or complementary methods?

After leaving school my first job was in a bank. On the first day I was introduced to double entry book-keeping, a method where two accounting systems are employed simultaneously so that each provides a check on the other. Twice a year we had a major day, the dreaded half-yearly balance, when we checked the accounts to find if the books balanced, in other words to see if the figures produced by the two systems tallied, and if they did not we then spent hours, sometimes until midnight or after, trying to discover where things had gone wrong.

Perhaps in Christology we may use not the one method only but both, and use each as a check on the other. If Jesus Christ is both fully divine and fully human and at the same time one Person (in other words, if the Chalcedonian Definition is true), we should not arrive at different Christologies by the two different approaches.

We should then at least be open to the possibility that we may approach the Person of Jesus Christ both from the standpoint of his humanity and of his deity.

(c) What are the proper starting and terminating points?

We need to be clear from the start as to what we mean by 'below' and 'above', and this applies whether we are moving from above to below or vice versa.

We could of course treat this matter in a completely open way, allowing a multiplicity of starting and terminating points, so that we would raise a whole series of questions extra to those being treated in this paper. Such a study could certainly have its place, but it could not be undertaken within the scope of a paper like this, but would require treatment in a considerable book-length work.

We will then view Jesus as a man in the fullest sense of that term. A number of unsatisfactory views of his humanity prevailed in the early centuries of the church even among comparatively orthodox thinkers. Clement of Alexandria, for instance, held that Christ did not know any pain, sorrow or emotion. Origen certainly believed Christ had a human soul, for this was related to his peculiar concept of a pre-mundane fall, but his body appears to have been made of a more rarefied matter than ours, having a kind of ethereal quality. Hilary of Poitiers maintained that his body was really above pain by nature so that he could only experience it by a constant act of kenosis. He also said that his sufferings affected him as an arrow passes through fire and air.

Such views, inadequate as they seem to us, were never deemed heretical by the church of that period. Then came an explicit denial which had the effect of clarifying thought on the matter, for Apollinaris denied a human rational soul to Jesus, holding that the Logos took the place of the rational soul in him. This came to be condemned as heretical.

We will also be viewing Jesus as divine in the highest sense of that word. We will not think of him as a mere Demiurge, like some of the Gnostics, an exalted Angel, the first and greatest of God's creatures, as the Arians. Neither will we see him, after the manner of contemporary theological pluralists, as one of a number of legitimate ways to God. A pluralism which chooses Christ from a number of options as the way to God is at best a sophisticated form of monolatry or henotheism,[4] and it means that we are compelled to surrender our Lord's unique place within the Triune Godhead. We will not be satisfied either with John Hick's suggestion that 'God Incarnate' is a kind of metaphor. He says, 'We see in Jesus a human being extraordinarily open to God's influence and thus living to an extraordinary extent as God's agent on earth, "incarnating" the divine purpose for human life.'[5] This is a long way from what the church historically has understood the incarnation to be, and looks like a way of seeking to retain an honoured term after it has been evacuated of its meaning.[6]

So in terms of his divine life, he will be viewed as the uncreated

---

4. I have tried to show this in *The Christ of the Bible and of the Church's Faith* (Tain: Christian Focus Publications, 1998), pp. 265-68.

5. *The Metaphor of God Incarnate* (London, SCM, 1993), p. 12.

6. This kind of thing is all too common. Its classic and most influential example is to be found in the contents pages of F.D. Schleiermacher, *The Christian Faith* (ET, Edinburgh: T. and T. Clark, 1928), pp. ix-xii. Here traditional theological terms are used while the book's contents give many of them entirely untraditional meanings.

Creator, unchallenged in his absolute sovereignty over all things because by nature without an equal, except in so far as he may be viewed as an equal Partner with the Father and the Holy Spirit within the eternal Triune life of the Godhead.

In this study then we are setting up as a Christological goal the doctrine that this one Person unites in himself full deity and full humanity, and we ask whether this broadly Chalcedonian position can be reached, and if so whether the best route is that from above or below.

(d) Are there possible hindrances to progress from one to the other? Whether we start from above or below we may encounter hindrances to progress, usually of a philosophical kind, or from a theology deeply influenced by a particular philosophy. For instance, we may both begin and end with Jesus the man because we have already assumed, prior to our investigation, that no historical person can possibly be more than human.

There are some hindrances which stem from a misunderstanding or a caricature of the Chalcedonian Definition. J.A.T. Robinson, writing about the Chalcedonian formula, says that according to it, 'Jesus was a hybrid .... a sort of bat-man or centaur, an unnatural conjunction of two strange species.'[7] If this is truly the case, the whole idea of a Christology either from below or above, that may make real progress, is inconceivable. It is however a gross caricature, for it ignores the vital fact of the image of God in human beings. This has usually been understood to include the fact that human beings, by God's gift, possess a personal nature,[8] and so, even prior to the incarnation, there was something of quite central importance that God and human beings had in common.

It would be useful to trace the whole history of the two approaches throughout Church History particularly in relation to the influence on Christology of the shifting philosophical

---

7. In an article, 'Need Jesus have been Perfected?' in S.W. Sykes and J.P. Clayton (eds.), *Christ, faith and history* (Cambridge: CUP, 1972), pp. 39,40.

8. For full discussion, see P.E. Hughes, *The True Image: The Origin and Destiny of Man in Christ* (Leicester: IVP, 1989).

background, but this would make this paper inordinately long. The classic confrontation between these two types of Christology was undoubtedly that associated with the Schools of Antioch and of Alexandria, especially in the 5th Century, when Nestorius and Cyril of Alexandria confronted each other from either side of this theological divide. It was largely the clash between these schools which made it necessary for the Chalcedonian Definition to be formulated.

The approach of the Alexandrians and so of Cyril was very much a Christology from above, while that of the Antiochenes and so of Nestorius was a Christology from below. Most of the expressions in Cyril's writings to which Nestorius objected were those that seemed to play down the humanity of Jesus, while those in the works of Nestorius objected to by Cyril appeared to him to play down his deity.

There were of course non-theological factors at work as well, with personal and ecclesiastical antagonisms well to the fore, but the theological factors were of great importance. The difference of perspective when combined with personal antagonism was so far-reaching that it blinded both men to points of value in the outlook of the other and even caused each at times to condemn statements from his antagonist that bore considerable similarity to statements he had himself made! Before this debate got under way, the Alexandrian approach to Christology had been much the dominant one in the church as a whole, so that the Antiochene school's emphasis was a much-needed balance to it. There are links of thought between the Alexandrian approach and Platonism, while, if there was a philosophical influence in the School of Antioch, it was more Aristotelian than Platonic.

If we think in terms of a Christology from above, it must be said that the concept of Divine incarnation was a very difficult one for the Greeks. They were quite familiar with the idea of the gods appearing in human guise, but this was certainly never in terms of a true incarnation. The idea that the body was at least inferior and perhaps evil was deep-set in the Greek mind and this reached its ultimate point philosophically and theologically in Manichaeism. Then also both the Jewish and Greek inheritances of the church tended to incline the minds of thinking Christians towards an idea of God as so utterly different from man that the whole idea of incarnation became highly problematic. An incarnation doctrine was anything but a logical outcome of philosophical trends in the early Christian centuries; just the opposite. We can therefore applaud the early Fathers for holding to a Biblical truth which was alien to the general thought-world in which they moved.[9]

There are hindrances from the other end, plenty of them, especially in modern times. There is the general tendency to rationalism and to the denial of the miraculous element in the person and work of Christ. So David Strauss[10] and Rudolf Bultmann,[11] for all their differences, were united in their rejection of the miraculous in general and therefore in relation to the life of Jesus, whose proper deity they rejected as a mythological concept. For many moderns, God may meet us in Christ but Christ is not himself God, so that 'in Christ' really means 'through Christ'. Christ is the vehicle for divine action without himself being divine in the fullest sense of that word. He is 'the Man for others'.

The influence of Kant has been very powerful and has proved for many a very effective block to a Christology from below which will make real progress upwards. Kant rejected certainty by the path of metaphysics.[12] He denied that any assured knowledge could be obtained by moving upwards from the phenomenal to the noumenal worlds. There is no pathway between the two except in the moral sphere. Kantian thinking has permeated a great deal of modern thought, and has influenced the outlook of many who have never heard Kant's name.

The Ritschlian theology was essentially Kantian or Neo-

---

9. J.N.D. Kelly, *Early Christian Doctrines* (London, Adam and Charles Black, 2nd Edn. 1960) provides useful information on all the Christologies of the Patristic period which are referred to in this article.

10. *The Life of Jesus Critically Examined* (1835, 1836, ET ed. P.C. Hodgson, Philadelphia: Fortress, 1971)

11. It is a general presupposition of his many theological writings, for instance his *Theology of the New Testament*, (ET, London: SCM, 1952).

12. See e.g. the article, 'Immanuel Kant' in T. Honderich (ed.), *Oxford Companion to Philosophy* (Oxford, 1995)

Kantian in its philosophical background. Ritschl and his school maintained that Christ has the value of God for us, he does for us the kind of things we would anticipate that God would do, but whether he really is God we can neither affirm nor deny, for such affirmation or denial could only be based on metaphysical speculation and this is illegitimate.[13] The unsatisfactory nature of this position, both theologically and spiritually, became clear during the later history of the Ritschlian school, for some of them moved to an affirmation of the deity of Jesus while others moved further away. This was because two elements which were really incompatible, one philosophical and the other Biblical, were tied together and in due time worked against and then eventually broke loose from each other.

Without doubt a great deal of theology has suffered a Kantian captivity during the past one hundred and fifty years and the hesitation of many modern writers in relation to a clear affirmation of the deity of Jesus seems to be due to these philosophical assumptions.

Michael Polanyi,[14] Thomas Kuhn[15] and others have shown that all thought must begin somewhere. We have to begin with a religious root, a faith which provides deep convictions from which we start and to which we return in all our thinking. We cannot simply begin with a *tabula rasa*. Writers like Cornelius Van Til[16] and Herman Dooyeweerd[17] have constructed Christian philosophies which give full value to faith in Christ and in Scriptural authority, so that certain fundamental theological affirmations form a basis on which a Christian philosophy is built.

---

13. For a useful summary of the Ritschlian outlook, see C. Welch, *Protestant Thought in the Nineteenth Century*, Vol. 2 (New Haven, Yale University Press, 1985), pp. 1-30.

14. M. Polanyi, *The Tacit Dimension* (Garden City, NY: 1966)

15. T. Kuhn, *The Structure of Scientific Revolutions* (Chicago, 1962)

16. C. Van Til, *The Defence of the Faith*, Vol. 1 (Nutley, NJ, Presbyterian and Reformed, 1963)

17. H. Dooyeweerd, *A New Critique of Theoretical Thought* (n.p. Presbyterian and Reformed, 1969)

2. The question placed within a wider context

The issue before us has something in common with a wider theological/hermeneutical issue: the question as to how we are to understand the whole Bible. Are we to interpret it in terms of its historical development, beginning in Genesis, seeing the unfolding of a great Divine purpose, and allowing its truths to become part of our being in the way they were for the first disciples of Jesus, before going on to read and consider the New Testament? Alternatively, should we overleap this historical unfolding of truth, go right to the end and view everything in the strong light that streams from the risen and exalted Christ? To put it in yet another way, are we to interpret the Bible exegetically or are we to interpret it theologically? Do we approach it as Biblical scholars or as Systematic Theologians? There can be little doubt that there is often a fundamental difference of mentality between these two types of Christian academics.

Biblical Theology of an historical kind, the type of 'Biblical Theology' pursued by Geerhardus Vos in his book of that name, might appear to be a kind of bridge between the two. It is a discipline which relates to both, and so, despite the fact that it has often been neglected, it is difficult to exaggerate its importance. Biblical Theology presupposes all the exegetical disciplines but it goes beyond them. It is inevitably a systematizing discipline but it does not use classifying terms which are external to Scripture and which show the marks of theological debate down through the ages, but it employs actual Biblical terms in its construction of a system.

Whether our Christology is from below or from above, it ought to be possible to formulate it as an exercise in Biblical Theology, for if we cannot this means that we are giving assent to and indeed resting theologically and spiritually on a doctrine which is foreign to the Word of God, and this we dare not do. It is true that Biblical Theology is not concerned only with Christology, but this is central to its concerns.

3. Christology from below

Certainly Jesus came as the climax of the Messianic hope in the Old Testament. It is true that the actual term 'Messiah' is of rare occurrence there in relation to a great Figure of the future. In fact many identify it only in Daniel 9:25, 26. Nevertheless the concept is much fuller than has always been recognised in modern times. The whole idea of Old Testament messiahship comes into disrepute if Old Testament passages are mishandled in order to extract messianism from them. The volume, *The Lord's Anointed*,[18] which contains a good deal of careful exegesis and yet produces significant messianic conclusions, has pointed the way to a rehabilitation of Old Testament messianism on a proper exegetical basis. This volume is concerned mostly with messianism in kingly terms, but the preparation for Jesus in the Old Testament, 'messianism' in a very broad sense, was many-sided at the human level. Terms such as judge, prophet, priest, king, servant of God, Son of Man are all applied in the New Testament to Jesus. Even the last of these is a human-like figure in Daniel 7, although of course he is seen there in a heavenly setting.

Christology from below was the way the first disciples came. They encountered Jesus first of all as a Man, but through their experience of him they came to believe in him as Lord and Son of God. It came through their extensive contact with a Man whose uniqueness was of such a character that it demanded a higher explanation of who he was.

We can see the development of a deeper understanding of him in a passage like John 9, where we see, for instance in verses 11, 17, 25, 30-33, 35-38, how the man blind from birth came gradually, although over a fairly short period, to advance in his understanding from 'a man called Jesus' to the point where his faith led him to worship.

We note also the way Peter preached on the Day of Pentecost. He proclaimed Jesus as a Man approved by God and, through death, resurrection and ascension, this Jesus, whom the hearers crucified, was made both Lord and Christ. This is not

---

18. P.E. Satterthwaite, R.S. Hess and G.J. Wenham, *The Lord's Anointed: Interpretation of Old Testament Messianic Texts* (Carlisle; Paternoster, 1995).

adoptionism,[19] but it is an approach to the Lordship of Jesus through his humanity, his life and his sufferings. All the Petrine sermons to Jewish audiences recorded in Acts tend to move this way and this rings true as it was the way Peter and the other apostles had actually come themselves.

The case of Paul is however an interesting one. We know little of his pre-Christian experience but his vehement rejection of the claims of Christ initially, we can reasonably assume, was because he did not accept the transcendent claims made for him as well as the great stumbling-block of the cross. He did, he says, many things contrary to the name of Jesus of Nazareth, and we note that this description of him is simply in terms of his home town (Acts 26:9). Here was a man who does not seem to have been in contact with the actual human Jesus, although of that we cannot be absolutely certain, but who had some acquaintance with facts about him through hearsay, facts which could well have been distorted, and on this basis rejected his claims.

Here then is an example of theological assumptions preventing a movement upwards from Jesus as a Man to Jesus as Lord and Son of God. Yet something else needs to be said. The interested enquirer can hardly start anywhere else than with Jesus the Man. What we are saying to him or her is that a person known from history is in fact the Son of God and Lord of all. The evidence for this is found in the records of his life, confirmed by the theological interpretation given of him in the writings of the New Testament.

4. Christology from above

We should not overlook the fact that part of the Old Testament preparation for Christ is given in terms of the saving acts of God

---

19. There is an excellent brief discussion of the theological implications of Acts 2:36 in R. Longenecker's commentary on *Acts* in F. Gaebelein (ed.), *Expositor's Bible Commentary Vol. 9* (Grand Rapids: Zondervan, 1981) ad loc. He concludes that Peter 'is proclaiming not an adoptionist Christology, but a functional one with ontological overtones – viz., that the resurrection of Jesus from the dead is God's open avowal that the messianic work has been accomplished and that Jesus now has the full right to assume the messianic title; that the exaltation of Jesus is the proclamation of his lordship, which God calls all to acknowledge.'

himself. The Old Testament shows us that Yahweh is the only God and the only Saviour. He delivered the people from Egyptian bondage and this deliverance was preceded by other saving events (e.g. Noah and the Flood and Abraham and Ur) as well as being followed by others for which it is a kind of paradigmatic event. This must all be taken fully into account as part of the Old Testament preparation for Christ. The New Testament writers regarded Jesus as the incarnation of this God, for Luke 19:10, for instance, seems to take up the language of Ezekiel 34:11, 'I, even I myself, will seek for my sheep and find them.'

We find also that each New Testament book presents the transcendent greatness of Christ at an early point, not waiting for the reader to come to conclusions but presenting this fact usually in an unmistakable way.

Matthew and Luke both tell the story of the Virgin Birth, Mark in his introductory verse, describes Jesus as the Christ, the Son of God,[20] while John's Prologue commences the story in eternity. Certainly in Acts 1:1 he is 'Jesus', but in the quotation from Peter in 1:21 he is 'the Lord Jesus'. As we saw, Peter's sermons to Jews present Christology from below, but the message to Cornelius and his Gentile friends commences with an assertion that Jesus Christ is Lord of all.

It is true that there is a 'Christology from below' statement in Romans 1:3, 4 where he is said to be of the seed of David and to have been declared to be the Son of God with power by the resurrection from among the dead, although he is referred to here first of all as God's Son. In the introduction to nine of the epistles claiming to be by Paul, God the Father and the Lord Jesus Christ are joint Sources of blessing for the readers, as They are also in the opening verses of 2 Peter, 2 John and in the Book of the Revelation. 1 Corinthians 1:2 calls him, 'our Lord Jesus Christ – their Lord and ours', while in Galatians 1:1 we find Paul saying that his gospel came to him not from man nor by man but by Jesus Christ and God the Father. If we did not have clear evidence to

---

20. There are textual problems here in relation to the words, 'Son of God', which all the larger commentaries discuss, but most of them conclude that they were probably original.

the contrary, this might even have given us the impression that Jesus was to be considered only from above. Colossians lacks such an opening, but it certainly makes up for it by its most exalted teaching about Jesus (e.g. 1:15ff; 2:9).

Hebrews 1 applies to him Old Testament Scriptures which refer to him as Son, God, and Lord, while James 1:1 calls the writer the slave of God and of the Lord Jesus Christ. See also 1 Peter 1:3, where 'the God and Father of our Lord Jesus Christ' implies a special filial relationship to God, even though the writer refers later to new birth and to the fact that Christians are children of God. For 1 John 1: 1-4 Jesus is the eternal Life who was with the Father from the beginning and Jude writes to those who are loved by the Father and kept by Jesus Christ. The only book of the New Testament that does not make early reference to the divine greatness of Jesus is 3 John, and of course this consists of only thirteen verses. Revelation not only has such an opening but also moves immediately into a Trinitarian passage followed by the record of an encounter with Christ in majesty.

This means then that the transcendent greatness of Christ is taken completely for granted by all the writers and in all their writings. It is a presupposition of all they write. This is true even of the Gospel writers. These books were of course intended primarily for Christian readers, who would have accepted the same exalted Christology as the New Testament writers.

It could be argued that we should ourselves begin with a full Christology from above. Why traverse the ground trodden by the disciples when they have once traversed it? Moreover, can we stop at some intermediate stage? In terms of a Christology from below, would we preach a pre-Pentecostal gospel? If so, where would we stop? Just before Pentecost? Before the ascension? Before the resurrection? Even before Calvary? Surely not. So, it could well be said, we should present people with Jesus as Lord from the very beginning, not leaving them to move upwards from Jesus the Man.

For Aristotle, the seed could only be properly understood in terms of the plant into which eventually it grew, for this was an unfolding of the meaning which was enfolded in the seed. This means that in Aristotelian terms we might say we should interpret in terms of the (New Testament) end at which all things aim.

5. A clue from the Gospel of John

Over the years, there has been something of a change in the way evangelists, both platform and personal evangelists, have dealt with interested enquirers. At one time it was fairly standard practice to present such people with a copy of the Gospel of John, but this has given way more recently to an encouragement to read Mark or Luke. This might seem to be in line with the present tendency to a Christology from below, rather than from above. But is the Christology of John really from above? This needs a closer look.

It might seem at first sight as though this Gospel stands over against the other three as a Christology from above. Here John begins with Jesus as the eternal Logos and, after making a number of general statements about him as Life and Light, he asserts the fact of the incarnation. It is only after this that we get begin to get concrete information about Jesus the Man. When we look into the matter more fully, in fact, this understanding of John's Christology intensifies rather than the reverse. It is not just the Prologue but the whole of the first chapter which is strongly Christological. John almost bombards us with Christological titles and descriptions, such as Lord, Lamb of God, the One who was before John the Baptist, him who baptises with the Holy Spirit, etc.

Yet the statement of the purpose of the Gospel in 20:30 is really a classic form of Christology from below. John tells the readers to look at the evidence of the works of Jesus and to conclude from this that 'Jesus is the Christ, the Son of God', so that they may have life in his name. So, John says, look at the evidence, and this is the conclusion to which you should come. Chapter 1 however presents very little evidence, except for the words of Jesus to Nathanael in John 1:48, which apparently led Nathanael to faith in him, although the Gospel reader is left somewhat in the dark as to the full import of these words.

At the start of Chapter 2, however, the evidence begins, for here is the first of the signs that are meant to elicit faith. John therefore operates with both a Christology from above and one from below. He makes very high assertions for the Person of Jesus throughout the first chapter but especially in the Prologue. Will assertions of this kind actually produce faith? We cannot limit the Holy Spirit, but it would not seem likely. If you or I were to encounter people who had never even heard of Jesus and say to them, 'Believe in Jesus as the Word of God, the Son of God and the Saviour of the World,' we would not be surprised if they replied, 'But you need first to tell us something about him before we can embrace such a faith.'

Yet the fact remains that John did not begin his Gospel with Chapter 2 but with Chapter 1. This means that the reader is let into the secret of the transcendent nature of Jesus before he reads the Gospel, so that he is prepared for this element in it. On the assumption that it is John the Apostle who wrote this Gospel, he is saying, 'This is the faith to which I and my fellow-apostles have come and I now want to give you the kind of evidence we encountered and through which God led us to this faith.' He shows his readers first of all the conclusion to which he expects them to come, and then begins to present evidence which may lead them to that conclusion.

It could be argued that each of the Gospel writers does this, although not in the same way as John. The early chapters of Matthew and Luke present the Virgin Birth, while Mark not only asserts that he is telling the gospel of Jesus Christ the Son of God but almost immediately records God's own affirmation at his baptism that Jesus is the Son of God. So the readers of each of the Gospels are made aware of the transcendent greatness of Jesus before the facts of his ministry are given. As Colin Gunton points out, all the New Testament writers espouse both a Christology from above (in that they all believed in His deity before they wrote) and one from below (in that they tell of Jesus of Nazareth).[21]

Christology from below then has an important apologetic function, but this is not all. Brian Hebblethwaite says: 'Anyone who believes that the Christian religion stands or falls with the conviction that Jesus Christ comes to us from the side of God is bound to hold that Church Christology must in the end be

21. Gunton, *Yesterday and Today,* p. 45.

Christology "from above". But there is no need to dismiss Christology "from below" as an apologetic or justificatory method of substantiating the Church's faith and showing its origins in a real human life and fate. Indeed there are dangers of docetism and ideology and fantasy in ignoring the historical question and the real humanity of Jesus.'[22]

What will this mean for us then? It will mean that our Christology from above will be constantly subject to checking from below. Again we may take an analogy from the doctrine of Scripture. We may perhaps formulate our doctrine largely from the great statements of the New Testament about Scripture such as are to be found in 2 Timothy 3 and 2 Peter 1, and yet it is important that this doctrine be checked against the actual Biblical facts. This does not mean that the discovery of a few difficulties will lead us to a revision of our Bibliology from above, but it does mean that we will work at them seriously, in the conviction that a true doctrine must fit the actual phenomenal facts.

Paul may have tried the 'from below' perspective before he became a Christian, perhaps endeavouring to test the claims of Jesus for himself. But then came the Damascus Road encounter with the risen Christ, and the total reorientation of his outlook which this brought, and his perspective from then on was predominantly from above.

The interpretation of Philippians 2:6 has now become almost as important a *crux interpretum* as the verse which follows it.[23] It is of course part of a great passage often now regarded as a primitive Christian hymn. The exegesis of it turns on the meaning to be given to *morphē theou*. The traditional interpretation relates this to the deity of Jesus, to the fact that he was eternally, as the Son of God, in the nature of God. It is also however possible to understand it in terms of his human life, in which, as Adam originally was, he was the uncorrupted image of God. This is not the place to deal with the various arguments for the two points of

---

22. Ibid., p. 81.
23. See the discussion in R.P. Martin, *Carmen Christi: Philippians 2:1-11 in Recent Interpretation and in the Setting of Early Christian Worship* (Cambridge, CUP, 1967), pp. 161-164.

view. It is mentioned only to highlight the fact that the first interpretation is in line with Christology from above, while the second with Christology from below. It may be possible to argue that the first is the more likely if the passage is original to Paul but that if it is indeed pre-Pauline the case for the second is strengthened somewhat.

6. Divine illumination and Christology

There is a factor of great importance and which we may easily forget in this discussion. Peter's confession of Jesus as the Christ, the Son of the living God, recorded in Matthew 16, evokes from Jesus the words, 'Blessed are you, Simon, son of Jonah, for this was not revealed to you by man, but by my Father in heaven.' We may place alongside this Paul's affirmation in 1 Corinthians 12:3, 'No-one can say, "Jesus is Lord," except by the Holy Spirit.'

If there is to be a true Christology from below then the element of Divine illumination is of great importance. The facts about the life, death and resurrection of Jesus are indispensable, for we are not mystics, looking simply for the dawning of an inner light without the presentation of any objective facts. Neither, however, can we dispense with prayer. The word of God and prayer must go together if others are to recognise in Jesus the very Son of God and Lord of all, and so we can understand why the apostles, entrusted with the preaching of the gospel, said that they would give themselves continually to prayer and to the ministry of the word (Acts 6:4).

This means that the interested enquirer must be prepared to learn from God. It is easy for either the enquirer or the modern scholar to come to the evidence presented in the Gospels with his or her mind closed already to the possibility that the claims made for Jesus in this literature are actually true. There must be a willingness to put aside one's habitual philosophical or theological presuppositions and to look at the evidence in an open-minded way, prepared if necessary for a radical adjustment of outlook. Such a readiness is likely to be evidence that already at that stage the Spirit of God is at work.

4

The Christology of Chalcedon

Donald Macleod

Please note carefully the title of this paper. I have not been asked to speak on the Formula of Chalcedon as such, but on its Christology. That Christology was hammered out in the fires of controversy in the preceding centuries and inevitably it has a keen cutting edge. It emphatically repudiates Docetism, Arianism and Apollinarianism. Equally emphatically it repudiates Nestorianism and Eutychianism. But there is also a strong positive emphasis, laying down certain axioms and parameters that must forever govern our reflection on the person of Christ. These axioms, as you recall, are, first, the deity of Christ; secondly, the humanity of Christ; thirdly, the uni-personality of Christ. Although God and man in two distinct natures, he is one *prosopon* or *hypostasis*, the two natures running together (*suntrechouses*) in the one subject.

These emphases can be asserted independently of the precise language of Chalcedon and my concern is with the emphases themselves and not simply with the Formula. What is at issue is incarnational, two-nature Christology. Christ was truly and perfectly God; Christ was truly and perfectly man; and Christ was one acting agent and one suffering subject.

Sustained attack
I want to begin by reminding you of an obvious fact: this Christology has been under sustained attack for most of the twentieth century and still remains under attack. Why? What are the main objections?

First, that this Christology is culturally relative. It is set forth, we are told, in the language and concepts of the Greek church of the fifth century: *ousia, phusis, hypostasis, prosopon* and so on.

77

These are of dubious relevance and validity at the beginning of the twenty-first century.

One response to this that it is merely a matter of hermeneutics: the task of transporting meaning out of one language, time and place into our own language, time and place. We face that task with regard to the Bible itself and indeed with regard to all ancient documents. Similarly with the Christology of Chalcedon. We have to lift it out of its fifth century context into our own twenty-first century context. That may require a change in nomenclature. It may also require a resort to other, more recent schools of philosophy. But it is by no means an impossible assignment. Indeed, it is no more difficult to lift the language of *ousia, phusis* and *hypostasis* into our own time than it is to lift the language of St Paul (*morphe, homoioma* and *eikon,* for example). We might even argue, in fact, that it is no more difficult than the common examination question, 'Express in your own words ...'.

It also seems to me that the philosophy of Chalcedon, such as it is, is not some sort of strait-jacket confining us helplessly within the thought-world of the fifth century. The fact that the words are Greek does not necessarily imply that the concepts are Greek. Indeed, the words are sometimes used in a very un-Greek way. For example, at the heart of Chalcedon lies a distinction which is quite alien to Greek thought: the distinction between *physis* on the one hand and *hypostasis* or *prosopon* on the other. The Greeks were strongly inclined to the view that *nature* implied *person.* One person meant one nature. This appears, for example, in Cyril's use of *mia physis* as synonymous with *mia hypostasis.*[1] In the Chalcedonian Formula, that link is explicitly broken. It distinguishes clearly between *physis* on the one hand and *prosopon* and *hypostasis* on the other. Chalcedon does not use the exact word *anhypostasia,* but the concept of a non-hypostatic nature is clearly present. In drawing this sharp distinction between nature and person the Formula is boldly parting company with an axiom of contemporary Greek thought.

---

1. See, for example, Cyril's *Third Letter to Nestorius* (5) and his *Letter to Acacius of Melitene* (L. R. Wickham, *Cyril of Alexandria: Select Letters* [Oxford: Clarendon Press, 1983], p.31, 49).

It also seems to me that the resulting theology is radically un-Greek: antithetical, indeed, to the whole genius of Greek theology. Greek theology was sympathetic to the idea of theophanies (gods in human form) and to the idea of divine adoptions, in which a god might take control of a human personality. But the language of Chalcedon is the language of incarnation. It speaks of the enfleshment of a divine person. Here, God himself enters upon an earthly, historical existence, so that we can say that this man is the Son of God and that in this particular individual God lives a truly human life. That goes far beyond both theophany and adoption. It is an explicit assertion of incarnation: God himself coming not only into union with our nature but also into the stream of time and the vicissitudes of space and exposing himself to limitation, development, fragility, vulnerability and pain. That, as far as I can see, is a profoundly un-Greek concept.[2]

The second objection is that the Christology of Chalcedon is dualistic.[3] It appears to place side by side within the one person or *hypostasis* two natures, each of which retains its own distinct properties and appears to exist without any real ontological link with the other. There seems to be no psychological bridge between them. This appears at its plainest in Leo's *Tome*, according to which 'the properties of both natures and substances were preserved and co-existed in One Person' and 'the inviolable nature was united to a passible nature', with the result that Jesus 'was capable of death in one nature and incapable of it in the other'.[4] This laid the foundation for the practice of attributing some aspects of Jesus' existence to his human nature and others to his divine nature, without any obvious synthesis between them.

I would say two things in response to this. One is that we attempt

---

2. My language here echoes that of A. N. S. Lane: 'while the Fathers used Greek concepts, the resulting theology was profoundly un-Greek' (from an essay, 'Christology beyond Chalcedon' in H. R. Rowdon (Ed.), *Christ the Lord* [Leicester: Inter-Varsity Press, 1982], p.263).

3. This criticism is made even by conservative evangelical theologians. Cf. A. N. S. Lane, *op. cit.,* p.268: 'The Chalcedonian picture of Christ is unashamedly dualist.'

4. For the Latin text of Leo's *Tome* see H. T. Bindley, *The Ecumenical Documents of the Faith* (London: Methuen, 3rd edition, 1925), pp.195-204. The English translation is given on pp.279-291.

to answer this particular difficulty at our peril. In fact, it was the reckless compulsion to overcome the difficulty that made Chalcedon necessary in the first place, because elements in the church were taking one or other factor in the problem and pushing it to an extreme. The Monophysites, for example, argued that Christ had, after his enfleshment, only one nature. This was the position of Eutyches: before the incarnation there were two natures; afterwards there was only one.[5] The effect of this was to destroy the reality of both natures. The one *physis* of the Eutychian Christ was a mixture neither human nor divine. This certainly overcame the dualism, but it did so at the cost of imposing an intolerable synthesis.

The other approach was that of the Antiochene theologians: to over-emphasise the humanity of Jesus to the point where it had separate individual status. In my view, Nestorius never reached that point, but that was certainly the tendency of this school.[6] But, again, this was no solution of the problem. It moved towards a real dualism between two unintegrated agents, the Son of God and the Son of Mary.

To a large extent, then, Chalcedon is a warning against the search for a theory to overcome the dualism. Its real message is that we must safeguard the elements of the problem (the unity of the person on the one hand and the reality of both the divine and human natures on the other) and refrain from either fusing the natures or sundering the person.

The second thing to be said in response to the charge of dualism is that the Formula of Chalcedon insists very strongly on the existential unity of the person, Jesus.[7] It emphasises that although

5. This was the position attributed to Eutyches by Leo. See Bindley, *op. cit.,* p.289.

6. For the position of Nestorius, see J. F. Bethune-Baker, *Nestorius and His Teaching: A Fresh Examination of the Evidence* (Cambridge: Cambridge University Press, 1908). Cf. G. L. Prestige, *Fathers and Heretics* (London: SPCK, 1968), pp.120-149.

7. The precise words of the *Formula* are as follows: 'One and the Same Christ, Son, Lord, Only-begotten; acknowledged in Two Natures unconfusedly, unchangeably, indivisibly, inseparably; the difference of Natures being in no way removed because of the Union, but rather the property of each Nature being preserved, and both concurring into One Person and One Hypostasis; not as

there are two natures, there is but one *hypostasis* or *prosopon*. This means that, without claiming to solve the problem, it stresses the unity without pretending to explain it.[8] It insists that the two natures constitute one *hypostasis*. This means that all the actions of the incarnate Christ are actions of this *hypostasis*. At one level, he is the agent of all the actions. On another, *he* is the speaker of all the words. At yet another, *he* is the subject of all the experiences. *Prosopon*, in a way, emphasised the phenomenological: people saw one Christ. *Hypostasis* emphasised the fact of underlying agency and underlying subjectivity.[9]

This is something of enormous kerygmatic importance. We must avoid utterly all attempts to parcel out the Lord's actions, words and experiences as between the two natures. Instead, we have to keep asking, '*Who* did this? *Who* said this? *Who* suffered this?' The reply is invariably the same: '*He* did it. *He* said it. *He* suffered it. *The Son of God* did it.' It was the person who raised Lazarus from the dead. It was the person who preached the Sermon on the Mount. It was the person who suffered and died on the cross of Calvary. Chalcedon may not resolve the dualism, but it does, very certainly, repudiate it, insisting that at every point we are dealing with one Christ.

This is particularly important when Christian thought turns to the atonement. Remember the words of 1 John 2:2: 'And he himself is the *hilasmos* for our sins.' *He* is the expiatory sacrifice. It is not his human nature that dies, but himself. This man who is the Son of God dies precisely as the Son of God. He dies in a divine way, just as he is divine in a human way. But when it comes to his exaltation, the subject of the action changes: 'wherefore *God* highly exalted Him.' He himself went towards the abyss, but only God could raise him. Would he? Christ was confident he would. He knew the promises and he knew that the Father heard him always.

though He were parted or divided into Two Persons, but One and the Self-same Son and Only-begotten God, Word, Lord, Jesus Christ' (Bindley, *op. cit.*, p.297).

8. Cf. William Temple, *Christus Veritas* (London: Macmillan, 1925), p.126: 'The Church at Chalcedon virtually gave up the attempt to understand, while refusing to sacrifice either part of its apparently contradictory belief.'

9. On the relation between *prosopon* and *hypostasis* see G. L. Prestige, *Fathers and Heretics* (London: SPCK, 1968), Chapter VIII (pp.157-78).

But such assurance was by no means uninterrupted. Christ had to serve even through the mists of a sense of utter forsaken-ness, trusting everything to the God whom his people's sin had offended. Only that God could turn defeat into victory and death into life. Emotion is at the mercy of understanding; and it is quite wrong to assume that at every point the whole truth about his situation was present to Jesus' mind.

There is nothing in Chalcedon to pre-empt such language or to proscribe such exploration. Chalcedon says very plainly, 'Go and do full justice to the deity of Christ. Fall at his feet as dead!' But it also says, equally plainly, 'Go and do full justice to the humanity of Christ. It is the same as your own. It has the same anatomy, the same genetic code and the same psychology.' He was sinless, of course, but at the level of psychology the controlling factor is that he had a human (and therefore a limited) mind. Emotions, affections, choices: all these are functions of perception and information. Christ was human in his perceptions and therefore human in the whole range of his psychology. His responses are always those of one with limited information. The fact that he possessed supernatural knowledge does not negate this. Even supernatural knowledge may be limited.

Chalcedon allows us to do full justice to all this. He was no mere man, but he was a real man.

Gospel criticism

But the greatest challenge to Chalcedon today comes from the field of Gospel criticism. It is all the more serious because it is not a frontal attack on Chalcedon as such. The Chalcedonian fathers assumed the canonicity of the Gospels. They also assumed that through these Gospels they could have access to the truth about Jesus. They assumed that these Gospels recorded how the early Christians saw him. They also assumed that the Gospels recorded how Jesus saw himself. They were confident, therefore, that their formulations were all mandated by the Gospels and, indeed, demanded by them.

But all this has changed. We face not only a change in language or a change in philosophy, culture, or intellectual climate. We face a radical change in attitudes towards the Gospels themselves. Of course, much of our modern Gospel scholarship is coming from secular theological faculties which are not in the service of the church. These have their own validity: I don't question that. But some of this scholarship is also coming from within the church itself and it is raising the most radical questions. You all know Bultmann's famous comment that we can now know nothing of the life and personality of Jesus.[10] The story told by the Synoptics is, in his view, legend. None of it is verifiable.

If this is true, what are its implications for Chalcedon? Let me go beyond that: beyond the Synoptics. The most important background document for Chalcedon is the Gospel of John. The Chalcedonian fathers assumed its historicity. They assumed that here we hear the real Jesus talking and here we see real history and real geography. Today that position is universally discounted, apart from a few mavericks such as John A.T. Robinson (building on the work of J.B. Lightfoot).[11] The Gospel of John is not taken as serious history. John Hick describes it as a theological dialogue in dramatic form.[12]

The problem for us is that there is no single document to which the doctrines of the incarnation and the Trinity are more indebted than they are to the Gospel of John. Indeed, if I were into conspiracy theories, I would say that in launching a sustained attack upon this particular gospel the devil really has chosen his ground with consummate skill. In this essay I'm not even going to attempt to answer the difficulties raised by Johannine scholarship. I'm interested only in its bearings on Chalcedon. Chalcedon presupposes two things: that we have reliable access to what the early church thought about Christ; and that we have access to what Christ thought about himself. Current Gospel criticism threatens both of these assumptions. It tells us that we can know neither what the primitive church thought nor what Christ thought.

---

10. Rudolf Bultmann, *Jesus and the Word* (New Edition, London: Collins, 1958), p.14.

11. J. A. T. Robinson, *The Priority of John* (London: SCM Press, 1985). Cf. J. B. Lightfoot, *Biblical Essays* (London: Macmillan, 1893), pp. 1-198.

12. J. Hick (Ed.), *The Myth of God Incarnate* (London: SCM Press, 1977), p.171.

The fate of Chalcedon will depend ultimately on the outcomes of Gospel criticism, not on changes in the general intellectual climate.

Chalcedon today

But what of Chalcedon today? Let me air two different answers to that question, one from William Temple and the other from Eric Mascall. Temple once commented that Chalcedon marks the bankruptcy of Greek patristic Christology.[13] The two-nature Christology was a *cul-de-sac.*[14]

For the moment I will offer just one response to this: it is not true to history. As a matter of fact, Christological reflection continued long after Chalcedon; and it continued at the hands of those who held firmly to the doctrine set forth in the Formula. Indeed, some of the elements of even classical Christology are themselves post-Chalcedon. This is true, for example, of *anhypostasia* and the related idea, *enhypostasia.* It can be argued (successfully, I think) that the concept of *anhypostasia* is implicit in both Apollonaris and Cyril. But the word *anhypostasia* is extremely rare in patristic Greek and its use in Christology is certainly post-Chalcedon.[15]

I use that simply to underline the claim that Christological

---

13. This comment appears in Temple's essay, 'The Divinity of Christ' in *Foundations: A Statement of Christian Belief in terms of Modern Thought by Seven Oxford Men* (London. Macmillan, 1912), p.230. He qualified this view in *Christus Veritas*: 'It is really not the formula, but the history of the whole controversy, that leaves the impression of bankruptcy. The formula did exactly what an authoritative formula ought to do: it stated the fact' (p.134fn.).

14. According to Wolfhart Pannenberg, the Chalcedon Formula correctly expressed the elements of truth in both the Alexandrian and the Antiochene schools of Christology. As a result, it was suspected by both sides, the Antiochenes seeing it as a threat to the real humanity of Jesus, the Alexandrians as a threat to his unity with God. These opposing suspicions resulted from the Chalcedonian formula's inability to overcome 'the conceptual dilemma of patristic Christology'. 'The formula rather intended to maintain the elements of truth of the two mutually contradictory elaborations of the two-natures doctrine' (*Jesus: God and Man* [London. SPCK, 1968], pp.291ff.).

15. Apollinaris argued that Christ did not have a human mind (see H. M. Relton, *A Study in Christology* [London: SPCK, 1934]), p.11. Cyril held that although the Logos united himself to human nature he did not unite himself to a man. But the Christological use of the word *anhypostasia* is no earlier than

reflection did not stop at Chalcedon. The Formula was not a barrier to further progress. But I could also point to the Monothelite controversy. After Chalcedon there was a revival in Monophysite *n* Christology and this led to a vigorous prosecution of the Monothelite view that Christ had only one will. The debate raged with all the usual paraphernalia of intrigue and deceit well into the sixth century, till the church eventually convinced itself that in Christ there are two wills: a human way of choosing and a divine way of choosing.[16] Whether these sixth-century resolutions will satisfy the modern mind is a moot point. The word 'will' was not then defined as it is in modern psychology. It referred much more to appetite, acquisitiveness and desire than to choice and decision.

Nor did Christological reflection finish even then. What about John Calvin's long-neglected discussion of Christ's deity? Calvin himself never explicitly described Christ as *autotheos,* but he certainly maintained that he was God *a se ipso*: from himself alone. Calvin's strenuous insistence on the self-existent deity of Jesus was a significant enrichment of the Nicean Christology.[17]

Or take, again, the on-going debate generated by the nineteenth century Kenotic theories. Most of us, no doubt, reject these precise theories, but the stimulus they gave to Christology has been both remarkable and welcome; and it has not, by any means, been confined to those who have turned their backs on Chalcedon. There is still much to explore in the idea of Christ emptying himself, and there are clear kenotic ideas even in men of such impeccable orthodoxy as Hugh Martin.[18]

Leontius of Byzantium (485-543). See G. K. W. Lampe, *A Patristic Greek Lexicon (*Oxford: Oxford University Press, 1961), p.164.

16. For the Monothelite controversy, see R. L. Ottley, *The Doctrine of the Incarnation* (London: Methuen, 5th edition, 1911), pp.447-456.

17. See J. Calvin, *Institutes*, Bk I, Ch. XIII; and B. B. Warfield, *Calvin and Augustine* (Philadelphia: Presbyterian and Reformed, 1956), pp. 229-284. There is a brief survey of Calvin's contribution and the resulting debate in D. Macleod, *The Person of Christ* (Leicester: Inter-Varsity Press, 1998), pp. 149-152.

18. See, for example, Martin's words in *The Shadow of Calvary* (Edinburgh: 1875. New impression, Glasgow: Free Presbyterian Publications, 1956), p.26: 'remaining still, as he must ever remain, the same God unchangeable, he yet appeared in the form of a servant, not drawing on his divine might and energies, but denying himself their exercise and forth-putting – concealing, retiring out

These developments make plain that Chalcedon did not mark the end of Christology. If it did, we wouldn't be here today.

The other view I mentioned was that of E.L. Mascall: Chalcedon is the truth and nothing but the truth, but it is not the whole truth.[19] It is not a terminus, but it is an indispensable station along the road to final truth. It is our responsibility to check its axioms and then to build on their foundation an ever-deepening understanding of the Saviour.

If we accept this position of Mascall's, as I certainly do, we are left with certain questions which still require urgent reflection. Some of these relate to concepts inherent in Chalcedon itself. I want to look at two of them.

One is the word *theotokos*. Christ, we are told, was born of the virgin Mary, the *theotokos*. To what extent can we endorse this term and continue to use it?

At the very outset, there is a problem of translation. The rendering, 'the mother of God', has become more or less naturalised in Christian theology, but it is surely highly questionable. The idea of 'the mother of God' does not occur in explicit terminology anywhere in patristic Greek. *Theotokos* means 'God-bearer'. It is important to eliminate the mother-idea because it not only registers the Marian presuppositions of Roman Catholic dogma, but also endorses sub-Christian trends in our human religiosity, particularly the quest for some kind of earth-mother.

On the other hand, the word *theotokos* encapsulates an important theological truth: the person who was born of Mary was the Son of God. This is why such Scottish saints and scholars as John Duncan set great store by the *theotokos*.[20] They saw it as

---

of view, withdrawing from the field of action, those prerogatives and powers of Deity, which in the twinkling of an eye might have scattered ten thousand worlds and hells of enemies.'

19. E. L. Mascall, *Whatever Happened to the Human Mind?* (London: SPCK, 1980), p.29. Cf. G.C. Berkouwer, *The Person of Christ* (Grand Rapids: Eerdmans, 1954), p.91: 'there is no reason to make the pronouncement of Chalcedon a final mile-post in the history of the church, however gratefully we may confess its truth. For the Scriptures are richer than any pronouncement of the church, no matter how excellent it be and how faithfully it has been formulated in subjection to the Word of God.'

20. To those who accused him of blasphemy for daring to call Mary 'the

a custodian of Christ's deity over against all Arianising tendencies.
Who is this child of Mary's? Who is this baby? *Theotokos* says,
'This baby is the Son of God. He is God the Son.'

But although the word *theotokos* is theologically correct, is it
kerygmatically correct? I take the question from Karl Rahner.[21]
Something may be theologically true and yet kerygmatically
inappropriate. It may pedantically conserve a theological truth
and yet in its overall impact upon the church be unfortunate and
deleterious. Of course, Rahner would not agree that this was
applicable to the *theotokos*. He was thinking of such an off-the-
wall conundrum as whether Christ worshipped the second person
of the Trinity. If the Son prayed to God the Father who is
homoousious with God the Son, then there is plausibility in such
pedantry. Rahner did not endorse the implied answer to that
question, but let's ignore the initial starting point. The question is,
Can a term be theologically true and yet kerygmatically incorrect:
true among pedants, but misleading in Christian communication?
Nestorius certainly thought that the use of *theotokos* in the pulpits
of fifth century Constantinople was kerygmatically incorrect. He
did not object, at a theological level, to the term, but he disliked
it, and I think he was justified in his dislike because the term
creates entirely wrong impressions. The problem in essence is
this. *Theotokos* is theologically correct as a Christological affirmation, but the populace did not hear it as a Christological affirmation: they heard it as a Mariological one. It didn't prompt the

mother of God', Duncan (who earlier in his life had flirted with unitarianism)
responded, 'Dare, sir? I dare; and if you knew anything of church history you
would not venture to call that Popery, which is simply a word happily coined to
express one of the most glorious of all truths. Don't you know that of all the
heresies affecting the Person of Christ which the early Church had to struggle
against, none was more deadly than Nestorianism.' Referring to the use of
theotokos by the Council of Ephesus, Duncan declared: 'they were not making
the Virgin the mother of His Godhead – they were not such ignorant fools as
that – but the mother of *Him* who was God, and who as the Son of God was
born, lived, died, rose, and is now seated on the right hand of the Majesty on
high – all in our nature' (see D. Brown, *Memoir of John Duncan*, Edinburgh,
1872. Reprinted as *The Life of Rabbi Duncan*, Glasgow: Free Presbyterian
Publications, 1986, pp.171, 172).

21. K. Rahner, *Theological Investigations,* Volume I (London: Darton,
Longman and Todd, 2nd edition, 1965), p.129.

question, Who was Mary's child? It prompted the question, Who was Mary? and it led to the answer, 'Mary? She is the Mother of God!' From that point onwards, the impetus towards the current Marian dogmas was unstoppable.

It is important to be clear as to the dangers we face here. To the popular mind, 'God' is God the Father. In fact, in the New Testament, *ho theos* always means God the Father: Rahner himself has shown that very clearly.[22] To say, then, that Mary is the Mother of God is to be heard as saying that she is the Mother of God the Father. If so, is it not totally appropriate to worship her? And if your answer to that is, 'No! Not in the sense of *latria*', your distinctions are not being heard. A populace exhorted to accord to Mary the respect of *hyper-doulia* will respond by worshipping her. *Hyper-doulia*, like *theotokos,* is kerygmatically inappropriate.

Anhypostasia

Another concept which requires further reflection is *anhypostasia.* The concept has come under sustained attack in the twentieth century,[23] and that puts us under obligation to reassess it. Is it a valid way towards understanding the identity of Christ?

An-hypostasia is in its very form a negative. It is the denial of *hypostasis.* We must be clear, however, as to what exactly is being denied. It is most emphatically not being denied that Jesus Christ

---

22. See Rahner's essay, '*Theos* in the New Testament' (*Theological Investigations*, Vol. I, pp.79-148).

23. See, for example, R. C. Moberley, *Atonement and Personality* (London: John Murray, 1901), p. 93; H. R. Mackintosh, *Doctrine of the Person of Christ* (Edinburgh: T. & T. Clark, 2nd edition, 1913), p.207; D. M. Baillie, *God Was In Christ* (London: Faber, 1948), p.86; and J. A. T. Robinson, *The Human Face of God* (London: SCM Press, 1973), p. 39. In defence of *anhypostasia* see Barth, *Church Dogmatics,* IV.2 (Edinburgh: T. & T. Clark, 1958), p.49f.: 'it is hard to see how the full truth of the humanity of Jesus Christ is qualified or even destroyed by the fact that as distinct from us He is also a real man only as the Son of God, so that there can be no question of a peculiar and autonomous existence of His humanity ... in Jesus Christ we do not have to do with a man into whom God has changed Himself, but unchanged and directly with God Himself.' Cf. T. F. Torrance, *Theology in Reconstruction* (Grand Rapids: Eerdmans, 1965), pp. 130ff. Both Barth and Torrance insist, of course, that in assuming human nature to himself Jesus Christ is not only real man, but a man.

was an individual or that his humanness was markedly individual. He was not just some kind of amorphous mass of human-ness. His human-ness was distinguished from that of Peter and James and John and every other human being. He had personal traits just as we have ourselves. Remember, for example, how distinctive and individualistic were Jesus' teaching methods. His use of parable and aphorism, for example, were never replicated by the apostles. They were parts of an overall individuality. Christ served God as the specific man that he was. He dared to be himself at the human level. He was not somebody else. We can put it guardedly this way: Christ had 'personality' in the modern sense of the word. He had a quality and a style all his own.

Anhypostasia is not denying that. What it is denying is that the human nature of Christ stands as a person over against his divine nature. I am in no position to deal with questions on the details of Martin Buber's philosophy of relationships,[24] but his vocabulary is eminently serviceable: the human nature of Jesus does not stand in an 'I- Thou' relationship to his divine nature. The two natures are not individual agents able to act on each other as do, for example, two people who love each other. They are not able even to act *with* each other, as two independent individuals might. Far less are they able to act against each other.

This is the only function of *anhypostasia*: to rule out the idea of dual agency. If you deny *anhypostasia* and insist that the human nature is hypostatic you are left with only two options: either you must deny that the divine nature is hypostatic or you must insist that there are two *hypostases* or two individuals in Christ.

Nevertheless, *anhypostasia* need not be our final resting-place. There is merit in the alternative word *enhypostasia*, which came into Christological use in the late fifth century.[25] There is a risk in describing Christ's human nature as simply *im*-personal. *Enhypostasia* reduces this risk, avoiding the idea that the humanity of Jesus has no *hypostasis* and insisting, instead, that it belongs to the *hypostasis* of the Son of God. It is individualised as the humanity of God. The person, the Son of God, exists before he

---

24. M. Buber, *I and Thou* (Edinburgh: T. & T. Clark, 2nd edition, 1959).
25. For the details, see G. K. W. Lampe, *A Patrisiic Greek Lexicon*, p.486.

takes that human nature. In fact, it is the person who takes the human nature at the point of the conception. From this point of view, the incarnation is a dynamic act on the part of the person, the Son of God. Notice the precise language of John 1:14; '*The Word* was made flesh.' It was not the Trinity that became incarnate, nor the Father, nor the Spirit, but God the Son. It was not even the divine nature that became flesh, but the divine person, the Son of God.

But neither did the incarnation mean the divine Son taking or adopting a human person (the heresy of which Cyril accused Nestorius). He took the *form* of a *doulos:* he did not take a *doulos.* What he takes is human nature. But that human nature is never non-personal. It is always the human nature of the person, the Son of God. He will express himself through that nature. He will perform all his actions, speak all his words and suffer all his experiences as one who is enfleshed.

Hence the word *enhypostatic*. Its effect is to particularise the humanity of Jesus. This seems to me directly relevant to the idea that in the virgin birth human nature as such was sanctified. What was sanctified was not human nature as a universal, but human nature as hypostatised in Jesus: the human nature of the Son of God, not the human nature of Judas Iscariot.[26]

Modern debates

I want to close by suggesting that Chalcedon and its Christology are directly relevant to two of the key debates in modern theology: the debate on pluralism, and the debate on divine impassibility.

First, it is relevant to the debate on pluralism. Pluralism is totally sympathetic to Adoptionism. It has no difficulty at all with the idea of the spirit-filled man. You can have any number of spirit-filled men from the Buddha to Muhatma Gandhi. Scholars such as John Hick, John A.T. Robinson and Geoffrey Lampe[27] would

---

26. See, *contra,* Barth, *Church Dogmatics*, IV.2, pp.47ff.: 'In Jesus Christ it is not merely one man, but the *humanum* of all men, which is posited and exalted as such to unity with God.'

27. See J. Hick (ed.), *The Myth of God Incarnate*, pp.167-85; J. A. T. Robinson, *The Human Face of God*; G. K. W. Lampe, *God As Spirit* (Oxford: Clarendon Press, 1977).

take this position, arguing that what we have in Jesus is merely some kind of divine adoption. The Spirit came upon him. They might even allow that he was filled with the Spirit to a unique degree.

But pluralism cannot live with the idea of incarnation. That is why it is difficult to name a single incarnationalist who is also a pluralist. Pluralists are almost always going to be adoptionists. Hick, for example, speaks of two myths: the myth of Christian uniqueness and the myth of incarnation.[28] The two go together. In the incarnation, what we have is a specific person of the Trinity taking flesh; and he becomes flesh in one man, Jesus Christ. There cannot be a plurality of incarnations. We cannot have God enfleshed in a multiplicity of human beings, each claiming to be the Son of God. The incarnation is unique and specific. God the Son becomes flesh; and he becomes flesh only in this man, Jesus: only here. And because he is enfleshed in this man and only in this man, this man is the Way, the Truth and the Life. He, uniquely, is the revelation of God. In this man, and in this man alone, we see the form and the image and the glory of the Father. Besides, we see it in a way that is counter-intuitive: at the very point of revelation, this enfleshed God is washing feet and being crucified. He is revealing himself first as the God who obscures himself and who humbles himself. But it is only revelation because it is *self-revelation*. It presupposes his oneness with God. He is the revelation only because he is first of all the Logos, the Son of God. Revelation takes place in him because of who he is; and it takes place in no one else because no one else is the enfleshment of the Son of God.

Similarly, this man who is the incarnate Son of God is uniquely the way to God. Not only is he uniquely qualified as 'advocate towards the Father' by being God's Son, but he offers a sacrifice, a *hilasmos*, which is absolutely unique. He is himself the *hilasmos*. Not only does God offer the sacrifice. God sacrifices himself. Once this happens, there is no place for any further sacrifice. The way to God is open through the rent veil of God's own flesh.

---

28 Besides editing *The Myth of God Incarnate* Hick was also joint-editor (along with P. F. Knitter) of *The Myth of Christian Uniqueness* (London: SCM Press, 1998).

Autos hilasmos (1 John 2:2): not *autos*, a spirit-filled man, but *autos,* the Son of God incarnate. The *parakletos* (advocate) and the *hilasmos* are one and the same. The *parakletos* bases his argument upon the *hilasmos*. 'Who appears for this man?' 'I do,' says God's Son. 'What is your case?' 'I myself am the case. I am the *hilasmos* for this man's sin. Not only am I this man's advocate. I am his argument. I gave my life for this man: my life! I gave myself, the Son of God.' Only at Calvary did that take place and the uniqueness of Calvary derives from the prior uniqueness of Christ himself.

Secondly, the relevance of Chalcedon to the debate on divine impassibility. We have to admit at once that Chalcedon, the Formula, is explicitly opposed to the idea of divine passibility.[29] Nevertheless, the overall Christology of Chalcedon is one which I think allows us to accommodate the idea of divine passibility.

Let me start at this point: Is the relation of God to sin the same as the relation of God to pain? God cannot sin. That is why we cannot, in my judgement, have an incarnation that involves an enfleshment in fallen human nature.[30] But does that also imply that there can be no pain for God? Can God not go towards our pain? We are given an explicit parameter, ' ... yet without sin'. We are never given the parameter, '... yet without pain'.

What is the significance of the incarnation for the idea of divine passibility? Consider, first of all, the *homoousion*, which is integral to Chalcedon. It reminds us that when Christ suffers, he suffers as one who is *homoousios* with God the Father and with God the Holy Spirit. He suffers as one who is not simply generically identical with God, but as one who is *numerically* identical with God. They do not constitute two gods, but one God. That means that on the cross of Calvary the only God there is suffers and dies.

---

29. 'The Synod ... expels from the company of the priests those who dare to say that the Godhead of the Only-begotten is passible.' According to Leo, the incarnation consisted of the union of the *inviolable* divine nature with the *passible* human nature (Bindley, *Ecumenical Documents of the Faith*, p.282).

30. Cf. the words of Leo: 'Nature it was that was taken by the Lord from His mother, not defect' (Bindley, *Ecumenical Documents of the Faith*, p. 284). The language of Chalcedon itself is that Christ was 'like us in all things, sin apart'. As Bindley points out, 'This phrase is equivalent to Rom. viii.3, *en homoiomati*

Now, whether that is kerygmatically appropriate is another question. The whole notion of a crucified God is kerygmatically difficult. But you cannot ignore the *homoousion* when you speak of the crucified Christ. The one being who is God suffers on the cross. ♱

Or take again the idea of *perichoresis*: the co-inherence of the divine persons in each other. According to this concept, wherever the one is, the other is; wherever the one is, the whole Godhead is; wherever one person is, all three are. At the same time, Rahner has reminded us unforgettably of the importance of the internal distinctions between the persons to every aspect of the economic Trinity.[31] All three are involved in each *opus ad extra*, but each is involved in a different way. God creates in a three-fold way and God indwells us in a three-fold way and God redeems us in a three-fold way. I am suggesting that God suffers in a three-fold way.

On the cross of Calvary, God the Son suffers and dies. He is not only, at that point, *homoousios* with God. He is also in *perichoresis* with God the Father and God the Holy Spirit. They cannot be absent from Calvary, any more than they can be absent from the creation of the world. They are not suffering in the same way as God the Son: that would be patripassianism. The Father is not being crucified. But that is not the same as saying that the Father and the Spirit are not suffering at all. The cost of redemption cannot be confined to the one person, God the Son. There is a cost to God the Holy Spirit and there is a cost to God the Father in their communion with God the Son. At the very least, God the Father is present at Calvary as Abraham was present at the sacrifice of Abraham on Mount Moriah. We have to allow the concepts of *homoousios* and *perichoresis* to illuminate the cross. When the *anomia* (1 John 3:4) which is sin enters the world, it carries other anomalies with it: most dramatically the anomaly of pain for God himself. My position is that sin is impossible and that pain in God is impossible, but that when the one impossibility becomes reality

---

sarkos hamartias. Our Lord took *perfect* Manhood, not *fallen* manhood. His was not "flesh of sin," but like it in every respect, except its sinfulness' (Bindley, *Ecumenical Documents of the Faith*, p.239).

31. K. Rahner, *The Trinity* (Tunbridge Wells: Burns & Oates, 1970), pp. 34ff.

it makes the other impossibility reality as well. Sin, which cannot be, brings divine pain, which cannot be. Is it not the ultimate gravity of sin that it brought Calvary into the experience of God?

5

The Way From Chalcedon

Mark W. Elliott

Introduction

Most students of early Christian doctrine, if they retain nothing
else, remember that 'Nicea, 325' was about God the Father and
God the Son being of the same essence (*homoousios*) and that
Chalcedon insisted on Jesus Christ as 'one person, two natures'.[1]
However one often hears reference made to 'Chalcedonian' and
'Nicene' Christianity in ways which seem to construe these two
conciliar symbols or formulae confusingly. One such way is to
conceive of Chalcedon as buttressing the Nicene defence of the
deity of Christ, whereas it seems much more the case that the
later council's overall intention, by its insistence on 'two natures'
(*duas naturas*) was to safeguard the humanity of Christ.[2] Another
suspect tendency is that which describes the Chalcedonian formula
'two natures, one person' as 'a metaphor'. Now Nicea's
homoousion is not metaphorical, not only in the intentions of those
who framed it, but also as it stands, attempting as it does, to

---

1. See B. Studer, *Trinity and Incarnation* (ET; Edinburgh: T&T Clark, 1993)
of *Gott und unsere Erlösung* (1985); F. Young, *Nicea to Chalcedon* (London:
SCM, 1983), with their common thesis that Christological soteriology demands
prior Trinitarian understanding. For a more specifically Christologically driven
account, see: A. Grillmeier, *Christ in Christian Tradition* [Jesus der Christus
im Glauben der Kirche. English] *I*; 2nd rev. ed. - *Vol. 1: From the Apostolic age
to Chalcedon (451)* (London : Mowbrays, 1975), and II/*1 Christ in Christian
tradition ; Vol. 2: From the Council of Chalcedon (451) to Gregory the Great
(590-604): Part 1: Reception and contradiction: the development of the
discussion about Chalcedon from 451 to the beginning of the reign of Justinian*
(London : Mowbray, 1987).

2. So J. Hick, in *The Metaphor of God Incarnate* (London: SCM, 1993, 101),
writes: 'In earlier centuries the main stress was often upon Jesus' deity, although
during the last hundred years or so more often upon his humanity.'

describe God in terms such as substance and *hypostasis*. So, Rowan Williams, in 'The Nicene Heritage'[3] argues that Nicea deliberately departed from the picture language of Gnostics in which God 'became' in his own story; the Nicene doctrine denies that God had to metamorphose so that humans could understand him. Thus the incarnation shows what was 'already' going on within God; it shows that God was not simple then developed, isolated then relational. In other words, there was no need to change his nature in order to save us. Nor was there a need to posit the Son as the worshipper or agent of God, but as God in his freedom to be more than some divine consciousness who has to react to what is demanded by his masterscheme.

For its part Chalcedon describes the situation within the mystery of the inner human being, and a mysterious human being at that, Jesus Christ, and yet remains non-metaphorical in that it does not attempt to describe that situation by reference to something else (the essence of metaphor). In fact, the declaration that Christ had two natures was for them the closest approximation to the reality of the situation. That he was 'one person, two natures' is not a metaphorical statement, but a description, albeit in fairly imprecise terms, of what they believed to be the case. By 'nature' they meant 'essential being' and Christ had two of these, since he certainly was not a God pretending to be a man.

Evidently there were metaphors in circulation many of which the fathers indeed employed to help them understand the mystery, and the favourite was that of the human soul in a human body – in an analogous way, in the case of Christ, a divine nature which lodged in, was closely connected to his humanity.[4] Yet possibly because it is so obviously open to misinterpretation (a soul may be understood to dominate the body or get mixed up with it, or may keep itself from being too closely associated… according to one's philosophical anthropology, so as to suggest that Christ's divinity may envelop or be mixed in with humanity or might be

---

3. In J.M. Byrne (ed.), *The Christian Understanding of God today*, (Dublin: Blackrock, 1993). Williams' 'Barthian' reading of Athanasius is itself an interesting example of an attempt to rescue tradition for modernity.
4. See especially F. Gahbauer, *Die anthropologische Modell* (Würzburg, 1984).

quite separate from it) the soul-body metaphor is not used in the conciliar formula.[5] All that can be said is that *a posteriori* (i.e., from a reading of the Scriptures), Jesus Christ was one person and that he was equally composed of two natures. The question of how he could have two natures and still be one of us has an answer beyond Chalcedon, as we shall see. Suffice it to say here that the retreat to spirituality in the works of Baillie and Hick – that what Chalcedon points to is a human being supremely filled with grace, can meet a rejoinder. However they are by no means alone in having seen Chalcedon as the end of pre-modern attempts at Christology.

The Question of Heresy

Of course there may well have been and continue to be Christological 'readings' which run into the desert sands of heresy. For example, Adoptionism represents the belief that the one who 'grows into God' is not God as the Father is God. The implications for Christmas are that the child in the manger has not yet exercised his God-potential. According to the theory, whether articulated by D.M. Baillie, John Hick, or John Bowden, he only fully realises his 'Jungian' potential not at the resurrection but at the Cross where he is most truly the nature of God as Love – most adult – whereas in the manger he is most human, grasping like any baby. Jesus is a man on the way to full love and thus full humanity by God's grace. There is no need to talk of divinisation as becoming God any more than any believer might hope to become 'god' by theosis. Thus Chalcedon is redundant.[6]

My rejoinder to this would not be to delve into New Testament

---

5. Bernard Lonergan, *The Way to Nicea: the dialectical development of trinitarian theology* (London: Darton, Longman & Todd, 1976), argues that symbols were 'apt to be somewhat ambiguous vehicles of the truth', e.g. Isa. 6:1 was dangerous for it seemed to encourage an 'angel Christology'.

6. Disappointingly, Pannenberg stops at 'Chalcedon' and shows little sign of having 'read to the end of the story'. Jesus did not have the divine qualities from the start – that is what is meant by leaving the Father/the Father's share – but had to work back to get them; so there was no *communicatio idiomatum* of Jesus on earth (see p. 432 of the German *Systematische Theologie* II – 'Die menschliche Natur Jesu Christi hat also teil an der Gottheit des Logos, aber nur durch Vermittlung der Selbstunterscheidung von Gott').

exegesis, but rather, to point out that one could say that Adoptionism is heretical simply because it is a denial at the level of the story of Jesus Christ, that there is little continuity between the child in manger and the One on the Cross then Resurrected. This heresy is a mis-telling of the story, rather than a poor grasp of metaphysics. Also, by borrowing heavily from orthodoxy ancient and not so ancient it may be affirmed that the Virgin Birth is a sign that everything which seems naturally good is inadequate for human participation in God, and thus eternal life. However, in order to be such a sign (in biblical understanding of the term) there has to be an element of historical and not just conceptual 'contradiction'– it has to involve a real interruption in the world by God. In Christ God breaks out of swaddling of infancy so as to permeate a willing humanity in increasing movements – but the divinity is Christ's own which enables him to love because God is truly love; transcendent love however pure would not qualify one for divine status since that always includes other qualities.

An adoptionist reading of the New Testament, while at points plausible, involves a selective reading of the New Testament, a ruling out of assertions of the earthly Jesus as already divine as 'mythological', and so on. If however it can be shown that such a belief lacked the power of endurance, such as a loss of Christian identity in which such groups as the Ebionites could be absorbed by Islam after the seventh-century conquests, then, while a modern-day adoptionist might argue that such a loss is no great loss, it is evident that it has forfeited its demand to be taken seriously as a tradition within the Christian tradition. It has not stood the test of time of the classic explanation. This does not exclude the Ebionites from consideration as *contributing to* the Christian tradition, since that does not depend either on overall doctrinal 'soundness' or on 'endurance', and their value was to put the Church's mind to the test.

Of course if doctors or scientists had tried to locate Jesus' divinity or even his humanity by running a battery of tests they would have failed. Such is the kind of argument which many implicitly work from, on the assumption that the simple human nature of an ordinary person could be 'found' or evinced by using a check-list of DNA, appearance, linguistic capacity, etc. For that reason many today are unwilling to allow that Christ could have had two natures in that these would not have been open to empirical enquiry and because, supposing it could be shown that he did have two natures, Christ would be a very strange thing. So 'nature' is then understood for today as a metaphorical term which must be reducible to a literal meaning.

Modern versions of the 'two natures' theory have discussed what the cash value of 'two natures' might be. Perhaps he had 'two consciousnesses'? A.T. Hanson[7] takes this as a literal possibility – Jesus switched from one consciousness to the other, while Thomas Morris[8] is much more circumspect and prefers to talk more equivocally – that Jesus' having two natures was *something like* having two 'tracks' running in the brain, the divine one with access to the human, the human without access to the divine. John Hick, in *The Metaphor of God Incarnate*, has attacked Morris' theory, largely on the grounds that according to such a model the perfect humanity of Jesus is compromised. So in that sense Morris' new metaphor leads him into more problems; better to say vaguely that Jesus somehow was possessed of two natures than to say Jesus had two consciousnesses in the sense of two tracks which worked like some computer. Hick goes on to mention that Athanasius shared with the rest of the Fathers a naive belief that the incarnation was meant literally, that God took human form (which Athanasius did believe), and that Christ had a divine mind in a human body (which is a gross misrepresentation of Athanasius as an Apollinarian).[9] For Hick it is better to follow D.M. Baillie in regarding the incarnation as 'the supreme instance of "the paradox

---

7. 'Two Consciousnesses: the Modern Version of Chalcedon,' *SJT* 37 (1984) 471-83.

8. *The Logic of God Incarnate* (Ithaca: Cornell UP, 1986.)

9. On p104 of *The Metaphor of God Incarnate* Hick suggests: 'Let us consider the alternative possibility that "incarnation" in its theological use is a metaphor. It is an unusual kind of metaphor, since it began as literally intended language. The more usual transition is in the opposite direction, a metaphor "dying" as metaphor to become literal speech. But in the case of divine incarnation the initial idea has proved to be devoid of literal meaning and accordingly identified as metaphor, functioning in a way that is continuous with its non-religious uses.'

of grace".' Thus Jesus was the first man to be totally transparent to the workings of divine grace.[10] 'According to them [D. Baillie and Lampe] Jesus was conscious of the environing divine presence, and was responsive to the divine will, to such an extent that he could be said (in a natural metaphor) to have incarnated a love that reflected the divine love.'[11] The paradox (Baillie followed an Augustinian observation) is that a person is never so free as when s/he can say that whatever good was done was God's. This accords, in Hick's view with the earliest (and purest?) understanding of Christology as Christ the man moved perfectly by the Spirit. Yet for us this may mean that Jesus is not necessarily unique; there may be other 'incarnations' of 'Deity' which can be supported by religions other than Christianity.[12]

In any case, that which Hick calls 'metaphor' is a case of moving from the ultimately mysterious to the not quite so mysterious; it is to try to explain the unknown (the divine working of grace in a human being) by the Unknown (the mystery of the person of Jesus Christ). Unfortunately, metaphor usually works by clarifying and bringing the object into the range of the comprehensible by a more familiar object-model.[13] The approach of many today with respect to the Chalcedonian formula is to see it as something primitive or as something over rationalistic. Either way William Temple's statement that 'Chalcedon showed the bankruptcy of Greek metaphysics' springs to mind. However, the long track of development in the area of the doctrine of Christology did not find its terminus at Chalcedon, merely its grand junction. As Meyendorff put it: 'Dans l'histoire de la pensée chrétienne

---

10. See Hick, 'The Christology of DM Baillie,' *SJT* 11 (1958):1-12, 10.

11. John Hick, *The Metaphor of God Incarnate*, 53.

12. It is interesting that Hick has changed his mind since his article on Baillie, largely, he tells us (*Metaphor,* 106, n. 4) by the persuading of M. Wiles. The earlier article had shown that while resolving the problem of Christ's humanity, the 'grace-paradox' notion did not really explain what it meant for God to become human; for we end up treating God as a common noun rather than a proper name.

13. See J. Martin Soskice, *Metaphor and Religious Language* (Oxford: OUP, 1985); P. Ricoeur, *The Rule of Metaphor* (Toronto: Univ. of Toronto Press, 1977); E.F. Kittay, *Metaphor* (Oxford: OUP, 1987).

orientale, le Concile de Chalcédoine (451) ouvrit un chapitre nouveau.' Rahner in his influential article asked the question: 'Chalcedon – end or beginning?', although he made it seem that it was a jumping-off point for his, or at least mid-twentieth century, theology in which Jesus was special because in him the Word assumed human history,[14] and a jumping-off that meant a jumping *over* of so much Christological thinking that went on between 451 and 1951. This is all the more surprising in that Rahner helpfully noted how the incarnation was not a surprise, but a high-point in the time-long process of interaction between God and the world. If God works to reveal himself over a duration, would he not do the same in illuminating the mystery of the special 'moment' of incarnation through the years of the history of the Church?

The Route from Chalcedon barred
One reason why Christology between Chalcedon and, say, Schleiermacher has been neglected is partly because of the poor standing of some ecumenical councils. While Rome and the Eastern Churches recognise the first six (up to Constantinople III), after that point there is disagreement – this is despite the crucial teaching (inspired by the theology of Maximus the Confessor and accepted by the orthodox 'Eastern' churches) that Christ formed a new humanity, restoring to humans free will 'in Christ', yet a true and complete one so that his human action is God's human action.[15]

Meanwhile Protestants remembered how undemocratic and

14. 'In Christus ist der Logos nicht nur (statisch) Mensch geworden, er hat menschliche Geschichte angenommen' Karl Rahner, 'Ende oder Angfang?' in Grillmeier (ed.), *Das Konzil von Chalkedon* Vol III (Freiburg, 1957), p19.

15. Christoph Schönborn in his article, '681-1981: Ein vergessenes Konzilsjubiläum – eine versäumte ökomenische Chance' in *Freiburger Zeitschrift für Philosophie und Theologie* 29 (1982), 157-174, adduces three reasons why the Western Church ignored the 3rd Council of Constantinople (681): its condemnation of the former Pope Honorius (625-38) as a monothelite heretic – agreed to by the contemporary Pope Leo II, but a problem for the dogma of Roman infallibility; the widespread ignorance that Christology had developed since Chalcedon (451); and also that the notion of free will as a reality even for the baptised was not acceptable in hyper-Augustinian circles in the early medieval West.

even dangerous councils were for the likes of Jan Hus who was promised safety if he came to Konstanz. Calvin (*Inst* IV ix,8) mentions 'Nicaea, Constantinople, Ephesus I, Chalcedon, and the like' in 1543; and Bullinger (*Decades*, 1550) also limited 'the councils' to these four. There was of course a great interest in Christology among early Protestant theologians, implicit in Luther (with his 'Catholic Christology'[16]) and as the repercussion of the Eucharistic controversies. Carried out by thinkers of no mean ability, nevertheless the Lutheran-Calvinist split along the lines of Alexandria-Antioch suggests that even those Confessional Protestants who cared deeply about the truth of the matter remained, to some degree 'stuck' at Chalcedon, beyond which it felt unsafe.[17] Luther in his *Von den Konziliis und Kirchen* (1539) recognised only the first four ecumenical councils. Schönborn suspects that this is due to the Protestant refusal to give humanity its due in salvation, keeping its role wholly passive, rather than seeing Christ's human will as moving the human Christ to agree with the divine will.

Since the glory days of sixteenth and seventeenth century Protestantism, when a creative connection was made between the theories of the *extracalvinisticum*[18] and of *kenosis*, there has been

16. Franz Posset, *Luther's Catholic Christology* (Milwaukee: Northwestern, 1988).

17. H. Heppe, *Reformed Dogmatics* (also Schmid-Pohlmann *Doctrinal Theology of the Lutheran Church*); see also K. Barth, *Göttingen Dogmatics* (ET; Grand Rapids: Eerdmans, 1991), 156-60. As has been observed of Barth, he was pre-modern in his Christology: 'I myself do not see why we should not say what the creed says along with all the early church' (161); 'For some 200 years the scientific tradition of Protestant dogmatics has been broken off.....We can rightly bring many criticisms against the older orthodox. But they did at least know what they were talking about' (167). For the older orthodox Christology gets summed up under the heading in Heppe (Ch. 17) of the Mediator of the Covenant, rather than God-Man as such; we get enhypostasis and something like the one theandric energy in the notion of *unio apotelesmatum* (the mediatorial operations).

18. 'Wonderfully, the Son of God came down from heaven in such a way that he did not however leave heaven. Wonderfully he willed to develop in the womb of the virgin, to be turned out into the world and to hang on a cross in such a way as always to fill the world just as from the beginning' (Calvin Inst II, 13,4, cited by Barth CD IV/1,180f: 'it was the abstract Lutheran denial of being

little development of the theology of the incarnation.[19] In Anglicanism, *Lux Mundi: on the Religion of the Incarnation* was about many things, but a defence of orthodox Christology was not particularly high on the agenda. Even within the Catholic Church there is not so much as one would like: perhaps in part due to the cutting-off from Neo-Chalcedonianism after the Lateran Synod of 649 and a love of the simpler, purer theology of Chalcedon expounded by Leo, then Boethius; perhaps in part due to the feeling that sterile medieval debates can only be presented in a sterile way. The German language *Handbuch der Dogmengeschichte* has yet to get round to covering the history of Christology. So when Rowan Williams gives his bibliography in his *Theologische Realencyclopedie* article 'Jesus Christus III: Mittelalter', the only general work which covers the period between 500 and 1500 in the West is Josef von Bach's work from the nineteenth century.[20] Likewise, for the East, John Meyendorff's *Le Christologie Byzantine* is neither detailed nor beyond suspicion in some of its judgements and seems to peter out somewhere around John of Damascus with a chapter on Gregory Palamas as a not wholly pertinent after-thought.

It is perhaps worth remembering that the period from the fathers

---

a Logos *extra carnem* which was the real innovation.. [while for Calvin] He who becomes a creature and exists in that *forma servi* does not cease to be Lord and Creator and therefore to exist in the *forma Dei*.'

19. A. McGrath, *The Making of German Christology* (Leicester: Apollos, 1994):44, is *not* the place to find a discussion of the Incarnation of God, but only of the human Jesus conceived of in various ways. Jüngel offers hope, for unlike Barth he does not detach dogmatics from the historical Jesus, but in his 'Thesen'-*Unterwegs zur Sache* – the Einmaligkeit of the resurrection of Jesus suggests something 'odd' uncanny about him. C. Gunton has argued that Jüngel focuses too much on the immanence of God which is his 'humanity' (following Hegel) rather than the humanity of Christ as such: 'It is God the Spirit as the focus of the relationship of God the Father whose office it is to maintain attention on the particular human being, Jesus of Nazareth, as the one mediator between God and the world.' 'The being and attributes of God. Eberhard Jüngel's dispute with the classical philosophical tradition,' in J. Webster (ed.), *The Possibilities of Theology* (Edinburgh: T.&T. Clark, 1994), 7-22, 21.

20. *Die Dogmengeschichte des Mittelalters von christologischen Standpunkt oder Die mittelalterliche Christologie vom 8. Bis 16. Jh.*, (2 Bde., Wien 1873-75).

to the Enlightenment was full of Christological reflection from which our own thinking might well benefit.

Nine Steps from Chalcedon

1. Henry Chadwick observed: 'Basil of Seleucia declared that Christ is "known in two natures", a formula which in effect echoes Cyril's proviso that the dual nature of Christ is discerned only in the abstract by the reflective mind, not in the concrete by the worshipping soul.' But 'known in two natures' would be the downfall of Chalcedon.[21] This was not so different from Theodore of Mopsuestia's view, that in reality Christ was two and is one only when he is worshipped. In both cases, the appearance is unity, under which a deeper reality lies. Whatever the reasons for the failure to 'sell' Chalcedon to the 'Monophysites', there is a suspicion that soteriological concerns were always to the fore in the emphasis on the duality of Christ: there simply had to be a full humanity if humanity were to be saved. But, as commonly observed since Lebon, there was a heavy Cyrillian 'spin' put on Chalcedon in the century following it. Thus, against the Apthartodocetists, Leontius of Byzantium insisted that Christ's true humanity experienced all suffering but dealt with, or processed it, differently since the Word himself co-suffered ('impassibly').

2. After all, it was the *hypostasis* (indivisible subject) not the divine nature as such which suffered. Both Leontius of Byzantium and Leontius of Jerusalem insisted that no *physis* could be without a *hypostasis*. For the latter Leontius, in Christ there was a synthesis of characteristics or idiomata; which meant that the one *hypostasis* was a synthetic *hypostasis*. Here he employed a new definition of hypostasis as 'being by itself' rather than the Boethian definition of 'being according to each'— as if a divisible being shared out or carved out into individual shapes from a common block. In Christ the divine person can

---

21. H. Chadwick, Intro, to A.-M. Festugière(ed.), *Actes du Concile de Chalcédoine*, (Paris, 1982), 11, 14.

be the hypostasis (the true personal reality) without downgrading his human-ness: the human nature is still complete, yet 'borrows' and resides in (*en*) the hypostasis of the Word and relies on the latter for its personality, its expression, its becoming (Leontius of Jerusalem). However, surely createdness is not part of divinity? Indeed not, but if createdness is understood as a non-uncreatedness then it is not the case that humanity has some attributes divinity lacks but rather that it lacks something divinity has and which, in Christ, divinity supplies. Humanity is only divinity minus.[22] It might appear to be divinity plus sin, but in fact since sin is a defect, not an attribute, humanity has a 'minus' in that.

At the Second Council of Constantinople (553) there was a fairly successful attempt made to reconcile the two Christologies of Alexandria and Antioch along these lines.[23] Any unity is only in the hypostasis; so any danger of mixing or of domination is avoided.[24] One might like to speak of two sources of energy but also of only one output. But *enhypostasia* does not mean a lessening of the humanity as *anhypostatic,* as if it was always 'borrowing' the divine hypostasis, as Reformed theology (from the seventeenth century to Barth) has sometimes insisted.

---

22. For Leontius of Jerusalem's doctrine of *enhypostasia* see A. Grillmeier, *Christus,* 2/2, 302-13. Analogously, the likeness of human flesh can be maintained if 'sin' is construed as (that which is on the way to) non-being, a lessening of humanity; Christ in being sinless did not lack anything human.

23. Meyendorff, *Le Christ dans la theologie byzantine*, (Paris: Cerf, 1969).

24. K-H Uthemann, in 'Der Neuchalkedonismus als Vorbereitung des Monotheletismus. Ein Beitrag zum eigentlichen Anliegen des Neuchalkedonismus,' *Studia Patristica* (Leuven: Peeters, 1993), 373-414, argues that by the mid-sixth century, the flavour of neo-Chalcedonian was truly Chalcedonian rather than hyper-Cyrillian in that it continued to balance one person and two natures and to continue to fight against monophysitism. What it *did* let in was the concept of one *hypostatic* energy; Leontius of Jerusalem came to speak of a physical union of Logos and sarx: 'Auf Grund dieser Enhypostasie sind die Idiomata der sarx Christi göttlich, wohl besser gesagt, vergöttlicht, da sie so eine Bindung an die göttliche Natur haben' (388). It would take Maximus to warn against this 'synthetic' version of Christ.

3. In Jesus' saying: 'Your will be done', the implication is that, as
the Antiochene theologians would put it, it is his human will
that is expressing this wish.[25] Christ is so much under the
influence of the Father that he 'automatically' follows the
Father's will due to the energetic effects of the divine nature;
there is no indecision of the gnomic will: it does not have to
choose over against the divine purpose. Maximus expresses
the belief that the humanity of Christ is made more perfect for
its being associated intimately in Christ with divinity, or more
accurately God the Word. The Word perfected Christ's
humanity; that humanity, made according to the image of God
(the Word himself), even at its most mature (e.g. at the
resurrection of Jesus) expands as the divine power removes
the obstacles to expansion. He can then be fully human because
he is fully divine. The two natures do not mix to form some
third thing but there is a tight *perichoresis*, literally a pouring-
around, an inter-penetration resulting in the joint end-product
of a holy way of being. Thus there are not 'two tracks' in
Christ's mind but rather a human consciousness which prays
in Gethsemane that the Father's will be done, but since that
consciousness is also divine he is able to obey such a calling
fully, perfectly.[26] Maximus wrote to Pyrrhos: why, given that
Christ is without sin should twoness of will in him mean
conflict? For something different does not mean something
opposite.[27] As the Third Council of Constantinople (AD 681)

---

25. See A. Louth, *Maximus the Confessor* (London: Routledge, 1996); Lars
Thunberg *Microcosm and Mediator* (Chicago and La Salle: Open Court), 227f.

26. Schillebeeckx wants to argue that Jesus' hypostasis was the Father
himself, since Jesus was so turned towards him. 'This implies that the centre of
Jesus' being-as-man was rooted not in himself but in God the Father – something
borne out also by the historical evidence about Jesus; the centre, support,
hypostasis, in the sense of what confers steadfastness, was his relationship to
the Father with whose cause he identified himself' (p. 658). He concludes:
'Deeper than the Abba experience therefore, and its ground, is the Word of
God, the self-communication of the Father' (p. 666f.). For Schillebeeckx, as for
many Western theologians, the Trinity has no ontology; God *really* is one; the
Word and the Father are identified as one and the same and God 'needs' to have
man if he is to have anyone to relate to.

27. PG 91,292A ; cf. Guido Bausenhart, *'In Allem uns gleich außer Sünde'*:

affirmed, the will of the man Jesus, 'when he is considered as Saviour, is not in opposition to God, being made divine in its entirety.'[28] Divine energies transform the human nature/being from the moment of conception in Christ's case. Thus there is no place for any idea that Christ may ever have been ignorant of anything (since ignorance very soon becomes sin). Rather the iron in the fire became fully fiery.[29] Contact with God is given through Christ's glorified humanity, the only mediator, which is a point which Gregory Palamas would emphasise.[30]

4. The rise and fall of so-called 'Adoptionism' in Spain is an all too neglected point in the development of Christology. Also on closer inspection Chalcedon and the Spanish adoptionists saw the personal unity in Christ in quite different ways.[31] John Cavadini has argued that for the adoptionists, the Islamic ruling culture was not such a compromising force as many think. The Spanish did not play down Christ's divinity but emphasised that he was the agent in the incarnation.[32] For humanity to be adopted meant something like its being assumed. What may have sounded heterodox was the idea that Christians are meant to become 'Christs', which merely meant like Christ.[33] He

---

Studien zum Beitrag Maximos' des Bekenners zur altkirchlichen Christologie (Mainz: Matthias-Grünewald-Verlag, 1992), 125.

28. N.P. Tanner (ed.), *Decrees of the ecumenical councils* (London: Sheed & Ward; Washington, DC: Georgetown University Press, 1990), 129.

29. See R. Maloney, 'Approaches to Christ's knowledge', in T. Finan and V. Twomey, *Studies in Patristic Christology* (Dublin: Four Courts, 1998).

30. See J. Meyendorff, *A study of Gregory Palamas* (London, 1964).

31. Jesus Solano, 'El concilio de Calcedonia y la controversia adopcionista del siglo VIII en España', in Grillmeier *Das Konzil*, 841-71, 849.

32. John C. Cavadini, *The Last Christology of the West: Adoptionism in Spain and Gaul, 785-820* (Philadelphia: University of Pennsylvania Press, 1993), 8. The roots of this Spanish theology were in North African Latin theology, Isidore of Seville and the Council of Toledo. See José Madóz, *Le symbole du Ive Concile de Tolède* (Louvain: Spicilegium sacrum Lovaniense, 1938). Also, Gary B. Blumenshine, *Liber Alcuini contra Haeresim Felicis* (Vatican City: Studi e testi 285), 1980.

33. Löfstedt (ed.)*CCCM* 59 (Turnhout: Brepols, 1984), 29; 1083-5: 'et cum adoptivo adoptivi, et cum advocato advocati, et cum Christo christi, et cum parvulo parvuli, et cum servo servi.'

became firstborn (*primogenitus*) by assuming, not an adopted one, but adoption. 'The point is much more subtle, namely that *by assuming* flesh or a body, etc., the Word, the "Only-begotten" with regard to nature, becomes the "First-born" in adoption and grace.'[34] The change is that from being Son by nature he, through emptying, needs grace to be the Son by grace. Beatus' problem was his concern that Christ's humanity should come between the divine and Christian souls and that the historical Jesus never went so low as to be in a position of weakness and bondage, as Elipandus seemed to suggest. 'The point is that since the human being *is* the self-emptying of the Word, he must be a human being perfect and complete, otherwise the self-emptying of the Word would not be perfect and complete.'[35] Both agreed in the belief not that Jesus as a man is now only the adoptive Son of God but that as a man he is the Son of God (naturally). 'There is in Alcuin's report and analysis of Elipandus no hint at all of what we have proposed as Elipandus' true positions, namely that by the self-emptying of the Word, by his assuming of a human nature, he – the Word himself – becomes "full of grace" or adoptively a son".'[36] For Elipandus there is no question of a man who was adopted into sonship. That is a caricature of his position. Elipandus thought of Beatus as guilty of docetism. Sonship for the adoptionists had to mean the sonship of nature not just relation – he must actually be a human son of God. Both forms of Spanish Christology eschewed the 'two natures, one person' system – which was why the educated and ecumenically minded Alcuin rejected both. However the Spanish did set out a Christology which focused more on the relationship of the Incarnate Son to the Father and Spirit and less on the combination of natures within the Son.

---

34. Cavadini, 33.
35. Ibid., 60.
36. Ibid., 87.

5. The pressing importance of soteriological considerations, the central question of the early middle ages – how could humanity be saved? – led to the view of Christ's humanity as primarily *the way* to salvation. With such an emphasis there was a loss of how Christ could have been divine and human. In fact, there may have been a loss of balance, an inability to find the Chalcedonian Golden Mean and a tendency to deviate both ways and have to work hard to get to where Chalcedon had long before arrived. More detailed soteriological considerations included the question: where did the Word go when the soul departed from the body on the cross? The contemporaneous growth of Christ-mysticism in the twelfth-century Renaissance led to consideration of *assumptus homo* Christology, one which started from the reality of the human being who was then assumed by the Word.[37] By the grace of union the Christ man becomes God. Abelard promoted the opposite to the *assumptus homo* theory, the *habitus* theory (the humanity was a garment, a 'habit') which came to be associated with the nihilianistic theory – that Christ's humanity was, substantially speaking, in itself, nothing since it was not a person. The West's most crucial link with the thinking of the Greek fathers was the encyclopedic works of John of Damascus; in 1150 Eugenius III had *De fide orthodoxa* translated; although an earlier partial translation had been achieved in Hungary (by Cerbanus/Szigeti), which Peter Lombard used first before correcting it in light of the Papal one. The results for Lombard (and the many he influenced all the way up to the Reformation) were a superhuman Christ who largely works upon believers by example, although he rejected the Abelardian nihilianism: there was still a human soul and body, a humanity: 'Peter holds that the Word was joined to human nature both in the sense of being joined to a concrete human being and in the sense of being joined to humanity in general.'[38] The *assumptus homo* theory is little better for 'in emphasizing the intimate union between the divinity and the

---

37. L. Ott, 'Mittelalterliche Christologie' in Grillmeier (ed.) Das Konzil von Chalkedon.

38. See M.L. Colish, *Peter Lombard* (Leiden: Brill, 1994), II, 738.

109

humanity of Christ, in effect it absorbs the human nature into the divine nature in such a way as to blur the distinction between the two natures which proponents of this theory claim to be defending.'[39] The humanity is integrated into the divinity but not so as to be changed by it, for it must play its Anselmian role as the perfect human; yet by grace Christ was exempt from any learning process as a human being.

6. Aquinas spoke of the beatific vision, available to saints after death, as that which gives us the light by which we can see God (cf. the use of Psalm 35:10 'In your light we see light', especially in *Summa Contra Gentiles* III, 53). Christ's soul experienced this on earth, since it was omniscient in all things except of the essence of God. Yet, despite having this perfect vision, Christ's human knowledge grew in as much as he was head of the Church and was the distributor of grace (*Summa Theologiae* III,8.1,48.1). It has been asserted that something in Thomas' Aristotelianism meant that it is with him that the agency of the humanity of Christ begins to be re-affirmed, as distinct from earlier Platonic theologies which had played it down. Whereas Chalcedon misleadingly had the idea of the Person as the one essence, and has no room for the being-in-action (*Seinsakt*) of the humanity, Thomas made such room.[40] So, if the vision of God equals 'nothing else but the primal, unobjectified consciousness of being Son of God', which is simply there as soon as the Hypostatic Union takes place, then he could not have been conscious of it. For in the 'unmediated vision' there is no 'thing in front of the thought' and thus the vision is not knowledge that he has the hypostatic union. Moreover, the basic condition of immediacy comes to consciousness during his life in his gradual self-possession of it; therefore we should not define it as *scientia certa* as Ott

---

39. *Ibid.*, 739.

40. See Francis Ruello *Le christologie de Thomas d'Aquin* (Paris: Beauchesne 1987), 343: 'Christ' comes logically before Jesus because he is united to God before he saves. Jesus is thus not an abstract humanity but always a human nature joined to God. Also, Ott in A. Grillmeier and R Williams, *Jesus Christus V* (TRE. 16 (1987).

does: better as Thomas puts it in *Summa Theologiae* III,q10,a.1 – the earthly Christ did not have the kind of comprehension that the human soul will have of God in paradise. This guarantees Christ's real humanity and its creaturely freedom: 'Freedom in the space left open for decision is indeed better than the filling up of this space for freedom by a knowledge which would suffocate this freedom.'[41]

7. According to Aquinas (*STh* III.17.2), 'the human nature shares in the existence of the divine person; and it does this by having the same sort of relation to the divine person as a concrete part has to its substance.'[42] Aquinas seems to make the human nature into an essential part of the Trinity. However, the alternative, that the human nature is an accident of the divine substance was preferable to Scotus. Christ the man had full and complete knowledge from the start (Scotus), and any change in the humanity's circumstances was one merely of an ascent from duality into unity, or, more accurately, the transformation and harmonisation of divine and human characteristics. The Word did not control humanity – otherwise Christ would not really have been human: what it does is to preserve the humanity from being dominated by any other reality. That's what is meant by the concept 'person' (*Op. Oxon.* III.1,1); there has to be individuation as well as uniqueness – there needs to be ongoing 'for itselfness': a nature subsisting in its own *suppositum*, even though Christ's human independence was *actualiter* dependent on the Word's independence. But the human nature is not a person because it is not independent.[43] As Rowan Williams asserts in his article, this is not so much to contradict Thomas

41. Ibid., 265.
42. Richard Cross, *Duns Scotus* (New York-Oxford, 1999),114.
43. See Cross, 120f.
44. TRE, 16, (1990); see further, Maria Burger, *Personalität im Horizont absoluter PrädestinationUntersuchungen zur Christologie des Johannes Duns Scotus und ihrer Rezeption in modernen theologischen Ansätzen* (Münster: Aschendorff, 1994) Scotus stressed the completeness of humanity did not mean independence from God: it is Christ who realised this. 253: 'Er fragt weiter, warum diese ontologische Moeglichkeit realisert wurde; und hierfuer legt er in

as to take him further.[44] Their main disagreement was on the ground of, the reason for, the work of the Incarnation;[45] however that did seem to imply a number of differences in their respective Christologies. Christ's human nature had no more grace than anyone else's. 'The human nature which he assumed was in itself able to sin, since it was not blessed as a result of the power of the union, and had free choice' (*Ord.* III.12. un, n. 3); the human will was not dominated by the Word since it was the will of the human nature (*pace* Aquinas); the human will *chose* to have grace and beatific vision. Thomas had been a bit more circumspect about Christ's non-experiential knowledge; even in this area he had to learn things, and did have genuine acquired knowledge through his mind's gradual self-exploration. Nevertheless, he was not taught anything by anyone else.[46]

8. For William of Ockham, the humanity which is sustained by the Word is not the same as any other humanity. Only in Christ are 'man' and 'humanity' distinct because in Christ 'man' stands for the Son's substance as a divine person, and 'humanity' for the human nature sustained by the Son as a divine person.[47] Thus in Christ, the man (*homo*) does not equal humanity (*humanitas*). The incarnation is about an uncreated person with a created nature which could have been a donkey,

---

der Lehre von der absoluten Prädestination eine sehr eigenständige Antwort vor Nicht das zufällige Ereignis des sündenfalls löste diese Realisierung aus, sondern das sich aus dem gottlichen Wesen ergebende wollen von Mitliebenden' – a dynamic perspective of love – 'Jesus Christus ist zu höchster Gnade und Herrlichkeit praedestiniert, die ihm durch die hypostatische Union zuteil wird' 254: 'Aus der ontologischen Unabgeschlossenheit menschlicher Personalität läßt sich nicht die Forderung nach Annahme durch eine göttliche Person ableiten... Scotus macht gerade deutlich daß das Eintreten der Möglichkeit der hypostatischen Union kontingent erfolgt.'

45. Cross, 127, traces this back to Rupert of Deutz, *De glor.13* (CCCM 29:409-10). But of course it is there in Eriugena, and is more likely to have reached Duns Scotus by the mediation of Robert Grosseteste.

46. See STh III.q12, a2

47. *Reportatio* III, q.1, B-S, as paraphrased by G.Leff, *William of Ockham*, (Manchester: Manchester University Press, 1975), 434f.

stone, etc., because the uncreated is as different from a brute
as it is from a created human. Scotus had already suggested
this on the grounds of God's power. In nominalist thought one
cannot think of *humanitas* as a collective concept or a universal;
rather it only refers to the 'human' characteristics of any one
person, so that Ockham did not mean that the whole of the
human race was thus united to the Word.[48] God is so much
subject of the incarnation that one can say 'God is able to sin'.
'If he took on human nature without any gifts [of grace] and
the nature were left to itself, he would be able to sin. And this
is no more unfitting than to say that Christ suffers, is beaten
and dies. But since people shudder to hear such and that it
sounds bad, I deny it.'[49] Against Scotus who had said that
Christ's soul had the maximum grace possible, for Ockham,
the Word is in charge of a human who is only by degree not by
status different from us. In fact God the Word as subject
becomes man/body/capable of sin; but this is only meant
denominatively. Since personality is a defect of non-
dependence on God, Christ's anhypostatic human nature lacks
nothing and is therefore perfect. Against any *assumptus-homo*
Christologies, it was a non-dependent human nature which gets
united to the Word.

9. According to R. Riedinger, Nicholas of Cusa was the first to
have direct knowledge of the contents of the Council of
Constantinople, 681.[50] (Although Thomas Aquinas had partial
knowledge through their transmission by the Ps-Isidorean
decretals.) Cusa stressed God's ability to join the created and
the uncreated. The possibility of a 'coincidence of opposites'
meant that God can be both infinite and tiny (infinitesimal),
and in the Son God became open to movement. 'Jesus is thus
the absolute creative power of God and in Him as in the Son,

---

48. See Williams, TRE 16, 753f: the nominalist emphasis was on a
communication of terms, not of a real exchange: it became that God is man, not
God became man.

49. I b III, q X (350).

50. See R. Riedinger, 'Griechische Konzilsakte auf den Wege ins Mittelalter'
in *Annuarium Historiae conciliarum* 9 (1977): 253-301.

the middle person, the eternal Father and the Holy Spirit dwell. All things are in the Word; in that most high and most perfect human nature which mightily embraces all creatable beings, all things exist, that all fullness may dwell in Him.'[51] The human intellect where this contact between God and creature is made exists in its fulness when it grows to fill the space of the divine nature, becoming fuller by the vision of that divine perfection. 'The intelligence of Jesus, altogether the most perfect in existence, can be personally supposited only in the divine intellect, which alone is actually all things. Intellect in man is potentially all things and grows by steps from potency to act, so that the further it grows the less it is in potency. But the maximal intellect, the actually full term of the potency of every intellectual nature, could not exist unless it were also in God who is in all things. It is as though a polygon inscribed in a circle were human nature and the circle were divine nature. If the polygon were to become the maximum, than which no greater could exist, it could never exist by itself in finite angles, but only as a circular figure. In consequence it would not have a figure of its own proper being separable even intellectually from the eternal circular figure itself.'[52] There is a sense that when the human being has transcended the limits of its own species, then in order to keep moving it must move on 'up' into God.[53]

Jesus' vision of God in post-enlightenment terms

The modern, existential approach to Christology goes back to Luther with his refusal to divide Christ up into natures, or spirit/soul/body. Thus, on account of its silences and non-speculative discourse Luther's Christology appears fairly orthodox, only

---

51. Nicolas Cusa *On Learned Ignorance* translated by Fr. Germain Heron ; with an introduction by Dr.J.B. Hawkins.(London: Routledge & Kegan Paul, 1954), III/4; 139. Also R. Haubst *Die Christologie des Nikolaus von Kues* (Freiburg, 1956).

52. Ibid.,140.

53. See R. Haubst, 'Der evolutionsgedanke in der Cusanischen Theologie', in G. Santinello (ed.) *Nicolo Cusano agli inizi del mondo moderno* (Firenze, 1971), 295-307, 304.

veering towards 'monophysitism' in his accounts of the post-resurrection Christ who is present in the Eucharist, although it may be read as a voluntarist Christology in which the key factor is the 'biblical' one of 'will' as something which is common to God and humans.[54] Add to this the legacy of the enlightenment, the Kantian turn to humanity and one obtains a transcendental Christology of the kind represented by Karl Rahner. According to Rahnerian anthropology, 'among those forms of knowledge there is a knowledge, concerned with itself, which is *a priori* and not concentrated on an object, and which is a basic condition of existence for the spiritual subject. In it the subject is present to himself, and at the same time is aware of his transcendental relation to the totality of possible objects of knowledge and freedom.' Also, there is a positiveness of ignorance which the Greeks did not appreciate: *docta ignorantia*: 'a certain amount of not-knowing is essential to the free act of man' so that Jesus was able to risk. Even the beatific vison, if Jesus had it, was the clear vision of an incomprehensible mystery. Can we really say that Jesus had bliss all his life like that of the blessed in heaven? Rahner has insisted that the biblical Jesus had a *visio* that was *immediata* but not *beata*: in fact, the nearness of God caused him pain. This vision was not so much added on to the hypostatic union but was very much part of it, if we are to understand the hypostatic union 'ontologically' as well as 'ontically'.[55]

Returning to the concerns of the present day, the cry is often heard: 'how can so much Christological speculation help one

---

54. Marc Lienhard, *Luther: témoin de Jésus-Christ: les étapes et les thèmes de la Christologie du Réformateur* (Paris: Cerf, 1973), esp. 388: 'Le Réformateur n'a guère parlé d'une "co-opération" entre les deux natures. Cette conceptualité est étrangère à sa pensée. Mais il a beaucoup souligné l'activité humaine de Jésus-Christ qui traduisait en même temps l'attitude du Fils éternel... Si notre interprétation est exacte, il semble qu'il ait admis une volonté purement humaine du Christ traduisant dans l'histoire et dans les conditions d'une existence humaine la volonté éternelle du Fils'

55. Rahner, ('Knowledge and consciousness in Christ' in Vorgrimler (ed.) *Dogmatic versus biblical theology*, (ET: London: Buns & Oates, 1964), 247. Also, at 256 'In other words, only in this unique, subjective unity of the human consciousness of Jesus with the Word, in the most absolute nearness, uniqueness and definitiveness, does the Hypostatic Union take place in its full reality.'

encounter the living Christ of the gospel?' Even in modern theological philosophising, and despite its protests, there is just too much Platonism! In so much thinking we read of a Platonic universal 'humanity' being changed by a particular 'Jesus'. 'If the "humanity" that Christ shares with all other human beings is not an individual entity, then how can the Incarnation change or effect it?'[56] A simple, if not simplistic answer to this is that it is not so much that the Word assumed a universal humanity (as Ockham and Cusa, for example, have demonstrated), but it is because the Logos himself is the Universal principle of everything that the particular man was not so particular – the divine logos is so much there.

Back to the Bible

Yet again, how does all this metaphysical sophistication help people believe any more in Jesus Christ as divine? Why has Christianity endured? Is it only because as a myth it goes deep into the collective unconscious, a myth of one who was claimed by the Church to have died for humanity, or is it that the truth always wins out? Synoptic studies about whether 'Son of Man' is or is not a special title relating to Daniel 7 have come to an impasse, and it seems clear that Jesus is only explicitly 'the Son of God' in the later Gospel of John. Yet there is something to be made from recent treatments of the concept of Messiah. By that is meant someone who has existed before taking up earthly life. One who is hoped for as the one to put a final end to the reign of evil (in Qumran the eschatology is literally meant, in the New Testament it is not so clear – N.T. Wright); one who is like a Son of Man, in the likeness of human flesh. William Horbury in his recent work has pointed to the figure of Josiah in later parts of the Hebrew bible – at the heart of the idea of the Isaianic ideal king and in 2 Chronicles 35.25: 'a messianic prototype who is defeated and slain, rather than continually victorious.'[57] Particularly important in the New Testament is the attestation of Romans 9:5 which connects

---

56. R. Sturch, The *Word and the Christ*, (Oxford: Clarendon, 1991), 35.

57. W. Horbury, *Jewish Messianism and the Cult of Christ* (London: SCM, 1998), 21. 'An element in this argument has been the presentation of a case for

the Messiah with the one who is over all, God blessed for ever; whether there is, for Paul, total identification is open to question, a question of punctuation.

If one can speak of a Messianic trajectory, it can be seen in the concern of the Syriac-speaking church not only to argue for Jesus's Messiahship, but also for the fulness of his deity.[58] Both are included in Aphrahat and in the Christology of Ephraim; there is not only a love of describing Jesus in material and 'human' images which relate to his place in salvation-history, but also an insistence on his divine status.[59] From this background emerges the long practice of praying to Christ 'as to a god' (Pliny), as reported in Josef Jungmann's important work.[60]

Two things argue for seeing the Messiah in divine terms: the facility of pouring out the Spirit and the authority and power to drive out evil.[61] For the post-Pentecost church, Acts strongly suggests that this must be 'in the name of Jesus'. For James Dunn,

widespread recognition of a "spiritual messiah" with superhuman characteristics, e.g. from Nu 24:7. Recognition of this phenomenon tends to modify the sharp contrasts often drawn between a "human" Jewish Messiah and a "divine" Christian figure' (151).

58. M. Hengel, 'Christological Titles in Early Christianity' in J. Charlesworth (ed) *The Messiah . developments in earliest Judaism and Christianity: the First Princeton Symposium on Judaism and Christian Origins* (Minneapolis: Fortress Press, 1992), 425-48, 443: 'Secondly, it is clear that the glorification of Christ, the doctrines of his preexistence, creation mediation and exaltation did not remove the scandal of his shameful death, but rather deepened it..a crucified *God* was for every educated person in antiquity a shameless impertinence, indeed an absurdity; this pre-existence meant it was no pagan apotheosis.'

59. ' "Arius Hellenizans?": Ephräm der Syrer und die neoniceanischen Kontroversen seiner Zeit' *ZKTh* 101 (1990):21-57: Edmund Beck, *Ephrams Trinitatslehre im Bild von Sonne/Feuer, Licht und Warme* (Louvain: Peeters, 1981). [Series title:Corpus scriptorum Christianorum orientalium; 425. Subsidia; 62.] Peter Bruns (ed.) *Unterweisungen/Aphrahat*; (Freiburg: Herder, 1991). I. Ortiz de Urbina, *Die Gottheit Christi bei Afrahat* (Roma: Pont. institutum orientalium studiorum), 1933: [Series title: Orientalia christiana; 87].

60. J.A. Jungmann, *The place of Christ in liturgical prayer* (2nd ed; London: G. Chapman), 1989.

61. Max Turner in *Power from on high : the Spirit in Israel's restoration and witness in Luke-Acts* (Sheffield: Sheffield Academic Press, 1996) has written how in the Lucan source of Luke 4:18-19 there is no doubt that liberation is not just equated with 'forgiveness from sins'; rather it is equated with 'deliverance

there was an 'influence of messianic ideas on Jesus in several ways. (1) Some ideas he reacted against. In particular, the current view of the royal messiah was one which he did not find helpful as a means of understanding or informing his mission. (2) Some he drew on and used to inform his own vision of what he had been called to.[62] If Jesus was understood to be the Messiah in at least a semi-divine way, or to pre-exist in a way analogous to archangels, and yet is confessed as one who was higher than them but is only for a season made lower than the angels (Heb 1:5-14), then we can see 'Messiah' as a concept which takes us a good part of the way towards Nicea.

Tom Wright has spoken of the vocation of Jesus as constitutive of his divinity: 'Jesus' conviction that it was his task and his role, his vocation, not only to speak of this kingdom, but also to enact and embody it…. He was coming to Zion, doing what YHWH had promised to do. He believed himself called to do and be what in the scriptures only Israel's God did and was.'[63] My response to this would be that the term 'incarnation' fits with the story of a

from captivity to Belial'….'It is Jesus' role as the Isaianic soteriological prophet that dominates the conceptual foreground.'

62. J. Dunn, 'Messianic Ideas and their influence on the Jesus of History' in J. Charlesworth (ed.), *The Messiah: developments in earliest Judaism and Christianity: the First Princeton Symposium on Judaism and Christian Origins* (Minneapolis: Fortress Press, 1992), 365-381, 380.

63. N.T Wright, 'Jesus and the Idea of God,' *Ex Auditu* 14 (1998): 42-56, 51-53. Wright quotes from the conclusion of *Jesus and the Victory of God*: '"Awareness of vocation" is by no means the same thing as Jesus having the sort of "supernatural" awareness of himself, of Israel's god, and of the relation between the two of them, as is often envisaged by those who, concerned to maintain a "high" christology, place it within an eighteenth-century context of implicit Deism where one can maintain Jesus' "divinity" only by holding some form of docetism. Jesus did not, in other words, "know that he was God" in the same way that one knows one is male or female, hungry or thirsty, or that one ate an orange an hour ago. His "knowledge" was of a more risky, but perhaps more significant, sort: like knowing one is loved. One cannot 'prove' it except by living by it. Jesus' prophetic vocation thus included within it the vocation to enact, symbolically, the return of YHWH to Zion. His messianic vocation included within it the vocation to attempt certain tasks which, according to scripture, YHWH had reserved for himself. He would take upon himself the role of messianic shepherd, knowing that YHWH had claimed this role as his own. He would perform the saving task which YHWH had said he alone could

man called to become increasingly aware of his pre-existent identity and his vocation to eschatological dominion; it need not mean deism or docetism as Wright suggests.

A feminist challenge

However objections to the absoluteness of Jesus Christ come from other directions. Two shall be mentioned. First, there is the feminist challenge to Christology as posed by Daphne Hampson: '(T)he framework of thought that made it [the patristic solution] possible is no longer open to us...' [and there is] 'the problem that the symbolism of Christ is somehow male. Even though it may be said that what is taken on in the incarnation is a humanity in which we all share, it is still the case that the form in which this human nature is said to have been taken on is that of a male human being.'[64] Five years on, Hampson turned to criticise the Christian account of soteriology. 'I do not have the least desire that God should take on our condition.' [Better that God be] 'a power and a love which lifts us out of our suffering and which heals us.'[65] One may be excused for wondering then if it is a problem that the one who reveals God is a male human being, if in fact it is the Spirit's energy (and the power of the Word perhaps) which effectively renders salvation. After all, the human element for Hampson is central to the New Testament: 'The focus is not so much on the man Jesus, but the life praxis of the Jesus community....' An inter-personal reality, the community (of faith?) takes over, as symbolised by the tree of life of Revelation 22.2: 'If there is a dominant Christology here today it is one where Christ comforts, consoles and enables us to live with the system and still be Christian'. What we need is destabilizing kyriarchy: 'Thus, a Christology that disowns the hero concept. (When, in his earthly life, did Jesus give a crumb of encouragement to his being made a hero?)'[66]

Yet Hampson here comes close to the mediocrity of Ivan

achieve. He would do what no messenger, no angel, but only the "arm of YHWH" the presence of Israel's god, could accomplish.'

64. Daphne Hampson, *Theology and Feminism* (Oxford: Blackwell, 1990), 58.

65. Daphne Hampson, *After Christianity* (SCM, 1995), 146.

66. Ibid., 202, quoting Mary Grey.

Karamazov's version of Christianity as that of a lowest common denominator which can be accepted by 'ordinary people'. Orthodox Christology demands the imitation of Christ, reveals the status of human beings as extraordinary, and promotes more than a merely passive admiration for the work of the Superman. Jesus as the hero of the faith relies, as the western medieval tradition emphasised, on grace: what he is and does thanks to the immediate presence of the Word and the direction of the Spirit.

Second objection: pluralism

Theology in the latter part of the twentieth century has swung between the need to recognise particularity and the concern to acknowledge that this may be scandalous. Fewer people seem interested in a particular God, yet that seems to encourage a retreat to the 'language' of traditions while maintaining the universality of a public God. The problem is at least as old as the Hebrew prophets.[67] The recent and controversial book by Jacques Dupuis rejects the notion of the 'absoluteness of Christ', even in its Rahnerian formulation (that believers in other faiths may be 'implicit Christians'). 'The reason is that absoluteness is an attribute of the Ultimate Reality of Infinite Being which must not be predicated of any finite reality, even the human existence of the Son of God-made-man.'[68] So, he is a universal Saviour as the Word but not the absolute revealer as the Incarnate One.

Against this one can make the obvious comment that in the same sentence that Christ calls himself the way (of salvation), he also says he is the truth (and the life).[69] Dupuis' pluralism is based in part on the idea that revelation has not ceased. 'In fact, as will

---

67. Cf. F.-W. Marquardt, *Von Elend und Heimsuching der Theologie: Prolegomena zur* Dogmatik (Munchen: Kaiser, 1988), 145: 'Es lehrt uns: Die jüdischen Zeugen Gottes sind unersetzbar für die christologische Integrität seines Wesens, dafür, daß wir ihn in seiner Einheit als wahren Gott und wahren Menschen und über alles Fleisch ausgegossen, es zu belebenden Heiligen Geist, erkennen können.'

68. J. Dupuis, *Toward a Christian theology of religious pluralism* (New York: Orbis, 1997), 8.

69. Le comité de rédaction de la *Revue Thomiste,* 'Tout récapituler dans le Christ' in *Revue Thomiste* 98 (1998): 591-630, 603 with reference to Thomas Aquinas, *Expositio in Ioannem,* 14, lect. II, 1868 (Marietti).

be observed later, the case of Judaism may be viewed as paradigmatic for a Christian theology of the relationship between Christianity and other religious traditions. This is due to the special link which exists between the two biblical traditions and to their common heritage in God's revelation to Israel. A theology of other religious traditions will seek to apply – insofar as is possible *and mutatis mutandis* – what can be said concerning the relationship of the two biblical religions.'[70]

Joseph O'Leary has recently taken this further. For him, Christianity needs to be supplemented by Buddhism just as Judaism and Islam challenged it before. For incarnation means God entering into relationship and relativity (allowing himself to be partially understood). In 'Buddhist' language, Jesus was so purely selfless as to be the universal person. Furthermore Kenosis meant an outpouring of his influence and ideas, as he emptied himself out into all cultures and religions. Therefore 'Christian mission could be interpreted as part of the Gospel's quest for its own full meaning, through contact with the other.'[71]

R. Schwager agrees that religions can learn from each other from the 'dramatic' conflict that arises between them. Only this way can the darkness in each of them be challenged; truth matters as part of love, and as the gospel asks these other religions about what their answer is to oppression, it allows itself to be criticised in turn.[72] Jesus takes on enmity and unforgiveness and in that sense is universal as the universal scapegoat. This universality is built on the idea of R. Girard of a common primeval drive towards violence and scapegoating, though even Girard regrets that the Christian religion tended to undo Christ's opposition to and overcoming of sacrifice by fixing on Jesus' death as a sacrifice. And yet, purification (of sin, not just regret) had to take place on

---

70. J. Dupuis, *Toward a Christian Theology of Religious Pluralism* (Maryknoll, N.Y.: Orbis Books, 1997).

71. J. O'Leary *Religious Pluralism and Christian Truth* (Edinburgh: Edinburgh University Press, 1996), 26.

72. 'Offenbarung als dramatische Konfrontation' in *idem* (ed.) *Christus allein? Der Streit um die pluralistische Religionstheologie* (Freiburg-Basel-Wien: Herder, 1996), 95-106. See also his *Jesus and the Drama of Salvation* (ET; New York: Crossroad, 1999).

the inside of humans, in the realm of their spirituality.

For that reason Hegel complained about the reduction of Christology to the merely human level. It is a divine history which happened 'on the inside' of the human Christ, at the level of reason.[73] The inwardness is what is detected from a contemplation of the gospel evidence, and the Church took a while to take it in (GS, XIV, 137[16]) since such a solution was so unexpected. For Hegel, the spirit alters the nature of man so as to enable a new relationship – enclosing the nature of God in humanity. Human subjectivity finds itself in God, and from then on there is an identity of the two, as the divine-human opposition is removed. It is the evangel about *Jesus* that matters, the individual as the concrete reality of Christianity: not just general ethical teaching.[74] There is revelation of God himself, in a tone that foretells Barth's theology. Of course, Hegel did not speak of a pre-existence of Christ or a virgin birth, but thought of these as somehow optional, 'accidental' details, as something that helped the early church explain God in Christ, a point that anticipates Bultmann.[75]

Yet Jaeschke has argued that Hegel saw the unity of divine and human as really present in the world: 'Thus this self-consciousness is not imagination, but is *actually the case*.[76] Nevertheless Hegel would not build anything on as flimsy a structure as the historical Jesus, and we are back to Melanchthon brought up-to-date: to know Christ is to know his benefits[77] of self-consciousness,

---

73. 'Es ist nicht die Geschichte eines einzelnen, sondern Gottes, der sie vollbringt' (XIV, 160.16); the man who carries the form of the Spirit.

74. 'For this reason the Hegel of Berlin days dismisses the comparison of Jesus and Socrates as an idle consideration over which one need not linger' , W. Jaeschke, *Reason in Religion: the foundations of Hegel's philosophy of religion* (ET; Berkeley-Los Angeles-Oxford: Univ. of California Press, 1990), 315.

75. E. Schmidt, *Hegels System der Theologie* (Berlin: de Gruyter, 1974), 175f. Cf. Hans Küng, *The Incarnation of God* (Edinburgh: T&T Clark, 1987); James Yerkes, *The Christology of Hegel* (Missoula, Mont:Scholars Press, 1978.). Also, R.D. Williams, 'Logic and spirit in Hegel' in Philip Blond (ed.) *Post-secular philosophy* (Oxford: Blackwell, 1998), 116-130.

76. Jaeschke, 318, and translators' note, n. 57: 'The last sentence reads in German: "So ist es nicht Einbildung, sondern es ist *wirklich in dem*" .'

77. *Loci Communes* (1521), 63; cf. R. Schafer, *Christologie und Sittlichkeit in Melanchthons Frühen Loci* (Tübingen: Mohr, 1961).

the realisation that humans are not meant to be independent and left alone, subject to fate. Faith consists in Christ's being born in the heart; the religious life is a spectating one in order to be a liberating one; to understand is to transcend, be resurrected, to be Faustian in a good sense.[78] Perhaps it is better (with Kierkegaard) to meet Christ in the present or near-future than to look back and recollect as Hegel seemed to in order to have a solid base for enjoying the present. Yes, but who are we looking for? Do we need a Kantian-Hegelian identikit picture built up by a plurality of witnesses, a concept to be informed so that we can think on him in faith, even if he is strictly beyond our reason's ken? This is instead of resorting to our Kierkegaardian fantasies of what Christ might come to mean to us. The flipside of the 1950s debates in Catholicism about the psychology of Jesus was the nihilism of Kazantzakis in trying to recreate the inner life of Jesus in *The Last Temptation of Christ*.[79] Psychology is not necessarily the best way to approach Christ. But, and this is the point to be made with regard to a 'history of religions' approach to Christology, certain things happened in Christ which were self-consciously unique and which, although in their re-counting they are glossed heavily with ideological human interpretation, it was at a sub-conscious, even a cosmic level where these things made a difference.

Affirming the Tradition

Is everything in the tradition sacred, best left alone out of the highest respect or the utmost indifference? Three modifications seem appropriate:

(1) For instance, surely it is better to say that Jesus had 'one will' as the monothelites insisted – what human could have two wills?

(2) The late patristic dogma that the pre-existent Son is the person of the man Jesus can be upheld without too much difficulty,

---

78. See Stephen Crites, *In the Twilight of Christendom: Hegel vs. Kierkegaard on Faith and History* (AAR Studies in Religion, 2: Chambersburg, PA, 1972).

79. See William Hamilton, *A quest for the post-historical Jesus* (London: SCM, 1993).

although, as the nineteenth century noticed, it required some theory of divine kenosis to work.[80]

(3) Likewise, the theme of 'the humanity of God' in the work of E. Jüngel reminds us that *posse non peccare* can be said (analogically) about God just as of humans: he has the power not to sin rather than it is impossible for him to sin; logically the choice is there for God. Or, as R. Feenstra puts it: 'Of course the Incarnation included no other or independent hypostasis besides the eternal divine one, but this in no way entails that the incarnate person is not a human person. For a divine hypostasis is just a hypostasis with a divine nature, and a human hypostasis is just a hypostasis with a human nature, and a divine-human hypostasis is just one with both.'[81]

When it comes to matters of 'the historical Jesus' as a stumbling block for faith in Christ the divine Saviour, the recent work of Bernard Sesboüé proves helpful.[82] The Jesuit from the Centre Sèvres in Paris argues that the stronger temptation when it comes to Christology is to think of Jesus as merely a man. It is clear that John Paul II's *Redemptor Hominis* (1979) is more about Christ as the way to a new humanity as we reflect on his moral character than on any discussion of Jesus standing in the Trinity. Sesboüé declares that it is right and proper for Christology to start 'from below', but not to end there. Likewise Jacques Duquesne's book, *Jesus* (another example of journalists doing theological journalism – cf. R. Augstein's *Jesus: Menschensohn*; A.N. Wilson's *Jesus*), is criticised for failing to attend to questions of method. Appropriate to the subject investigated, maintains Sesboüé, is some amount of humble agnosticism as to whether there *could have been* a miraculous virginal conception, a realisation that Mary's perpetual virginity is not required to make sure the likelihood of that conception, that a portrait of Jesus is not the same as a

---

80. Cf. Thomas Morris ('The Metaphysics of God Incarnate' in R. Feenstra and C. Plantinga (eds.), *Trinity, Incarnation and Atonement* (Univ. of Notre Dame Press, 1989), echoing Thomasius, about the loss of the relative rather than essential properties: omnipotence, omniscience, omnipresence.

81. R. Feenstra in Intro to *Trinity, Incarnation and Atonement,* 10.

82. Bernard Sesboüé: *Jésus Christ à l'image des hommes* (2nd edn. Paris: Desclée de Brouwer, 1997).

photograph, that if some reported event is symbolic it may also be historical, that everyone is affected in what we see in a story by what views or prejudices we bring.

To avoid the post-Easter, high christological titles, some modern scholars have insisted on telling the story from the beginning, and resisting the putting of a grid of 'the End' on it. Such 'narrative christologies' also eschew Platonist two-tiered ontologies. Likewise in P. Schoonenberg's christology there is a wish to emphasise 'nature' as 'Wirklichkeit' (efficacy) and to reaffirm the tensive features of the 'narrativity' in the story of Jesus. Surely, however, this is all a little naive, and a-historical in that those who read then and read now do know the ending of Jesus' story.[83] Rather, with Wolfhart Pannenberg, we realise that who Jesus is at the end of the story we know as the same during the story; there may be character development, but it is a development of the same character, even in and through death and resurrection. What develops, surprises us, is the receptivity of the reader-worshipper's imagination and will. Through being a man for others (so, W. Kasper) who redefines what human being is, he is also the revelation of the Trinity, and as both he is where human and divine meet in divine energy.

---

83. See J. Moingt, *L'homme qui venait de Dieu* (Paris: Editions du Cerf: Cogitatio fidei; 176, 1996). B. Sesboüé in his *Jésus Christ à l'image des hommes* (Paris: Desclée de Brouwer, 1999), offers a critique of recent attempts to cut the figure of Jesus down to size and wants to combine the forces of biblical ('narrative') Christology and systematic insights from the Christian tradition of Christology.

6

A Reformation Christology:
The *Formula of Concord* (1577)

David F. Wright

It is well known that Lutheran and Reformed streams of sixteenth-century evangelical Protestantism followed somewhat different courses in Christology, although each believed that it was faithful to the church's traditional dogma, chiefly the Definition of the Council of Chalcedon of 451. It is well known also that the 'supper-strife' – the Protestants' internal disagreements about the nature of Christ's presence in the eucharist – was a major locus, whether as cause or effect, of this Christological discord. In very broad terms, Lutherans leaned in an Alexandrian or Cyrilline direction, the Reformed to an Antiochene or quasi-Nestorian approach. One critical reason why the breach over the Lord's supper proved so resistant to healing was deepseated suspicion, at least on the Lutheran side and already evident at the Colloquy of Marburg in 1529, of Christological – and perhaps therefore also Trinitarian – unorthodoxy on the other side. It may have been not wholly unfounded. Calvin in his day never, to my knowledge, explicitly endorsed *theotokos*, the Greek word meaning 'God-bearer' (not 'mother of God') whose rejection contributed significantly to Nestorius' condemnation in 431 at the Council of Ephesus.

So eucharistic engagements between Lutheran and Reformed normally included a Christological leit motiv, even if in the earlier decades hardly any treatises specifically devoted to Christology were produced. These began to flow, however, from the 1560s, with major works by Johannes Brenz, the Württemberg Reformer, and Martin Chemnitz, a Brunswick pastor-theologian.[1] The efforts

---

1. Brenz, *De Personali Unione Duarum Naturarum in Christo* (Tübingen, 1561), and *De Majestate Domini Nostri Jesu Christi ad Dextram Dei Patris et*

of Chemnitz and others such as Jacob Andreae and Nicholas Selnecker lay behind the *Formula of Concord* of 1577 (first published 1580). Its primary aim was the resolution of internal Lutheran disputes,[2] but insofar as these had been infected by the plague of the 'Sacramentarians', that is, the Swiss or the Zwinglians or the Calvinists, its teaching also established Lutheranism's distance from Reformed emphases. The introduction to Article VIII of the 'Solid Declaration' of the *Formula* reads as follows:

[A]fter [Luther's] death a few theologians of the Augsburg Confession, not quite ready to commit themselves publicly and explicitly to the Sacramentarians in the doctrine of the Supper of the Lord, did operate with and use the same basic arguments about the person of Christ with which the Sacramentarians ventured to eliminate from the Supper the true, essential presence of the body and blood of Christ.

How did they venture to do so?

They said that nothing is to be attributed to the human nature in the person of Christ that transcends or contravenes its natural, essential properties, and they went so far as to load down Luther's teaching ... with accusations of almost all the monstrous old heresies.[3]

From these extracts from Article VIII's introduction several points emerge. First, the way into this lengthy discussion of the Person of Christ is unambiguously eucharistic. No other reason is given for the attention that Christology receives. The *Formula*

---

de Vera Praesentia Corporis et Sanguinis eius in Coena (Frankfurt, 1562); Chemnitz, *De Duabus Naturis in Christo* (Leipzig, 1578), transl. J.A.O. Preus, *The Two Natures in Christ* (St. Louis, MO, 1971). In 1570 Chemnitz had issued a shorter work (*libellus*, he calls it) with the same title.

2. Thus the *Formula*'s title presents it as 'A Thorough, Pure, Correct, and Final Restatement and Explanation of a Number of Articles of the Augsburg Confession on Which for Some Time There Has Been Disagreement ...', transl. T.G. Tappert, *The Book of Concord* (Philadelphia, 1959), 463 (cited hereafter as Tappert).

3. Tappert, 592. The Formula comprises an Epitome and the Solid Declaration. Unless otherwise indicated references in this paper are to the latter.

has no place for Trinity. The question immediately arises whether Christology is determining eucharist or vice-versa. What kind of interaction is operative between the two?

In the second place, the argument is advanced in terms of ancient truth and ancient error. The categories are traditional, although subject to some refinement and development. So in part this is a debate about the patristic heritage, to which for other reasons both Luther and Melanchthon had contributed earlier treatises on the authority of the councils of the church.[4]

Appended to early printings of the *Formula of Concord*, although never officially part of it, was a *Catalogus Testimoniorum*, a dossier of witnesses setting out what Scripture and 'purer antiquity' handed down 'not only about the person and divine majesty of the human nature of our Lord Jesus Christ elevated to the right hand of God's omnipotence but also which expressions (*loquendi formulis*) each used to speak of them'.[5] This *Catalogus* is not widely available in English translation, but merits further study in its own right.

Quite apart from this appendix, Article VIII cites the Fathers or the early ecumenical councils at several points. Furthermore, characteristic of its style is a combined appeal to both Scripture and the Fathers: 'the Holy Scriptures and the ancient Fathers on the basis of the Scriptures'; 'statements which the ancient orthodox church made on the basis of sound passages of the Holy Scriptures'; errors 'condemned in the ancient approved councils on the basis of the Scriptures', and so on.[6] The *Formula* thus illustrates the manner in which *sola Scriptura* was deployed so often by magisterial Reformers – not *sola* strictly but together with the

---

4. Luther, *Disputatio de Protestate Concilii* (1536) and *Von den Konziliis und Kirchen* (1539). The latter is translated in *Luther's Works*, vol. 41 (Philadelphia, 1966). Melanchthon, *De Ecclesia et Autoritate Verbi Dei* (1539).

5. For Latain and German, *Die Bekenntnisschriften der evangelisch-lutherischen Kirche*, 11th edit. (Göttingen, 1992), 1101-35; both with English also, ed. F. Bente and W.H.T. Dau, *Concordia Triglotta/Triglot Concordia. The Symbolical Books of the Evangelical Lutheran Church* (St Louis, MO, 1921), 1105-49. I am grateful to the Revd William O. Harris of the Luce Library, Princeton Theological Seminary, for providing me with a photocopy of the latter.

6. Tappert, 600, 601, 602, 603, etc.

elucidating or confirming witness of early tradition. The *Formula* is an exposure of our roots. Even though we may not be Lutherans, here is the rock whence we were hewn. Do we still adhere to it?

Thirdly, the *Formula* 'summed up the basic intentions of Lutheran Christology and thus became the basis for Lutheran orthodoxy'.[7] It posed no challenge to the Augsburg Confession, which said too little about Christology for the needs of later intra-Lutheran debate, for the simple reason that in 1530 Christology was not at issue between the Old Church and the new Protestants. Here in the *Formula of Concord* is a text which still enjoys high standing for those sections of the Lutheran communion that care about its heritage in more than a narrowly Luther-focused manner.

This paper will now proceed to highlight the distinctive and problematic features of Article VIII. Its foundation is laid with a restatement of Chalcedon: one person, the person of Christ, i.e. 'the unity of the person of the Son of God' (VIII:7), and two natures united in him, unseparated, unblended, 'unmingled and unabolished' (VIII:8). The incarnate Christ is one person in whom subsist both the divine nature and the human nature. Without his humanity Christ the Son of God is not complete (VIII:11). We note that on the issue of the person of Christ in the strict sense, the *Formula* shows no trace of post-Chalcedonian refinements.[8] The concerns to which Chalcedon's Definition gave rise do not surface here, where we find simply statements such as 'the Son of God ... took the human nature into the unity of his person' (VIII:6), 'the human [nature] which was assumed in time into the unity of the person of the Son of God' (VIII:7).

Although the essential properties of one nature, for example the infinitude of the divine, never became the essential properties of the other (VIII:8-10), nevertheless the human nature, in addition to retaining its essential properties, has been elevated to the right hand of majesty through personal union with the deity and its

---

7. Karl-Heinz zur Mühlen, 'Christology', in Hans Hillerbrand (ed.), *Oxford Encyclopedia of the Reformation*, 4 vols (New York, 1996), vol. 1, 314-22 at 320.

8. The *Catalogus* depends very largely on pre-Chalcedonian writings, the exceptions being John of Damascus, Theophylact (eleventh-twelfth-century commentator) and Nicephorus (fourteenth-century church historian).

exaltation or glorification (VIII:12). Furthermore, Christ received this majesty not only after the resurrection but from the time of his conception onwards (VIII:13). This is a central insistence of the *Formula*, and much of the Article is devoted to drawing out its implications and defending it. Thus the human nature in Christ received this majesty 'according to the manner of the personal union, that is, because the fullness of deity dwells in Christ' (VIII:64).

How then is this 'personal union' understood in the *Formula*? Not, to be sure, according to the error of Nestorius, by the combining of divine and human natures 'like two boards glued together' (VIII:14). The followers of Paul of Samosata are credited with the same error, on the authority of an obscure writer named Theodore, the presbyter of Rhaitu (VIII:15).[9] The compilers of the *Formula* are almost certainly dependent for their knowledge of Theodore on a Greek and Latin edition by Theodore Beza in 1576 made from a manuscript recently brought from Constantinople. Theodore's work is entitled *Preparation*, i.e. Introduction, on how the divine incarnation took place. It lists errors condemned in the early centuries before explaining the Definition of Chalcedon. To Theodore's text Beza provocatively appended a comparison of orthodox Christology with the views of leading Lutherans, Brenz, Andreae and Andreas Musculus.[10]

According to Article VIII, the union took place such that the

---

9. Theodore is a writer of uncertain date (perhaps late sixth or seventh century) and even uncertain identity: see M. Geerard, *Clavis Patrum Graecorum* III (Turnhout, 1979), 417 no. 7600. The text in Migne, *Patrologia Graeca* 91, 1484-1504, is incomplete.

10. Theodore's work was first published, in Latin translation only, by Godefridus Tilman at Paris in 1556. This was reprinted next in M. de la Bigne, *Bibliotheca ... Patrum*, 8 vols (Paris, 1575-9), vol. 8, 659-68, in 1579 and so after Beza (correcting F. Diekamp, *Analecta Patristica*, Orientalia Christiana Analecta 117, Rome, 1938, 178. Diekamp gives a critical edition.) Beza was the first to publish the Greek (although his text finishes a few lines before the incomplete text in Migne, *PG*) and he provided his own Latin version. He entitled the work *Libellus adversus haereses....* Interestingly enough, Theodore's little-known treatise became one of the very first works of any Father edited by a Scot. Robert Balfour, professor at Bordeaux, in 1599 issued it with Gelasius of Cyzicus's history of the Council of Nicaea.

divine and human natures have true communion (Gemeinschaft, *communicatio*), whereby they are 'blended' (gemenget, *conveniunt et commiscentur*) into one person (not into one essence). The *Formula* claims to be able to cite numerous patristic testimonies before and after Chalcedon in favour of this use of 'mixture' (Vermischung, *mixtio*), which the Fathers illustrated by analogies of body and soul and of fire and iron (VIII:17-18). Yet the Article proceeds to rule out Vermischung (*confusio*) or 'equalization' of the two natures as when mead is made out of honey and water (VIII:19). The Latin at least maintains a differentiation of terms, but the German uses Vermischung, mixing, in both acceptable and unacceptable senses. Unfortunately Tappert's widely used English version makes things more difficult still by its inconsistency. The *Catalogus Testimoniorum* provides no patristic texts to substantiate the *Formula*'s assertion about widespread favourable use of 'mixture'.[11]

The *Formula* favours the expression 'personal union and communion' (in Greek, *henosis* and *koinônia*). By virtue of this union and communion of the two natures it was not the human nature alone that suffered and died, for 'the Son of God himself has truly suffered (although according to the assumed human nature) and ... has truly died, although the divine nature can neither suffer nor die' (VIII:20). By virtue of this union and communion Mary conceived the Son of the most high God, who demonstrated his divine majesty in being born of a virgin without violating her virginity (VIII:24). By virtue of this union and communion Christ manifested his divine majesty in performing miracles as he willed, which the human nature could not have done without being personally united with the divine (VIII:25). We will return later to the issue of the divine majesty, but meantime note in greater detail the *Formula*'s endeavours to explicate *communicatio idiomatum*, the exchange of the properties between the two natures:

> [E]ach nature retains its essential properties and ... these are not separated from one and transferred to the other as water is poured from one container to another (VIII:32).

11. *Die Bekenntnisschriften*, 1022 n. 3 gives six references, but they include the *Contra Apollinarem* which virtually all scholars regard as Pseudo-Athanasian.

[T]he power to give life is not in the flesh of Christ the way it is in his divine nature, that is, as an essential property (VIII:61).

This exchange or communication did not take place...in such a way that the human nature in Christ...is now either transformed into the Godhead or...has become intrinsically equal with the Godhead, nor in such a way that the natural, essential properties and acts of both natures are henceforth of the same kind or even identical (VIII:62).

But because of the personal union, any property belonging to only one nature is ascribed not to that nature alone as though separate but to the whole person, the God-man, whether he is called God or man (VIII:36).[12] Hence Scripture says that 'The Son was descended from David according to the flesh' (Rom. 1:3), 'Christ was put to death in the flesh' (1 Pet. 3:18). The *Formula* cites Luther's *Great Confession* on the supper:

The person (pointing to Christ) suffers, dies. But this person is truly God, and therefore it is correct to say: the Son of God suffers. Although, so to speak, the one part (namely, the deity) does not suffer, nevertheless the person who is true God suffers in the other part (namely, the humanity). For the Son of God truly is crucified for us ...according to the humanity (VIII: 42).

Luther is quoted again, from *On the Councils and the Church*:

According to his nature God cannot die, but since God and man are united in one person, it is correct to talk about God's death when that man dies who is one thing or one person with God (VIII:44).

The person (Christ) 'does not act *in, with, through* or *according to* one nature only, but *in, according to, with*, and *through* both natures, or as the Council of Chalcedon declares, each nature according to its own properties acts in communion with the other' (VIII:46).[13] This statement in fact belongs not to Chalcedon's own

---

12. The English translation follows the German original. The Latin conveys a different sense: 'ascribed not to the other nature as though it (the other nature) were separate but ...' Cf. Tappert, 598; *Bekenntnisschriften*, 1028. Yet the Latin undoubtedly makes better sense in the context.

13. Cf. also Formula VIII:64, 66, where 'in, with and through' are repeated.

Definition but to the *Tome* of pope Leo I, which the Council canonized. It was in truth one of the three elements in Leo's *Tome* which the Alexandrians baulked at for a time until persuaded that they could be read in a Cyrilline sense.

Article VIII of the *Formula of Concord* justifies the eucharistic expression 'in, with and under' the bread and the wine in terms of scriptural parallels in explicating 'the Word became flesh', for example, 'God was with him' (Acts 10:38) and 'God was in Christ' (2 Cor. 5:19). No parallel is adduced for 'under'. Thus Christology is an analogy for Christ's presence in the supper.

> For as in Christ two distinct and untransformed natures are indivisibly united, so in the Holy Supper the two essences, the natural bread and the true, natural body of Christ, are present together here on earth in the ordered action of the sacrament, though the union in question here is not a personal but a sacramental one (VII:35-8).

The *Formula* seems to recognize, however, that it may appear to have been arguing not for an exchange of properties between the two natures but for the deployment of each nature's properties in and by the person Christ. Hence the Article faces directly the question whether the natures in the union have anything more than their own natural and essential properties (VIII:48). Its answer is that they do, although its interest lies almost exclusively in what the human nature has above its natural properties. After exaltation to the right hand of God's majesty, 'after the form of the servant had been laid aside', the human nature received 'special, high, great, supernatural, unsearchable, ineffable, heavenly prerogatives and privileges in majesty, glory, power, and might above every name that is named' (VIII:51). For the compilers of the *Concord*, as for Luther himself, God's right hand is not a specific place in heaven, as the Sacramentarians are accused of claiming without biblical proof, but 'precisely the almighty power of God which fills heaven and earth' (VIII:28).

The time reference of Article VIII:51 to post-exaltation is clear, but the ensuing paragraphs just as clearly have in view the whole span from the incarnate union onwards. 'Created gifts' alone 'do not measure up to the majesty' which Scripture and the Fathers ascribe to the assumed human nature in Christ. For to give life, to execute all judgment, to have all authority in heaven and on earth, to have all things given into his hands, to have all things under his feet, to cleanse from sin, and so forth are not created gifts but divine and infinite qualities (VIII:54-5).

A string of scriptural references attest that all 'these properties have been given and communicated to the man Christ' (VIII:55). They include 'the power to make the dead alive ... given to Christ because he is the Son of Man and inasmuch as he has flesh and blood' (VIII:59). There follows an interesting exegesis of 1 John 1:7, 'The blood of Jesus his Son cleanses us from all sin': This does not refer only to the merit that was once achieved on the cross. John is saying in this passage that in the work or matter of our justification not only the divine nature in Christ but also his blood actually *per modum efficaciae* cleanses us from all sins.

As John 6:48-58 and the Council of Ephesus declare, Christ's flesh is life-giving (VIII:59). The German original includes the Latin phrase, meaning 'in an efficacious manner', but the import of the sentence remains elusive. The text apparently takes cleansing from sin of real purification, but is still referring it to justification.

The *Formula* carefully guards 'real exchange or sharing' (*realis communicatio*) against misconceptions. Divine properties were not granted to Christ's human nature in a manner analogous to the Father's communicating his very essence to the Son. There took place neither 'an essential or natural outpouring of the properties of the divine nature into the human' nor a transformation of the human nature into divinity or equality with the Godhead. These and similar errors were condemned by the ancient councils on the basis of Scripture. In fact, the *Formula* insists, 'real exchange' has been used only to exclude the opponents' reductionist 'verbal exchange' (VIII:60-63). To recap, as it were, 'the human nature in Christ has received this majesty according to the manner of the personal union, that is, because the fullness of deity dwells in Christ..."bodily", as in its own body' (VIII:64).

The *Formula* then picks up a point which had been made earlier. The divine majesty shines forth in the assumed nature spontaneously and when and where he wills.... During the time of the humiliation the divine majesty was concealed and restrained, but now, since the form of the slave has been laid aside, it takes place fully, mightily, and publicly before all the saints in heaven and on earth (VIII:65).

'He had this majesty immediately at his conception even in his mother's womb but...he laid it aside...and he kept it hidden...and did not use it at all times but only when he wanted to' (VIII:26). On this basis Christ performed all his miracles, manifesting his divine majesty 'according to his good pleasure, when and how he wanted to' – but not only at the wedding in Cana but also in Gethsemane, for 'he died not just like another man' but in order to conquer sin and death (VIII:25).

Article VIII now brings the Holy Spirit into the picture, but no more happily.

> Since Christ according to the Godhead is the second person in the holy Trinity and the Holy Spirit proceeds from him as well as from the Father,...it follows that through personal union the entire fullness of the Spirit (as the ancient Fathers say) is communicated to Christ according to the flesh that is personally united with the Son of God. This fullness demonstrates and manifests itself spontaneously and with all power in, with and through the human nature (VIII:73-4).

It is the Father's outpouring on him of the Spirit of wisdom and power which ensures that 'as a man, through the personal union, he really and truly has received all knowledge and all power' (VIII:74). This role for the Holy Spirit in the incarnate Christ is a dislocating factor in Article VIII, almost displacing the second Person. Perhaps it reflects the composite or compromise character of the *Formula*.

Having begun with the supper, the Article returns to it in the final paragraphs. The *communicatio idiomatum* means that 'things are attributed to Christ according to the flesh that the flesh, according to its nature and essence outside of this union, cannot intrinsically be or have' (VIII:76).

The presence of Christ to his church on earth – 'Where two or three are gathered together ...' – is the presence of his entire person:

'also according to and with this same assumed human nature of his, Christ can be and is present wherever he wills' (VIII:78).

To make certainty and assurance doubly sure on this point, he instituted his Holy Supper that he might be present with us, dwell in us, work and be mighty in us according to that nature, too, according to which he has flesh and blood (VIII:79).

Entailed here, it seems, is not the omnipresence (ubiquity) of the humanity but only what Chemnitz rather than Brenz called its multivolipresence or ubivolipresence, or more simply, its multipresence. None of these terms is used in the *Formula of Concord*. Among the errors condemned at the end of Article VIII is not only the omnipresence of Christ's human nature 'in the same way as the Deity, as an infinite essence, through an essential power or property of its nature' (VIII:90) but also its local extension into every place in heaven and earth, which ought not to be attributed even to the deity.

Without transforming or destroying his true human nature, Christ's omnipotence and wisdom can readily provide that...Christ can be present with his body, which he has placed at the right hand of the majesty and power of God, wherever he desires and especially where he has promised his presence in his Word, as in the Holy Communion (VIII:92).

We have already observed 'wherever he wills' affirmed of the divine majesty communicated to the human nature. But other elements in the *Formula* point towards omnipresence. Luther is quoted as asserting that 'Since he is a man like this – and apart from this man there is no God – it must follow...that he is and can be everywhere that God is' (VIII:81). The preceding Epitome VIII:16 declares of the ascended Christ that 'He exercises his power everywhere omnipresently, he can do everything, and he knows everything.'

Furthermore, omnipresence fits better the framework of the *Formula*'s Christological elaboration. As Friedrich Mildenberger puts it,

If the humanity of Christ really participates in the omnipresence of the divine-human person, we clearly must think of it doing so in the same way that we think of the divine omnipresence. An 'unmodified doctrine of ubiquity' would have been neater.[14]

If there is an element of inconsistency in the *Formula* between multipresence and a stricter omnipresence, the same may also hold of the intermittent use of the divine majesty. The Epitome, simply because of its shortness, is inevitably sharper and crisper than the Solid Declaration. Furthermore it emerged at an earlier stage in the consultative process than the Solid Declaration, which is normally taken as the real text of the *Formula*.[15] The Epitome states bluntly that 'in the state of his humiliation [Christ] dispensed with [the divine majesty] and could therefore truly increase in age, wisdom and favour with God and men' (VIII:16). It also asserts that only after the resurrection 'not only as God but also as man he knows all things, can do all things, is present to all creatures' (VIII:16), which does not square at first sight with the Holy Spirit's imparting fullness of wisdom to Christ according to the flesh (Solid Decl. VIII:74). But we have already identified the place accorded the Spirit as one of the *Formula*'s weaknesses.

Another area of unclarity was briefly mentioned earlier: was it the person or the appropriate nature that received the properties of the other nature? The problem arises because the person is the divine Word-Son, not a new *tertium quid* that is a composite of human and divine. It is therefore easier to conceive of the human faculties being attributed to the person of Christ (according to his human nature) than of the divine properties being so attributed. Thus we can say, as the *Formula* does, that the divine Son suffers in his human nature – without the divine nature itself becoming passible or being turned into humanity or receiving passibility intrinsically (cf. VIII:20). But perhaps there is not much difference between saying that the divine person receives a property according to his human nature and saying that the divine nature receives it by virtue of personal union with the human nature.

---

14. F. Mildenberger, *Theology of the Lutheran Confessions* (Philadelphia, 1986), 180.

15. See briefly Tappert, 463-4.

Yet in this field of discourse one may say that 'the man is God' and 'God is the man' on the grounds of the genuine 'communion' of the two natures with each other, as Epitome VIII:10 of the *Formula* affirms, but not that 'the humanity is divinity' nor 'the divinity is humanity'. For the compilers of the *Concord* it was far less problematic to speak of the person (the incarnate Son) receiving majesty (and hence ubivolipresence) in respect of his human nature than to assert bluntly that the human nature receives it – if only because of the repeated stress on the *communicatio* of properties only in the personal union. Nevertheless, the result sometimes surprises the reader. Epitome VIII:17 quotes Luther to the effect that Christ's true body and blood are present in the supper 'not according to the mode or property of the human nature but according to the mode and property of God's right hand'. Odd though this may sound on first reading, is it saying anything more than that the human nature of Christ – its presence, properties and works – is never to be conceived of except within the personal union of the incarnate Son?

Other questions may be registered about the *Formula*, first about its relation to the Definition of Chalcedon. It professes to be faithful to Chalcedon, and indeed part of the challenge it poses for us may be that it is so only too scrupulously. Or to put the issue rather differently, it stretches or extends Chalcedon without developing it, or it develops it without maturation. So Mildenberger can claim that the *Formula*'s Christological endeavours 'almost destroyed the frame' of Chalcedon.[16] Edmund Schlink simply notes as an unavoidable question 'whether this Christology is to be considered an interpretation or an abrogation of the christological formulations of Chalcedon to which the church of the Augsburg Confession always felt obligated'.[17] The Catalogue of Testimonies was appended to the *Formula*, so it states 'To the Christian Reader', because some people alleged that, especially in Article VIII on the person of Christ, it departed from the forms of expression in the Fathers and councils of the ancient pure church.[18]

---

16. Mildenberger, *Theology*, 178.

17. E. Schlink, *Theology of the Lutheran Confessions* (Philadelphia, 1961), 192.

18. *Bekenntnisschriften*, 1105.

A more searching question asks whether the relationship between the two natures in the *Formula* 'increasingly becomes an independent theological concern, separate from the redemptive act'.[19] Werner Elert, an extensive writer on the Christology of emerging Lutheranism, repeatedly emphasizes that the impact or standpoint of the gospel ('evangelischer Ansatz') drives this kind of Christological exposition.[20] Yet his analysis is not uncritical of the *Formula*. On the one hand he argues that it is not predetermined by the need to vindicate omnipresence (for, as we have seen, it mostly does not), yet on the other hand its definition of the divine nature is one-sided:

> To be almighty, to be eternal, to be infinite, to be everywhere at the same time naturally (that is, according to the property of the nature and of its natural essence), to be intrinsically present, and to know everything are essential properties of the divine nature (VIII:9).[21]

Such attributes, Elert continues, are no less attributable to the pre-incarnate God than to the God revealed in Christ. An altogether different picture would emerge 'if in accordance with the impact of the Gospel (evangelischer Ansatz) God's inexhaustible will to confer grace...had been made not the cause but the decisive content of the "assumption of the human nature" '. Then, when God suffers in the incarnate Son, 'What thus appears to be a breakdown of the "absolute" omnipotence of God is, on the other side, the *revealed* omnipotence of His mercy.'[22]

Yet Elert is, I believe, on safe ground in pointing to the *Formula*'s summary of the divine properties communicated 'to the man Christ' as standing in 'the closest connexion with the impact of the Gospel':[23]

> [T]o give life, to execute all judgement, to have all authority in heaven and on earth, to have all things given into his hands, to have all

---

19. Schlink, *Theology,* 192.
20. W. Elert, *The Structure of Lutheranism* (St Louis, 1962), 223, 225, 229.
21. Cf. Elert, *Structure* I, 231-2, 229.
22. Elert, *Structure* I, 230.
23. Elert, *Structure* I, 233.

things under his feet, to cleanse from sin, and so forth are not created gifts but divine and infinite qualities. Yet according to the statement of the Scriptures these properties have been given and communicated to the man Christ (VIII:55).

Is not this Christological exposition, for all its seeming nascent scholasticism, not truly evangelical at heart? To quote from the last paragraph of Article VIII proper,

> to deprive Christ according to his humanity of [his divine] majesty...robs Christians of their highest comfort...[Christ] has promised that not only[24] his unveiled deity, which to us poor sinners is like a consuming fire on dry stubble, will be with them, but that he, he, the man who has spoken with them, who has tasted every tribulation in his assumed human nature, and who can therefore sympathize with us as men and his brethren, he wills to be with us in all our troubles also according to that nature by which he is our brother and we are flesh of his flesh (VIII:87).

---

24. Mildenberger, *Theology*, 180, evidently reads a simple negative here – 'The sinful human being is never confronted by God's "unveiled deity"...' – but both German (nicht alleine) and Latin (*non modo*) exclude this. But refining Tappert's rendering we might translate: 'promised that his unveiled deity ... will not alone be with them.'

7

The Christology of Edward Irving

Graham Macfarlane

It is, perhaps, the quest for the trinitarian Jesus that best typifies current interest in Christology. Putting it bluntly, if we were talking computer software, this would be the Microsoft of Christology. And no one puts the entire project better in focus that Pannenberg when he describes the christological and trinitarian agenda in the following terms. Concerning the explicitly *theological* task he states in volume 1:

> To find a basis for the doctrine of the Trinity we must begin with the way in which Father, Son and Spirit come on the scene and relate to one another in the event of revelation. Here lies the material justification for the demand that the doctrine of the Trinity must be based on the biblical witness to revelation or on the economy of salvation. On this approach there is no material reason to append the doctrine of the Trinity to that of God's essence and attributes. The latter can be relevantly dealt with in the context to the Trinitarian relegation of God as Father, Son and Holy Spirit.[1]

And concerning the explicitly *christological* task, he states in Volume 2 of Systematic Theology:

> The task of interpreting the appearance and history of Jesus in relation to God, as the act of God, must be to the fore when we deal with Christology within a total presentation of Christian doctrine. Since the overarching context in which we handle Christology has a more or less explicitly trinitarian structure according to the church's confessions of faith...the result for Christology is that it depicts the

---

1. W. Pannenberg, *Systematic Theology*, Vol. 1 (T&T Clark, 1991), p. 299.

appearance and history of Jesus of Nazareth as the action of the trinitarian God for human salvation.[2]

It would appear that it is both theologically and politically correct to use trinitarian language when referring to Jesus Christ. God-talk and Jesus-talk are mutual partners in the academy today, thanks due largely to the Rubicon crossed by Barth and the further advances made by the likes of Pannenberg. What is less clear, however, are the foundations on which one bases such a partnership post-Schleiermacher, despite the ground regained by Barthian scholarship. Even more opaque is the much more immediate solution to the modern twin problems of modalism and tritheism.

Of course, the former has plagued Western theology almost from its genesis. It always has been much easier to talk of God in the abstract as a divine 'Monad'. As a consequence of such thinking, the relationship between the One, the Three and the Many, as Colin Gunton puts it, has been lost, by and large, within the Western tradition.[3] Put bluntly, our Achilles' heel has always been in the area of relating the humanity with the divinity within a Chalcedonian Christology. Historically, Christians in the West have tended to get round this problem by assuming a closet form of docetism, albeit with a dash of *communicatio idiomatum* for flavour. To a large extent this solution works until one asks the basic questions beginning with 'How....?'

Tritheism, on the other hand, has always been the *bête noire* of Eastern Christianity, or so we are told. And yet, we must admit that even the simplest application of discourse analysis to the god-talk of the average modern, western Christian reveals an alarming degree of tritheism. That aside, the Achilles' heel within the eastern tradition has always been in the area of relating the three divine persons without falling prey to pluralistic expressions of God. It is far easier simply to address Father, Son and Spirit as three model representatives of the perfect English gentleman. However, as with the former, so with the latter, to a large extent this solution works

---

2. Pannenberg, *Systematic Theology*, Vol. 2 (T&T Clark, 1994), p. 289.
3. See Colin Gunton, *The One, The Three and the Many* (Cambridge: CUP, 1993).

until one asks the basic questions beginning with 'How....?'

In the face of such contemporary issues, the present resurgence in trinitarian reflection as stated above serves the interests of the church well. Much good is yet to be gained from such an endeavour. Yet we would be mistaken were we to presume that such reflection is a mid to late modern phenomenon. Further, we would be mistaken were we to think the problem of the 'How?' is well addressed and answered merely by virtue of such enquiry.

It is at this point that I can introduce the subject in hand, namely, the Christology of Edward Irving, a Presbyterian minister from central Scotland who lived out the majority of his ministerial vocation in London in the earlier half of the nineteenth century. For Irving the 'How?' questions concerning the manner in which the economic modes of relation between humanity and divinity within incarnation relate as well as the immanent modes of eternal relation had very real pastoral cash value.

For the purposes of this brief paper focus will turn in three areas. Each unpacks Irving's understanding of Jesus Christ, the eternal Son of the Living God:

his relation to the Father in whose name he came;

his relation to us for whom he came;

and what these two tell us about his own identity.

1. Irving's understanding of Christ's relation to the divine

Perhaps one of the most significant aspects of Irving's Christology is the way in which his context moulded both his theological and subsequent christological development. His primary interests began as engagement with the Socinianism he confronted as he took up ministry in London. This was a form of unitarianism which thrived in the cultural melting pot of eighteenth-century London. Irving arrived on the scene at a point when the notion of a unitarian God was beginning to take root once again. Irving's friendship with Coleridge, in turn, would have exposed him to the influences crossing over from Germany. Indeed, even the briefest of comparisons reveal Irving to share one thing in common with his most immediate theological contemporary, Schleiermacher: both explicitly describe the doctrine of the Trinity as the foundation stone – the coping stone – of all subsequent doctrine, and yet with very different hermeneutical application. For Irving, his Christology stands or falls on how he unpacks the relation between Father and Son.

Thus, Irving sets out to establish the identity of the Son. He begins by arguing for the priority of Christ's identity as Son over Word. For Irving, the description of Jesus Christ as Word fails to express the true nature of God. Whilst the notion of Word expresses the idea of will it cannot reveal one of grace. True, Christ as Word reveals the divine will but such a title cannot express the Father heart of God. The significance of Christ as Son, on the other hand, is that it is only as Son that Christ shares in and expresses the Father as Love. As Irving puts it:

> The Word doth express His participation of all the Father's counsels, and His office in revealing them all; but the Son is that which expresseth His full possession of the Father's undivided affections.... If it be an essential part of the eternal purpose of the Godhead revealed by Christ, that it contains the fullness of the Father's love in surrendering, as well as of the Father's wisdom in manifesting Christ, then I say that He who was surrendered must have been in the full possession of all the Father's love, as well as a sharer of all the Father's wisdom; or that he must have been Son as well as Word from all eternity.[4]

There are smacks here of Irving's friend, John McLeod Campbell. Indeed, the influence of Irving as well as Thomas Erskine of Linlathen are not lost in the following quotation from McLeod Campbell:

> Let us think of Christ as the Son who reveals the Father, that we may know the Father's heart against which we have sinned, that we may see how sin, in making us godless, has made us as orphans, and understand that the grace of God, which is at one the remission of past sin, and the gift of eternal life, restores to our orphan spirit their Father and to the Father of Spirit his lost children.[5]

---

4. Edward Irving, *Collected Works*, Vol.4, pp. 241-242.
5. John McLeod Campbell, *The Nature of Atonement*, 147, 6th ed.

Once this filial identity is established, Irving is then able to unpack the nature of this relationship. Again, the Socinian notion that the Son is a creature determines Irving's response. Irving identifies two issues: firstly, that if the Son is a creature, then the love showered on him will simply incite envy in all other creatures rather than amplify love. In addition, if the Son is a mere creature, then he affords only a *creature's* understanding and revelation of God. Given that the immediate significance of the incarnation for Irving is in its pastoral and salvific cash value, the identity of the one who did indeed become creaturely is of pivotal importance. As Irving puts it: 'If God be not known as Father, save to fallen men, nor Christ as Son, as what are they known?'[6]

However, when all is said and done, Irving's response thus far is merely a clever variation on an Arian theme. Rather, it is with his relation to the divine that Irving begins to develop his tradition. For here Irving reveals the *pneumatological* dimension to his Christology. After all, the christological discourses are clear in their priority given to the Spirit. But what does this mean, really? When the theological audit is performed, it is the pneumatic aspect of Christology that is, perhaps, the most lacking component in the western paradigm.

In his attempt to solve the trinitarian problem, Irving argued that God is indeed mystery, but not in the modern misrepresentation of apophaticism. Rather, our knowledge of God is known to the degree of his becoming: God makes himself known in his actions towards us in Christ. Admittedly, Western theologians from Augustine onwards have tended to play the *mysterium tremendum* card when it comes to the Spirit. Augustine slipped the Spirit in as the *nexus amoris*. After all, if all else fails, call the Spirit 'love'. And Richard of St.Victor expanded it well, in his own Scottish manner, albeit in a manner that tended to externalise the Spirit to the divine relations of Father and Son.

However, Irving plays another card arguing that the true locus of love is the relationship between the Father and the Son. No half-baked notions here. Rather, in a rather precocious and pre-emptying manner he anticipates the two most important

6. Edward Irving, *Collected Works* Vol.4, p. 260

contributions of the twentieth century in this area. On the one hand Irving pre-dates the Barthian notion of the incarnation as a dynamic 'event'. On the other, he relocates the Spirit in more Pannenbergian terms as the dynamic force-field within which the relationship between Father and Son takes place.

The Spirit, for Irving, is the *vinculum unitatis* – the uniting link – within the Trinity. Interestingly, relational unity is maintained neither on the grounds of a commonly expressed nature nor on the grounds of the Father's priority. Rather, within the divine relations themselves which constitute God as Father, Son and Spirit, the Spirit unites the Father and the Son in their eternal identities. This is *relational* rather than *substantial* unity. And with it Irving pre-empts any tendency to think of the three divine persons after the Boethian individual substance with a rational nature that is so prevalent today. With Irving's understanding of the Son's relation to both the Father and the Spirit, there can be no separating of the divine persons. Rather, there is radical *perichoresis.* Where the Son is, there, too, are Father and Spirit. For Irving, the maxim, *opera trinitatis ad extra indivisa sunt* – the external operations of the Trinity are indivisible – is consistent. Only through the Son do we ever meet the Father. Only through the Spirit does the Son reveal the Father within the economy of salvation. And only through the Spirit are the Father and Son ever one.

How, then, are the Father and the Son and the Spirit the one God? From within his tradition Irving affirms the substantial answer – because they share and constitute the one divine nature. Yet, from beyond his tradition, Irving argues at a relational level – because the Father and Son are united by the Spirit. Through the Spirit the Father's will is related to the Son: through the Spirit the Son's obedience is wrought.

Of course, the question has to be asked: On what grounds does Irving so argue? It was stated earlier that Irving's entire christological endeavour is motivated by pastoral or soteriological concerns. It is from them that the question can be answered. In order to do so we need to turn briefly to the second aspect of his theological enterprise:

The human condition

It should not come as a surprise that the relational dimension to Irving's thought continues. The purpose and end of creation finds its meaning not in human being itself but in the humans' dependency upon God who brings them into existence in the first place. Human beings are beings-in-relation: creatures dependent upon the Creator who is their very source of existence and being.

It is here that we discover the possible link between the Saviour and the creature. We are made beings-in-reflection: created to reflect the image of the image of God. We are created to reflect the Son who is the image of the invisible God. This reflection is located in the freedom of a will answerable to God. As the Son does not do his own will but that of the Father, as he is obedient to the Father's will, so we are created to exercise such freedom. Freedom of will in the human creature reflects the very character of God, who is himself perfectly free and uncaused. Consequently, we become truly human to the degree we relate to the one who made us. It is to the extent that we are free to will the will of the one in whose image we are created that we are pneumatic beings.

Irving's christology serves as the blueprint for his understanding of human beings and how we should exist. It is the Spirit who empowers us to will and thus to enter into the relationship of love which is the Father and the Son. If this be the case, then it means that we are 'ontologically relational', that is, relationality constitutes our very being. Our true identity, then, is corporate in that outwith this relationship we are condemned to the isolation of our own individualism. Our sin merely reflects the degree to which we do not relate correctly. It is a state *into which* we are born – our origin – which is then made *actual* by our own volition.

We have, as it were, established the axes around which Irving's christology operates. From 'an above' perspective, Irving unpacks the divine identity of Christ. He is the Son of the Father whom the Spirit enables to obey and thus reveal the Father's love. From 'a below' perspective, the purpose of incarnation is to rectify the human condition: a will enslaved to sin and therefore incapable of operating as *imago dei*.

It remains to outline the *how* of incarnation. To do so, we must first identify the locus of incarnation since this is decisive for Irving's understanding of Christ. Stephen Sykes identifies four possible *loci* to the bald statement that the divine Word took our flesh. Firstly, that at the moment of assumption it was 'instantly transformed to be a new type of humanity'. Secondly, that it was flesh weakened by sin but not naturally tainted by it. Thirdly, that it was sinful flesh. And lastly, that it was humanity as it was before the fall.

What has been overlooked by Irving's opponents is his intimate association between the place, agent and means of salvation. With this he develops a space within which to develop his own understanding of the Spirit's role in relation to the Son within incarnation and salvation. Irving's entire christology is built upon the belief that the 'work to be accomplished must always be the measure of the power necessary to accomplish it'.[7] And this is achieved by an understanding of both the Son and the Spirit. For if the work of Christ in redemption is seen only in terms of 'the bearing of so much inflicted wrath, vengeance, and punishment,' then there will be little place for the work of the Spirit. Rather it will be assumed that the divine nature itself is sufficient to bear 'the mighty load' and 'sustain the Sufferer'. Consequently, there would be little appreciation of the Spirit's relation to the Son which was, in effect, the power in which He performed His mighty works, and offered His blameless sacrifice.

For Irving, the Son takes to himself a humanity that is fallen – 'a fallen human nature' – sinful flesh in that he comes into the origin common to us all as inheritors of Adam's debt. His humanity is sinful in origin, but not in fact. Christ's is a solidarity with the common stock and oppressor of human nature. After all, the unassumed is the unhealed. Therefore, what we believe about the person and work of Christ must be worked out within the solidarity of fallen humanity. In relation to sin, he overcomes as one of us. It is about assurance: that what is attainable through Christ is possible because he has already overcome sin in the flesh and in so doing not only redeems a fallen creation back to God but brings about the means for all to attain such holiness. After all, it is no

7. Edward Irving, *Collected Works* Vol.5, p. 244.

source of comfort to the sinner to know that one who was unfallen upheld the law: what have we in common with such a saint?

The place of redemption, then, is in fallen humanity, which was assumed by the Son, in accordance with the Father's will, and accomplished through the agency of the Spirit. Whilst, then, the 'Who?' of salvation is the eternal Son, the 'How are you possible?' can only be answered with respect to the relation between the Spirit and the Son. The subject of Irving's christology is the Alexandrian Son but the manner in which this subject goes about his business is well and truly Antiochene. On the one hand it occurs by virtue of kenosis on the Son's part. It is the self-limitation of the Son as he identifies with humanity in its need of redemption. And this should not be understood in terms of divine impotence on the Son's part. Quite the contrary: it is an expression of willing obedience on the Son's part to bring about creation and redemption. As such it highlights his love for the Father in his capacity to follow human being into its own 'far country' in solidarity with that which requires redirection and restoration. It is a kenosis of will on the Son's part. On the other hand, the perichoretic hermeneutic continues in the manner by which the Son lives out a kenotic life. He does so as one sustained by the Spirit. And so, it is only through the Spirit that the human actions of Jesus become the acts of God: it is not a direct communication of attributes.

It would appear, then, that Irving manages to avoid both problems outlined at the beginning of this paper. He avoids the western predisposition to absorb the humanity of Christ within the divinity by redefining the dynamic of agency operating within the incarnation. The Son of God does not become man by his own brute power, as though it really did not matter which one of the three became flesh. Rather, if the economic manner of incarnation in some way corresponds to the inner relations then we see the Son relating to the Father through the agency of the Spirit.

In addition, Irving avoids the Eastern problem of tritheism by virtue of his robust understanding of perichoresis. Here, the Spirit is not an after-thought but central to the manner in which God relates in a thoroughly communitarian manner. The divine persons cannot be separated – the actions of any one are the actions of all three.

Conclusion

What can we say in conclusion? We can see how Irving safeguards the divine initiative in redemption: it is only God who can save. It is the Father who sends, the Son who comes, the Spirit who sustains. What Irving adds to the traditional themes of christology is the Spirit's relation to the Son, both in his eternal relation and in his temporal saving role. Without the Spirit's role, there is no meaningful and assuring doctrine of salvation. It is only as we receive the Spirit of Christ, who overcame the flesh and presented it holy before his Father, that we have assurance that we, too, may answer the *How?* question. In this, the *Who?* and the *How?* meet. For Irving, the person of Christ cannot be separated from what he came to achieve, from the whole question of redemption. And for Irving, that means a complete rethink concerning what is meant by the maxim, 'the unassumed is the unhealed'.

For him it meant that Jesus Christ is the true Mediator in both a general and a specific sense. Firstly, Christ assumes the general state of human being. As fallen human being he is one in solidarity with that which requires redemption. In his resurrection he is shown to be the prototype of a new humanity, the guarantor of its final outcome. Secondly, he assumes a specific human will, within the limitations of fallen humanity, and is seen to overcome the rebel nature and present himself unblemished before a holy God. And this he does with no advantage over us.

Irving's, then, is a christology that is *internally consistent* in that it makes sense of the entire paradigm of biblical and dogmatic witness. It is also *externally relevant* in that it presents an understanding of Christ that unites the person and work in a manner that meets the needs of those he came to save. To this end, in conclusion, Gordon Strachan was correct in his statement that Irving's christological position appears 'to be unique and deserves the attention which it has so far not received'.[8]

---

8. Gordon Strachan, *The Pentecostal Theology of Edward Irving*, p. 22.

8

The Christology of T.F. Torrance and the Formula of Chalcedon

John L. McPake

Introduction

In seeking to assess the distinctively Scottish contribution towards our understanding of the person of Christ, a useful point from which to draw our bearings is to be found in Donald Macleod's article on 'Christology' in the *Dictionary of Scottish Church History and Theology*. Macleod begins by contending that: 'There was no distinctive Scottish Christology until the emergence of Edward Irving in the middle of the nineteenth century. Nor was there much Christological controversy comparable, for example, to the Arianism which disturbed England in the late seventeenth and early eighteenth centuries.'[1] That is not to say that there was no clear statement on the understanding of the person of Christ in Scottish theology prior to this, and Macleod is clearly aware of earlier writers who remained resolutely within the parameters of Chalcedonian orthodoxy. Indeed, the inception of the reformed Kirk in Scotland in 1560 is marked by a clear and unambiguous statement in Chapter VI of the *Scots Confession* – 'Of the Incarnation of Jesus Christ' – in terms which are resolutely Chalcedonian. Similarly, the Church of Scotland's approbation of the *Westminster Confession* in 1647 places it firmly within Chalcedonian orthodoxy (VIII.2) and Scottish theology was little disturbed in this orthodoxy until the early nineteenth century.

Moving into the twentieth century, we see a number of significant developments in Christological thinking which have

---

1. D. Macleod, 'Christology', in, N.M. de S. Cameron, et al. (eds.), *Dictionary of Scottish Church History and Theology* (Edinburgh: 1993), 172-177, 172.

established a fine Scottish tradition, represented by such figures as H.R. Mackintosh, Donald Baillie, John McIntyre and T.F. Torrance. Each of these thinkers has made a lasting contribution to Christology and in all of their writings the problems raised by the formula of Chalcedon are ever present and they are all worthy of renewed study. However, I intend to focus only on the last of these and shall therefore offer a study of the Christology of T.F. Torrance (Professor of Christian Dogmatics, Edinburgh, 1952-1979) and his use of the Chalcedonian formula.

Intention
The intention of this paper is:
    1) To locate the Christology of T.F. Torrance with respect to the Chalcedonian formula and to indicate how he understands the significance of that formula. In so doing, I do not regard Chalcedon as the 'last word' on Christology, as if nothing else might be said from within the perspective of those who wish to hold to the orthodox formulation. However, I do take it as the first word!
    2) To offer an exposition and critique of Torrance's attempt to develop a Christology 'beyond Chalcedon'.
    In setting out my intention, I wish to clarify my understanding of the function of the Chalcedonian definition with some apposite guidance from D.M. Mackinnon. In discussing the role of the *homoousion* in Christological formulation, Mackinnon suggests that we ought:

> to see its significance as an instrument for advancing our understanding to enable us [to] see what it is that is at issue in the simpler, more direct, more immediately moving christological affirmations of the gospel. It is totally misunderstood if it is treated as a possible substitute or alternative to such affirmations. Its role is essentially complementary.[2]

I would see the function of the Chalcedonian definition in the same terms as Mackinnon assesses the function of the *homoousion*.

---

2. D.M. Mackinnon, ' "Substance" in Christology – A Cross-Bench View', in, S.W. Sykes & J.P. Clayton (ed.s), *Christ, Faith and History* (Cambridge: 1972), 279-299, 291. See also, 297.

Thus, what we find in Chalcedon are 'second order' propositions whose ideal function is to complement the 'first order' propositions which are found in the gospel affirmations about Christ. Mackinnon writes: 'That is, if we ask what it is about, we have to say that it is not about Christ, but about statements about Christ.'[3]

This is a distinction which we ought always to keep in mind. If we do so, we are then free to honour and receive Chalcedon as part of the living tradition of the Church, as well as being free to respond to the ever-renewed presence of Christ. Thus, there is an inherent dialectic in our receiving of Chalcedon *and* the calling to faithfully state our understanding of Christ in this present age.

Torrance on Chalcedon

Within the corpus of Torrance's early writings we find emerging a distinctive understanding of the person and work of Christ, which would later develop into one of the most original and distinctive contributions to Christology within Scottish Theology. In an attempt to chart this development, we shall survey his writings in order to draw together the themes which produce in his Christology an affirmation of the significance of Chalcedon allied to an unswerving determination to press on beyond Chalcedon. Christology, for Torrance, is not a theological locus which can be treated in isolation from other loci. Rather it informs, and is informed by, other central doctrines, e.g., Soteriology. Thus, we do not find in Torrance a treatment which focuses exclusively on Christology. Instead, we may anticipate his Christology emerging from the outworking of his overall theological position, and I would direct attention to an exhaustive study of the roots and development of that Christology by W.D. Rankin, whose *Carnal Union with Christ in the Theology of T.F. Torrance* fully treats all of the themes which we shall subsequently identify.[4]

At a relatively early stage in Torrance's published writings,

---

3. Ibid., 291.
4. W.D. Rankin, *Carnal Union with Christ in the Theology of T.F. Torrance* (University of Edinburgh: Unpublished Ph.D., 1997), esp. 1-145. The order in which the themes are presented and the manner in which they are treated reflects my own understanding of Torrance's position. Nevertheless, I would

we are met by an unambiguously stated affirmation of the contemporary significance of the Chalcedonian formula. Thus, he makes his position on Chalcedon clear, and his further intention, when he writes in 1954 that:

> There can be no doubt that the Chalcedonian formulation of the Union of Christ was one of the greatest and most important in the whole field of theology, and yet it was formulated in almost total abstraction from the historical life and work of Jesus Christ from his birth to his resurrection. It is one of the most pressing needs of theology to have the hypostatic union restated much more in terms of the mission of Christ...I do not mean that we would contemplate any change in the fundamental position adopted at Chalcedon or even in the terminology of Leo's Tome which conserves so wonderfully the mystery of the God-man. What I mean is that the Chalcedonian Christology needs to be filled out in accordance with its own fundamental position, in a more dynamic way, in terms of the incorporating and atoning work of the Saviour, for the only account the New Testament gives us of the Incarnation is conditioned by the perspective of the crucifixion and resurrection.[5]

Thus, it can be seen that what Torrance intends to do is to hold firmly to and to exegete the formula of Chalcedon, while filling it out 'in accordance with its own fundamental position'. Further, we see that the motivation for doing so is to be found in the fact that the formula of Chalcedon does not say enough about the nature of the reconciling work of Christ, 'for reconciliation is not something added to hypostatic union so much as the hypostatic union itself at work in expiation and atonement'.[6] I would contend that all of Torrance's subsequent Christological reflection is an outworking of the position stated above.

How then does Torrance understand the function of the Chalcedonian two-natures formula? He suggests that it:

---

acknowledge my indebtedness to Rankin's work throughout this section, even in the absence of any further direct citation of it. See also, D. Macleod, 'Christology', 174-6.

5. T.F. Torrance, 'The Atonement and the Oneness of the Church', *Scottish Journal of Theology* 7 (1954), 245-269, 246-7.

6. Ibid., 247.

is a compound existence-statement derived by tracing certain basic existence-statements back to their biblical sources and through them to an empirical relation, in worship and faith, to Christ Himself.[7]

Thus, in the first instance, Chalcedon is an attempt to faithfully state the impact of our encounter with the divine nature and with the human nature in the unity of His Person. Thereafter, the formula functions through 'analogical reasoning'. In so doing, it states its limitations through speaking only in negative terms – '*without* confusion, *without* change, *without* division, *without* separation' – and does so:

> in order that the transcendent fact of Christ Himself may continually disclose itself...unobstructed by statements that pretend to be able to reduce to a positive formula that which is more to be adored than expressed.[8]

At the same time, the formula uses 'the traditional logical distinction between statements of identity and statements of difference' to express, as positively as we are able under the conditions of our existence, 'the relation between the divine and human natures in Christ'. The fact that such statements are made via negation indicates that their positive character is necessarily curtailed, such that:

> It is made evident that the analogical form into which the understanding is cast is not in itself important – it is in fact expendable – but what does matter is Christ Himself, truly divine and truly human in His one incarnate Person.[9]

Thereafter, the resulting formula is to be understood as 'a *transparent medium* through which we may continue to discern the self-disclosure of Christ'.[10]

I take it that when Torrance states of the formula that 'it is in fact expendable', he means by this 'expendable' in principle, rather

---

7. Idem, *Theological Science* (London: 1969), 245.
8. Ibid., 245.
9. Ibid., 245.
10. Ibid., 245.

than indicating his intention to dispense with it. This may be seen, when he sums up the continuing value of Chalcedon in the following terms:

> As such the Chalcedonian Definition is a flexible and subtle analogue, provided with the means of its own correction, so that when used rightly it invites reconstruction in view of the fuller disclosure of the reality it serves and proclaims its own inadequacy by a logical suspension of form so that it cannot be made a substitute for the truth of the divine Word.[11]

Torrance's statement of his position and intention is clear at this point. Equally, his elucidation of the function of the Chalcedonian formula seems to me to be admirably stated in terms which serve as an exemplar of how we ought to use that formula, and I would commend this elucidation of the function without reservation.

Beyond Chalcedon

Thus, we note that Torrance regards Chalcedon as offering an account of the person of Christ which, while sufficient in itself, requires to be complemented by a sufficient statement of the work of Christ. Indeed, he suggests that:

> the Chalcedonian formulation does not say enough, for reconciliation is not something added to hypostatic union so much as the hypostatic union itself at work in expiation and atonement...we must give the hypostatic union more dynamic expression...We must think of Christ entering upon His active ministry as true God and true Man in one Person, in a union which penetrated into our sinful humanity and created room for itself in the midst of our estrangement, at once gathering sinful man into one Body with the Saviour, and opening up a new and living way into the Holiest.[12]

Once more, we may in principle commend an attempt to take us beyond Chalcedon which nevertheless intends to remain faithful

---

11. Ibid., 246.
12. Idem, 'The Atonement and the Oneness of the Church', 247.

to Chalcedon, especially one which specifically seeks to complement a focus upon the person of Christ with one upon the work of Christ. How then does Torrance seek to give a more 'dynamic expression' to the hypostatic union which is embodied in the Chalcedonian formula? He does so by taking the concept of *enhypostasia* and employing it in a theological couplet with the concept of *anhypostasia*. This integration of the two concepts into an inseparable bond, and the manner in which it is applied to the understanding of our redemption in Christ, constitutes the heart of Torrance's contribution to Christology. He writes:

> By *anhypostasia* classical Christology asserted that in the *assumptio carnis* the human nature of Christ had no independent *per se* subsistence apart from the event of the Incarnation, apart from the hypostatic union. By *enhypostasia*, however, it asserted that in the *assumptio carnis* the human nature of Christ was given a real and concrete subsistence within the hypostatic union – it was enhypostatic in the Word…. In the Incarnation the eternal Son assumed human nature into oneness with Himself but in that assumption Jesus Christ is not only real man but a man. He is at once the *One* and the *Many*.[13]

Thereafter, Torrance applies this to our understanding of the nature of the atonement and suggests that our holding together of the concepts integral to the couplet means that 'while atonement is throughout act of God for us, we are to understand it as act of God done in our humanity, wrought in our place and as our act'.[14] Thus, the humanity of Christ is integral to the very accomplishment of our redemption, as opposed to being merely instrumental. Further, he suggests that this leads us to giving a much fuller place to the notion of a 'concrete *substitution*', in which Christ's humanity is seen as effectively realising atonement. This takes place as a result of the fact that: 'He the sinless One incorporated Himself into our flesh of sin that through substitutionary atonement we who are sinners might be incorporated into Him as His body.'[15] This means, in effect, that the incarnate Christ shares in the act of

---

13. Ibid., 249-50.
14. Ibid., 250.
15. Ibid., 252.

atonement 'from both sides, from the side of God who is offended by man and from the side of man who is under the divine judgment of death'.[16]

Therefore, to summarise, we may suggest that Torrance intends to take us beyond Chalcedon's sufficient statement regarding the person of Christ by buttressing Chalcedon's account with a sufficient statement of the work of Christ. In particular:

1) Torrance complements Chalcedon's *anhypostatic* interpretation of the person of Christ with an *enhypostatic* interpretation. The complementary concepts now form an inseparable, and indispensable, couplet.

2) This theological couplet enables us to explain a) the manner in which Christ assumes our humanity, and b) the manner in which Christ effects atonement. The elements specified in a) and b) are inseparable, with this flowing from the fact that our humanity is now 'incorporated' into Christ, such that He effects a 'concrete substitution' in which our humanity becomes His humanity.

3) Following from 2), Christ's humanity is to be understood as a vicarious humanity. That is, Christ stands absolutely and fully in our place, to do for us that which we cannot do for ourselves.

4) Christ's assumption of our humanity is to be understood as the assumption of a fallen humanity, which is linked to a concept of incarnational redemption.

5) Christ's assumption of our humanity is to be understood as the assumption of a humanity, in which a corporate relationship is maintained between Christ and ourselves. This also links into the concept of incarnational redemption.

Further beyond Chalcedon

I have already offered an adequate exposition of Torrance's position with respect to 1) and 2). Let me now offer some fuller examples of the remaining elements.

a) The Vicarious Humanity of Christ

We have already noted that, for Torrance, Christ is to be understood as standing on both sides of the Divine-Human divide, inasmuch

---

16. Ibid., 251-2.

as He represents God to Humanity, and Humanity before God. How precisely is He to be understood as representing Humanity before God? According to Torrance, our trust and faith in Christ are grounded 'in his flesh', as well as in his 'spoken promises'. Equally, Christ is portrayed as having received from God all His blessings, and as having 'sealed' our 'reception' of these blessings in His life and death, such that:

> Faith is thus a polar concept that reposes upon and derives from the prior faithfulness of God which has been translated permanently into our actual human existence in Jesus Christ. We do not rely, then, upon our act of faith, but upon the faith of Christ which undergirds and upholds our faith.[17]

Thereafter, Christ is understood to have taken our place so concretely and completely that, in the humanity which He has assumed, He acts vicariously on our behalf, and becomes in that humanity 'the embodiment of our act of faith and trust and obedience toward God'. This vicarious action of Christ on our behalf toward God finds its own polar complement in the fact that, at the very same time, He is the 'embodiment of God's righteous and holy Act' toward us.[18] He writes:

> He stood in our place, taking our cause upon him, also as Believer, as the Obedient one who was himself justified before God as his beloved Son in whom he was well pleased. He offered to God a perfect confidence and trust, a perfect faith and response which we are unable to offer, and he appropriated all God's blessings which we are unable to appropriate. Through union with him we share in his faith, in his obedience, in his trust and appropriation of the Father's blessing; we share in his justification before God. Therefore, when we say that we are justified by faith, this does not mean that it is *our* faith that justifies us, far from it – it is the faith of Christ alone that justifies us, but we in faith flee from our own acts even of repentance, confession, trust and response, and take refuge in the obedience and faithfulness of Christ.[19]

---

17. Idem, *Theology in Reconstruction* (London: 1965), 159.
18. Ibid., 159.
19. Ibid., 159-60.

To summarise Torrance's position, we may say that, in the assumption of our humanity, Christ vicariously does for us that which we are unable to do for ourselves.

b) The Assumption of a 'fallen humanity' / Incarnational Redemption

Torrance unambiguously affirms that Christ establishes a '*union*...between our fallen human nature and his divine nature',[20] and contends that 'in taking Upon himself the form of a servant, the Lord transferred to himself fallen Adamic humanity which he took from the Virgin Mary, that is, our perverted, corrupt, degenerate, diseased human nature enslaved to sin and subject to death under the condemnation of God'. In so doing, he regards this position as essentially consonant with Paul's teaching in Romans 8:3.[21] Equally, he regards it as essentially consonant with that of such diverse figures as Athanasius[22] and Thomas Erskine of Linlathen.[23] Therefore, by uniting Himself to us, Christ effected a redemption and healing of our nature, such that 'he both took what is ours and imparted to us what is his',[24] and 'in assuming flesh from fallen and sinful humanity, far from being contaminated by it, Christ redeemed and sanctified it at the same time – the very assumption of Adamic humanity was essentially redemptive from the moment of its conception in the Virgin Mary'.[25]

Thus, in the face of such a realistic emphasis upon the character of the nature which Christ assumed, it is important to stress that Torrance maintains throughout that Christ Himself is without sin.[26]

Torrance's position is well summed up when he writes:

In this union he both assumed our fallen human nature, taking it from the Virgin Mary, and sanctified it in the very act of assumption and all through his holy Life he lived in it from the beginning to the

---

20. Ibid., 155.
21. Idem, *The Trinitarian Faith* (Edinburgh: 1988), 161.
22. Ibid., 161-2.
23. Idem, *Scottish Theology* (Edinburgh: 1996), 270-1.
24. Idem, *The Trinitarian Faith*, 162.
25. Idem, *Scottish Theology*, 270.
26. Idem, *The Trinitarian Faith*, 161.

end. Thus our redemption begins from his very birth, so that we must regard the Incarnation, even in its narrower sense, as redeeming event...In his holy assumption of our unholy humanity, his purity wipes away our impurity, his holiness covers our corruption, his nature heals our nature.[27]

A further development of this position is to be found in the emphasis which Torrance places upon the Eastern Patristic theme; that what 'Christ has not assumed he has not healed...'[28] This development is located within Torrance's forceful rejection of Apollinarianism, and is particularly directed towards establishing the reality of the fact that Christ assumed a human mind. That is, Christ assumed every part of that which is proper to humanity.

c) Christ – 'the One and the Many' / Incarnational Redemption
The suggestion that Christ assumed a humanity which involved a corporate dimension is open to misinterpretation, and Torrance marks out his position very clearly. He is not suggesting that Christ is to be thought of as assuming some kind of 'generic or universal ...humanity'.[29] Instead, he suggests that there is an ontological bond between Christ and all of humanity which comes about as a result of the Son and Word of God being the Creator. Thus, the 'carnal union' between Christ and ourselves is grounded in the fact that He who is incarnate is He who is the Creator. Torrance writes:

> the eternal Son and Word of God is He in whom all men cohere for He is the Creator who gives them being and through His Spirit holds them in being. There is thus an ontological relation between the creature and the Creator reposing upon His sheer grace, in which He gives them being as realities distinct from Himself, so that the ontological relation...is not reversible. That is, the Son and Word of God became man by becoming one particular Man, but because He is the Creator Word who became Man, even as the incarnate Word He still holds all men in an ontological relation to Himself. That relation was not broken off with the Incarnation.[30]

27. Idem, *Theology in Reconstruction*, 155-6.
28. Idem, *Theology in Reconciliation* (London: 1975), 154. See also, 167-8.
29. Idem, *The School of Faith* (London: 1959), cxi-cxii.
30. Ibid., cxii.

John L. McPake

Thereafter, having established that there is an ontological bond between Christ and humanity, Torrance draws out the soteriological significance of this when he writes that:

> it belongs to the very essence of the Incarnational life and work of the Son that in Him redemption penetrates back to the very beginning and reunites man's life to God's creative purpose. Redemption is no mere afterthought on the part of God, for in it the original creation comes to a transcendent realisation, and the one Covenant of Grace made with all creation is fulfilled.[31]

Thus, with an ontological bond having been established and the soteriological implications of this outlined, we see that, within Torrance's thought, Christ's assumption of our humanity involves a corporate relationship between ourselves and Him which has an inescapable significance for each person. As a result of this, we may say that there exists a 'polarity' within Christ's person, with respect to His relationship to ourselves, (*not* with respect to Himself). Therefore, Christ is; at one and the same time, a) the particular One who is objectively other than us, and b) He who is 'the Many', standing in a corporate relationship to each one of us through creation and redemption. He writes:

> It is because Christ is Himself "the One and the Many", the One who includes the Many, and the Many who includes each one, that He encounters men always and only in this two-fold way, within the corporate community of the Many, and within the life of each man.[32]

Truly beyond Chalcedon?
The attempt to journey beyond Chalcedon, while remaining faithful to Chalcedon is central to Torrance's contribution to the Christological endeavour, and for this he is to be commended unreservedly. In particular, his attempt to develop an understanding of the person of Christ which is complemented by a Soteriology which is integral to that understanding merits our full consideration. Indeed, as John McIntyre notes, the attention paid

31. Ibid., cxiii.
32. Ibid., cxxiii.

by the early Church to Trinitarian and Christological formulations is nowhere matched by a corresponding attention to the question of Soteriology. As a result, there is a relative lack of sophistication and nuance in our discussion of the latter.[33] Torrance attempts to remedy that lack, and does so in a form which draws upon the resources of the tradition in which Chalcedon stands. In so doing, the Chalcedonian formula, within Torrance's understanding, may be said to function as a catalyst for theological exploration. Thus, it is no end in itself. Rather, it is a medium through which we may potentially realise a fuller comprehension of the soteriological significance of Christ. Equally, the focus upon the manner in which Christ assumes our humanity affirms the integral place of that humanity in every attempt to comprehend Christ. Alongside this, the stress upon incarnational redemption potentially establishes the significance of Christ for every person in a form which is presented as having genuine ontological significance.

Nevertheless, whenever we attempt to extrapolate the significance of a relatively established position – such as Chalcedon – it is incumbent upon us to constantly refer back to that position in order that we may verify whether, or not, we have remained faithful to that position. It is here that we must question Torrance. That is not to say that Torrance's developed Christology may not in fact represent a coherent position in its own right. However, in looking at his Christology and comparing it to the Chalcedonian formula, it seems to me that we have moved beyond Chalcedon to the point where we might reasonably ask: Is Torrance's Christology a genuine development of the Chalcedonian position?

John McIntyre points to the fact that one of the tasks which Protestant theology needs to address more fully is that of relating the 'generic images...generated by conceptual theology' to the 'specific imagery' generated by the faithful reading of the Biblical narratives concerning Jesus. He suggests that it is the latter which should be pre-eminent, 'rather than the construct of the Councils'.[34] Following McIntyre, we may say that the adequacy of a conciliar statement is established only insofar as the 'generic images' which

---

33. J. McIntyre, *The Shape of Soteriology* (Edinburgh: 1992), 1-2 .

34. Idem , *On the Love of God* (London: 1962), 184-5.

it utilises resonate with the 'specific images' of Scripture. Similarly, we may say that a theology which intends to embody a conciliar position must be careful to ensure that, in its subsequent development, it maintains, or increases, that degree of resonance. I would contend that the 'generic images' found in Torrance's developed theology increasingly fail to maintain that necessary degree of resonance with Scripture. Indeed, for all that the intention is clearly otherwise, I would suggest that there is a diminution of that resonance. As an example, let us take Torrance's understanding of the vicarious humanity of Christ, and remind ourselves of his position. He writes:

> [Christ] stood in our place...as Believer...He offered to God...a perfect faith....Through union with him we share in his faith...when we say that we are justified by faith, this does not mean that it is *our* faith that justifies us...it is the faith of Christ alone that justifies us....we in faith flee from our own acts even of repentance, confession, trust and response, and take refuge in the...faithfulness of Christ.[35]

At first reading, this understanding of the role of Christ's faith within the concept of the vicarious humanity would seem to be an acceptable step back from the 'specific' to the 'generic', in order to provide a more comprehensive account of the person and work of Christ. Indeed, we *might* agree that it does represent an acceptable step! However, it only continues to be acceptable insofar as it is complemented by a distinct and adequate account of the role of faith in the life of person who responds to the Gospel injunction to place their faith and trust in Christ. However, where the latter is wholly subsumed within the former, then a distinct account is lost and its adequacy imperilled.

In particular, how would we make sense of the 'specific image' of Jesus' call to repent and believe (Mark 1: 15) if it is the case that only He can truly repent and believe? One theological explanation which we may wish to offer is to say that it is the grace of faith which enables us to repent and believe, and that prevenient grace thus given by God brings about our belief.[36]

---

35. T.F. Torrance, *Theology in Reconstruction*, 159-60.
36. *Westminster Confession of Faith*, X.2, XI.1, XIV.1, XIV.2, XV.1 , XV. 2.

However, that is not what Torrance says. Rather, he affirms that it is only Christ who can truly repent and believe with there being no genuine possibility of our so doing, and subsumes the account of our responsive faith within an account of the faith of Christ. It cannot be alleged of Torrance that an account of our responsive faith is not, formally speaking, present. Equally, we must affirm that he does intend to give substance to that formal presence. Thus, we may agree with Donald Macleod that, while Torrance's position 'appears to involve a thorough-going Christomonism in which the work of Christ is everything and that of the believer nothing', it is in fact heavily qualified by him so as to negate such an appearance.[37] Nevertheless, by resolutely placing that account within the work of Christ it becomes increasingly difficult to reconcile the 'generic image' of the vicarious humanity of Christ with the Scriptural 'specific images' of the evangelical injunction to repent and believe. Thus, the resonance between the 'generic image' and the 'specific image' of Jesus calling men and women to repentance and faith is diminished.

Therefore, I would contend that the 'generic images' utilised within Torrance's theology are not wholly consonant with the 'specific images' found in the New Testament. Why is this so? I would suggest that it is a direct result of the manner in which Torrance develops the *enhypostatic* interpretation of Christ which complements Chalcedon's *anhypostatic* interpretation. That is, Torrance overloads the concept of *enhypostasia* and, in effect, 'over-theologises' the concept, such that it takes on a significance far beyond its proper bounds. I would not myself reject the *enhypostatic* interpretation *per se*. However, it does not offer a limitless canvas upon which we may sketch the whole drama of Incarnation and Redemption. Rather, it has a potential significance insofar as it may be deployed to point towards the manner in which Christ assumed humanity. That is its proper, potential significance, and for that we may be grateful.

---

37. D. Macleod, 'Christology', 176.

Conclusion

If the above arguments are granted, the concept of vicarious humanity, as developed in Torrance's Christology, is undermined. Similarly, the suggestion that Christ assumed a fallen humanity, while hardly novel by Torrance's day, cannot be said to stand within the tradition of the orthodox understanding of the person of Christ. The suggestion that it does is misleading. Equally, the concept of incarnational redemption needs to be placed in a proper relationship to the Cross in order that the significance of the life of Jesus may be understood in the light of His death and resurrection, which is the perspective of the New Testament. Torrance, of course, intends to do nothing other than focus on the Cross. However, we may question if the concept of incarnational redemption does not, in fact, diminish that focus. Further, while Torrance is to be commended for magnifying the work of Christ for us, his understanding of the nature of our response to that work is stated in terms which seem less and less to resonate with Scripture.

Torrance clearly signals that his intention is to remain faithful to Chalcedon, and to develop his understanding of the person and work of Christ within the parameters of Chalcedon. However, while we may agree that Torrance does take us beyond Chalcedon, the question remains: Does he, albeit unintentionally, take us away from Chalcedon?

9

Images of Jesus Christ in the non-Western World: An Asian Reflection

Moonjang Lee

The purpose of this paper is to survey the prominent images of Jesus Christ in non-Western Christianity and then evaluate them from an Asian Christian perspective. I admit that this subject is so vast that I cannot properly perform the task unless I make it more specific. If we survey the literature on Christology produced by non-Western theologians, we may identify roughly two trends. The first focuses on the social stance of the historical Jesus to illuminate the social and political dimensions of Jesus' teachings and his earthly ministry. The other attempts to relate the Christ of faith to the religions or religiosity of non-Western people. What I attempt to do in this paper is not an overall survey of what non-Western theologians say about Jesus, but simply to examine the validity of the theological agenda behind those two different Christological constructions. It is assumed that there are various theological and contextual agenda hidden behind the presentations of the Christological images by non-Western theologians.[1]

1. The Quest of the Historical Jesus

One of the major enterprises for Christologies in the non-Western world is the quest of the historical Jesus. This question has been the source of fierce debates among biblical scholars in the West for a long time, and still we do not have the final verdict on this issue. In

---

1. Before we begin our survey, we need to be reminded of the fact that the Christologies in Latin America, Africa and Asia have been formulated in close dialogue with Western theologies. In other words, though the two different trends we identify within the Christological discourses in the non-Western world reflect local endeavours to present contextually relevant images of Jesus Christ, they also reflect the strong influence of political theology and the religious pluralism of the West.

non-Western theologies, however, apart from those biblical scholars who participate in the discourses of Western biblical scholarship, many theologians show an interest in the quest of the historical Jesus for different reasons. Their quest of the historical Jesus is neither to challenge nor to prove the historical authenticity of the biblical data about Jesus and his sayings. They are well aware of the history of the scholarly debates on the historical Jesus, but simply bypass it. They are not enthusiastic at all to prove the authenticity of the historical Jesus. Rather they attempt to present a new Christology in a new situation to find contextually relevant meanings of Jesus Christ. Given the context of their praxis of liberation in Africa, Asia and Latin America, research on the historical Jesus is accepted as valid insofar as it illuminates Jesus' praxis of liberation.[2] In other words, if the investigation of the historical Jesus strengthens theological and contextual themes such as liberation, preferential love and concern for the poor, the validity of the biblical data is not questioned.

We have a number of theologians who explore the historical Jesus not for 'an academic reconstruction of biographical details' but for 'the contextual relevance and the essential significance of Jesus'.[3] We cannot survey them all, but in this section I will examine the images of Jesus in Latin American liberation theology and in the Korean minjung theology. In Africa, we find South African Black Theology and more broadly African liberation theology in sub-Saharan Africa. These theologies, including other descriptions of the historical Jesus in Asia and Africa by individual theologians, generally echo the themes and messages of the liberation and minjung Christologies. The common concern of all these Christological constructions is to illuminate Jesus' mission for the poor and the oppressed and its implications for the construction of a just society.

Jesus as Liberator
One of the most conspicuous images of the historical Jesus is that of a liberator. The image of Jesus as liberator was first presented in a systematic way in the liberation theology of Latin America. It was Gustavo Gutierrez who initiated the discourse of theology of

---

2. Leonardo Boff, *Jesus Christ Liberator: A Critical Christology for Our Time* (New York: Orbis, 1978), pp. 282-86.

3. R.S. Sugitharajah, 'Prologue and Perspective,' in *Asian Faces of Jesus*, ed. by Sugitharajah (London: SCM, 1993), p. x.

liberation, but the liberation Christology has been substantially developed by Leonardo Boff and Jon Sobrino. The historical context that provided the motive and impetus for the development of liberation theology was the basic Latin American reality of underdevelopment and oppression. The acute awareness of the brutal reality facing the vast majority of people in Latin America was the starting point of theological reflection for some Latin American theologians.[4] As Gutierrez described the task of theology as a 'critical reflection on Christian praxis in the light of the word',[5] Latin American liberation theologians have given particular attention to the historical Jesus to obtain principles for their praxis of liberation. Thus the contextual agenda precedes their quest of the historical Jesus.

The primary concerns of the liberation theologians were the structural changes in their given socio-historical situation and the transformation of their oppressive reality through social action. What they needed to emphasise in the Latin American situation was a specific socio-political commitment to break with the situation of oppression. This social agenda prompted them to explore the historical Jesus in the hope of finding 'the norm of liberative practice and the prototype of the new human being for whom liberation strives'.[6]

Boff and Sobrino endeavoured to illuminate the historical figure of Jesus because he is believed to offer the key for liberation theology. For Boff and Sobrino, the ministry of the historical Jesus is characterised as the praxis for liberation. Therefore, the illumination of the various aspects of Jesus' liberating praxis has become the major concern in theology of liberation.[7] Then, on what ground is Jesus perceived as a liberator? In a nutshell, Jesus was a liberator because he showed his partisan love for and his solidarity with the poor and oppressed, proclaimed the liberation in the kingdom of God, and struggled for its realisation. Though Jesus was killed on the cross in the course of his liberating praxis by the political and religious authorities, through his resurrection he demonstrated that death could not separate him from the suffering people. According to liberation theologians, this Jesus calls upon us to participate in the struggle for

---

4. L. Boff, *Jesus Christ Liberator* (London: SPCK, 1980), p. 268.

5. Gustavo Gutierrez, *A Theology of Liberation* (New York: Orbis; London: SCM, 1973; rev. ed. 1988), pp. 6-15.

6. J. Sobrino, *Jesus in Latin America*, pp. 11-12.

7. Leonardo Boff, *Jesus Christ Liberator*, pp. 282-86.

liberation to establish a just society. Drawing on their discovery of the significance of Jesus in the socio-political and socio-economic situations at the time of Jesus, liberation theologians assert that the Christian churches today must copy Jesus' historical praxis of liberation: 'To worship and proclaim Jesus Christ as the Liberator is to ponder and live out our christological faith within a socio-historical context marked by domination and oppression.'[8]

In the Latin American context where people are fighting against poverty and oppression to build a just society, it is obvious that the liberation they fight for is a liberation from economic exploitation and from political oppression. It is natural for liberation theologians to equate salvation with the socio-political and socio-economic liberation. However, while emphasising the political dimensions of the liberating praxis of Jesus,[9] Boff and Sobrino note that Jesus did not offer social or political programmes to create a just society[10] or attempt to liberate Israel from the Roman colonial rule or destroy the oppressive social structures of Israel.

Boff and Sobrino are aware of the tension between the total liberation of humanity in the future and temporal/historical liberation. Boff states that the reign of God as a universal and transcendental reality has nothing to do with the nationalism of the Jews nor with the liberation from the political oppression of the Romans nor liberation from the economic difficulties of the people.[11] He also admits that liberation does not have socio-political dimension but possesses a universal and globalizing character.[12] However, what he argues is that, as the reign of God was already initiated in our world as a historical reality through the ministry of Jesus, liberation is partially realised in history. 'The total liberation proposed by God

---

8. L. Boff, *Jesus Christ Liberator. A Critical Christology for Our Time* (New York: Orbis, 1978), p. 264

9. Cf. see Jon Sobrino, *Christology at the Crossroads* (New York: Orbis, 1978), p. 211ff. He pays attention to the political significance of Jesus' words and deeds within Israelite society. He holds that, as there was no separation between religion and politics at the time of Jesus, Jesus' attack on the then Jewish religious leaders who possessed the power to control Jewish society inevitably carried political implications. Therefore, he asserts that Jesus' words and deeds are revolutionary.

10. Boff, 'Salvation in Jesus Christ and the Process of Liberation,' p. 90.

11. Boff, *Jesus Christ Liberator*, p. 55.

12. Boff, 'Christ's Liberation via Oppression,' p. 107.

must take the pathway of partial liberations. While the former is not simply the sum of the latter, the latter do anticipate and pave the way for the former.'[13] The historical liberations are anticipations and concretization of the salvation that will be full and complete only in eternity.[14] For Boff, the christological foundation for the liberating praxis today is the socio-political praxis of Jesus who showed partisan love to the poor. As Jesus' disciples we have to follow his cause, i.e., solidarity with the poor. Sobrino also refers to the tension between the future reign of God as utopia to be fulfilled by God and the present anticipation of the reign of God. He argues that the utopian goal of the reign of God gives impetus for Christian praxis in history and interprets discipleship as following Jesus in his liberating praxis.

Jesus as Suffering Minjung
In minjung[15] theology, a Korean version of liberation theology, the image of Jesus as liberator is strongly rejected. Minjung theologians emphasise the sufferings of Jesus as one of the poor and oppressed minjung. Being one of the poor and oppressed minjung, Jesus is presented as the personification of the people who can be designated as minjung. Jesus was a friend of minjung rather than their leader, educator or liberator. Liberation from economic exploitation and political oppression is achieved through minjung revolts. In this process of liberation, minjung must emerge as the subjects of history. Minjung theologians see that the presentation of Jesus as liberator is

---

13. Boff, *Jesus Christ Liberator*, p. 287.

14. Boff, 'Integral Liberation and Partial Liberation,' p. 19.

15. The term *minjung* is a combination of two Chinese characters: *min* and *jung*. The word *min* means 'the people' and the word *jung* means 'the mass', so the literal meaning of *minjung* is either 'the people' or 'the mass people'. The word minjung also designates a historical entity. The most clear description is given by Hyun Young-Hak, one of the pioneering minjung theologians, who states: 'When minjung theologians use the term minjung, they think of those currently living people like the poor farmers in the country, those who fled from the harsh country life to become either factory workers in the cities or the coal-miners, those who live in illegal shacks that can be demolished any time, a trash picker, a hoodlum, a day labourer, a street cleaner, a prostitute, the mistress of a brothel, the employees of small factories who suffer from lack of nutrition and sleep, and the prisoners, etc.' Hyun Young-Hak, 'Minjung, Suffering Servant and Hope,' in *Developments of Korean Minjung Theology in the 1980s* (in Korean; Seoul: Korea Theological Research Institute, 1990), p. 12.

incongruous with their notion of minjung subjecthood in history.

Like liberation theology in Latin America, minjung theology emerged within the historical context of economic exploitation and political oppression in Korea in the 1970s. Some Christian theologians began to pay attention to the unjust situation in Korea. As the phrase 'minjung theology' indicates, the theological focus in minjung theology is not on the historical Jesus but on minjung. Suh Nam-Dong, one of the pioneers of minjung theology, argued that the subject matter of minjung theology is not Jesus but minjung. According to Suh, the starting point of minjung theology is the premise that the historical Jesus is the means for understanding the minjung, rather than the concept of minjung being the instrument for understanding Jesus.[16] Ahn Byung-Mu, another pioneer of minjung theology, holds that minjung theology should illuminate the events that minjung and Jesus are making together, rather than dichotomise minjung and Jesus by the subject-object formula.[17] However, he argues that we should pay particular attention to the people surrounding Jesus.[18] For Ahn and Suh, including other minjung theologians, the discovery of minjung is the starting point of their theology.

Minjung theologians emphasise the low social status of the historical Jesus based on the following observations: (1) Jesus' origin in Galilee, a land of the poor and the oppressed; (2) Jesus' occupation as carpenter; (3) Jesus' lack of formal education and (4) Jesus' life as homeless.[19] Not only was Jesus himself one of the minjung, but he associated with people who belonged to the low class of Jewish society. Jesus showed his partisan love and concern exclusively for the poor and oppressed people, i.e., the so-called sinners of that time. Minjung theologians even argue that Jesus must be perceived as a collective symbol of the poor minjung, not as a historical individual.[20]

---

16. Suh Nam-Dong, 'Historical References for a Theology of Minjung,' in *Minjung Theology. People as the Subjects of History*, ed., by the Commission of Theological Concerns of the Christian Conference of Asia (London: Zed Press, 1981), p. 160.

17. Ibid.

18. Ahn Byung-Mu, 'The Subjects of History in Mark,' (in Korean) in *Minjung and Korean Theology* (Seoul: Korea Theological Study Institute, 1982), p. 180.

19. See Ahn Byung-Mu, *Jesus of Galilee* (in Korean; Seoul: Hanguk Theological Research Institute, 1990; Third Edition, 1993), pp. 15-40.

Therefore, minjung theologians interpret the suffering, death and resurrection of Jesus not as an individual but as a collective event. Jesus was not the liberator of the minjung but, as one of the minjung, participated in the historical process for the liberation of minjung. Liberation of minjung is realised through the collective struggle of minjung and at the end the liberated minjung emerge as the subjects of history.

Minjung theologians are adamant in rejecting that the historical Jesus played any leadership role in his struggle for a just society probably because of their pre-conceived idea that the poor and oppressed minjung *are* or *should be* the subjects of history. Given the context of bloody resistance against the unjust political leaders in the 1970s in Korea, they might have found it irrelevant to present Jesus as the leader or liberator of the poor minjung. Their political leaders for too long have deceived the Korean minjung. What they needed in that historical context was not an idle discourse about the ideal leadership but an active participation in the minjung revolts against the oppressive government. However, we can easily detect the inconsistency in their presentation of Jesus as a poor suffering minjung. If Jesus was a mere minjung, as minjung theologians argue, then why were the Jewish religious leaders scandalised by his association with tax-collectors and sinners who, according to minjung theologians, represent the minjung at the time of Jesus? If they describe Jesus as a mere minjung, the theological and historical agenda of minjung theologians will fail, for no radical message can be found in a minjung's association with other minjung. Another inherent problem in minjung theology is the tendency to de-historicize the historical Jesus. Though criticising Western biblical scholars (particularly Bultmann) for de-historicizing the historical Jesus, minjung theologians, by describing the historical Jesus as the projection of the collective minjung, de-historicized him.

Some Critical Reflections

The questions that liberation and minjung theologians bring to their Jesus research concern the significance of Jesus today, not the establishment of historical facts. We can readily endorse their contextual and theological agenda to build a just society and to

20. Cf. Song Ki-Deuk, 'The Identity of Minjung Theology,' (in Korean) in *Development of Minjung Theology in the 1980s*, p. 81.

discover the liberating messages of Jesus. The images of liberating and suffering Jesus have greatly contributed to the awakening of the churches in the non-Western world to the reality of injustice and human sufferings. However, what makes us hesitant to fully endorse their discourses as authentic ways of reading the historical Jesus is the fact that they are not quite successful in presenting contextually relevant and biblically faithful images of Jesus. As we have already pointed out, liberation theologians sense the tension between the total liberation in the future and the partial liberation in history, because the biblical data do not render full support to their idea of liberative praxis.

It is also the case with minjung Christology. Minjung theologians used the biblical data selectively to highlight the image of Jesus as a poor minjung. They too easily discredit those biblical data that suggest Jesus' royal/divine status as the product of ideological manipulation. One example of their misuse of the biblical data is found in their reading of the scene of the eschatological judgement in Matthew 25. Simply put, minjung theologians refer to the remark in which Jesus identified himself with the poor, the hungry, the thirsty, the sick and the outcasts from society, and regard this as concrete evidence of Jesus' minjung status. But a careful reading of this parable, far from supporting such an interpretation, actually reveals the opposite. I argue that the parable does affirm not the minjung status of Jesus but conversely the elevation of minjung into the royal status because the one who sits on the throne as the eschatological judge (v. 31) proclaims his identification with them and calls them his brethren. In this regard, as we have indicated earlier, the theological agenda of minjung theology is unlikely to stand if they make Jesus a mere minjung, not their saviour.

2. The Quest of Christ of Faith

The second trend in Christological discourse in the non-Western world focuses on questions concerning the identity of Christ as the object of faith. The major questions that are raised concerning the Christ of faith in non-Western contexts are the relationship between Jesus Christ and God; between Jesus Christ and other world religions; and between the human Jesus and Christ as a divine being. As Christianity became a world phenomenon with its expansion into other cultures and religions, Christian theologians from the West felt the need to articulate the relation between Christianity and world religions. Though the history of universalism in the West is long and complex, the radical discourses of religious pluralism, theologies of religions, and inter-faith dialogue emerged rather recently within Christian theological circles in the West, which have been encouraged through international conferences. Some Western theologians like Ernst Troeltsch (1865–1923), Wilfred Cantwell Smith (1916-1973), Karl Rahner, John Hick and Hans Küng paved the way for religious pluralism which is adopted, adapted and further developed by non-Western theologians. The consistent voice of these theologians is that no ultimate and unique self-revelation of God was given to humans and the gospel is merely one of many salvific encounters with God. Regardless of the Christian claim that God revealed himself only through Jesus Christ, they argue that other religions have worshipped God and possess the name of God in their own way. Therefore, Jesus Christ is only one of the many ways that God revealed himself and, in other religions, God made his self-revelation in other ways. In response to this shift in theological stance, a number of theologians in the non-Western world have interpreted Christ from within their local religious traditions and presented various images of Christ. In Africa, Jesus Christ has been perceived as the healer, the great or proto ancestor, the elder Brother, the Head and Master of initiation and many others. In the Asian multi-religious milieu, Christ has been perceived as the *Tao*, the Sage (the ideal humanity in Confucianism), the perfect realisation of *Yin* and *Yang*, the true *Yogi*, *Jivanmukta* (one who has attained liberation while alive), *Advaitin* (one who realised the non-duality with Brahman/God), *Prajapati* (Lord of creatures), Eternal *Om* (Logos) and many others.[21] The common agenda we find behind all these various perceptions of Jesus Christ is the effort to present him from within the various cultural and religious traditions using indigenous ideas and concepts.

The Cosmic Christ: Christology in Hindu Context
Let me first summarise the content entailed in the image of the cosmic Christ: (1) Christ is one of the *avatars* or incarnations of God. (2) Christ, as one of the incarnations of God, already exists in other

---

21. R.S. Sugitharajah, 'An Interpretative Foreword,' in *Asian Faces of Jesus*, ed. by Sugitharajah (London: SCM, 1993), pp. 4-5.

religions. So salvation is open to all humanity regardless of their religious allegiance. (3) Jesus is one of the humans who achieved or realised the *avatar*. Therefore, anyone who achieves the same *avatar* can be called Christ. We need to examine how they perceive the cosmic Christ in more detail.

Non-western theologians who embrace the ethos of religious pluralism reject the traditional confessional Christologies. Gnana Robinson in India recently argued that the various confessions of Jesus as Christ, Son of God, Son of Man, the eternal Logos and the Word were determined by the historical and religious contexts in which such formulas were formulated.[22] He also points out that to meaningfully communicate the gospel of Jesus Christ to people living in different contexts we need to formulate different types of Christologies.[23] Therefore, as P. Devanandan suggested, to interpret the gospel through pre-existing non-Christian philosophical and religious concepts, some Asian and African theologians have attempted to present Christ using traditional religious concepts. Indian scholars like Raimundo Pannikar,[24] M. M. Thomas,[25] Stanley J. Samartha[26] and Wesley Ariarajah[27] particularly have developed this theological stance. Though the languages they use to capture the image of Christ differ, we find that they express a similar understanding of Christ.

Stanley J. Samartha proposed to revise Christology by attempting to interpret Christ with the concepts of Brahman in Hinduism. He regards this as an expansion of Christology.[28] Israel Selvanayagam tried to revise Christology and suggested finding 'new ways for

---

22. Gnana Robinson, 'Jesus Christ, The Open Way and The Fellow Struggler: A Look into the Christologies in India,' *Asia Journal of Theology* (1994), pp. 403-15

23. Gnana Robinson, 'Jesus Christ,' p. 403.

24. *The Unknown Christ of Hinduism* (Darton, Longman & Todd, 1968)

25. *The Acknowledged Christ of the Indian Renaissance* (London: SCM, 1969).

26. *The Hindu Response to the Unbound Christ* (Madras: CLC, 1974) and *One Christ – Many Religions. Toward a Revised Christology* (New York: Orbis, 1991).

27. *The Bible and People of Other Faiths* (Geneva: WCC, 1985; Third Printing, 1989).

28. See his, 'Toward a Revised Christology,' in *One Christ – Many Religions*, pp. 92-111.

clarifying the nature and function of Jesus and confessing him in an appropriate way'.[29] By emphasising that the historically bound confessional formulas should not be repeated, he insinuates that the confession, Jesus is God, is an inappropriate way to confess Jesus in the Indian multi-faith context.[30]

It was Raimundo Pannikar who initiated a rendezvous between Christianity and Hinduism not on the doctrinal but on the existential level. The meeting point, according to Pannikar, is Christ, for Christ already exists in Hinduism. This Christ in Hinduism is an anonymous Christ. In Pannikar's Christology, the historical Jesus (particular Jesus) and the Christ of faith (universal Christ) are separated. The Christ who appeared through Jesus can also appear through Krishna or Buddha. Pannikar holds that the Christian God and Brahman in Hinduism designate the same Ultimate Being. As Brahman makes self-revelation in the form of *avatar*, Christ is to be considered as an *avatar* of God/Brahman. Therefore, the confessions 'Jesus Christ is God' and 'Jesus Christ is Brahman' mean the same. Christ is none other than the Brahman*ness* and the historical Jesus is one of those humans who attained such Brahman*ness*. Anyone who realises such Brahman*ness* on earth like Jesus becomes Christ. Gnana Robinson explained this Brahmanness as the self-realisation of non-duality with Brahman/God.[31] He states that the realisation of the non-duality in the self (*atman*), that is, the self realisation of *atman*'s identity with the ultimate Brahman is *moksha* (salvation). He describes Jesus Christ as the one who reached the self-realisation of such non-duality. It follows that to worship Jesus Christ is to deify a human being. This perception of the cosmic Christ can be described as a

---

29. Israel Selvanayagam, 'Who Is This Jesus? A Biblical outline for clearer self-understanding and communication in a multi-faith context,' *Asia Journal of Theology* 7:2, 1993, pp. 243.

30. We find echoes of this religious perception of Jesus Christ in many Christian theologians beyond India. In the Korean context, Ryu Tong-Shik expresses the cosmic character of Christianity in the following way: 'Regardless of their belief in the Gospel all humanity have become here and now the new children of God. If we call those saved people as Christians, there is no one soul on earth who has not become a Christian. If we call the place where Christ is a Church, then the whole world has become a Church.' Cf. his article, 'The Issue of Mission towards Other Religions,' in *Do and Logos* (in Korean) (Seoul: Daehan Kidokgyo Press, 1978), pp. 96-101.

31. Gnana Robinson, 'Jesus Christ,' pp. 403-15

panchristism,[32] a modified version of the pantheism of Hindu religion.

It is interesting to find two different ways of describing the relationship between the historical Jesus and the cosmic Christ in the Hindu context. When they perceive Jesus Christ as one of the *avatars* of the Brahman/God, it sounds like a Christology from above in that the emphasis is on Brahman/God's self-revelation rather than on the human Jesus. However, when they hold that Jesus was one of the human beings who attained the self-realisation of non-duality with Brahman/God, it sounds like a Christology from below in that the emphasis is more on the human endeavour to attain one's oneness with divinity.

Christ the Awakened: Christology in Buddhist Context
We find a similar description of Jesus Christ in the Buddhist context. Seichi Yagi explains the relationship between Jesus and Christ by using the concept of Buddha.[33] According to Yagi, God already exists unconditionally within each and every human being. This is described as 'first contact'. Gotama was the person who was awakened to this fact. That is, he came to have an enlightenment, which Yagi calls 'second contact', and became Buddha. Jesus is perceived to be the person who attained the same enlightenment and became Christ. A Korean thinker, Ryu Young-Mo, expressed a similar idea in a different way. He also separates the temporal life of the human ego (Jesus) from the eternal life of the spiritual Self (Christ). He states: 'Those who are in the Christian faith call Jesus the only Christ, but Jesus is not the only Christ. Christ refers to the eternal life and is given to human beings by God through the Holy Spirit. Christ is the ultimate life of the total human beings and therefore cannot be confined to a particular person at a particular period of time. Even before Jesus, Christ existed. Christ existed even before Adam. What is unique with Jesus is that he attained the full realisation of this Christ.'[34] According to Ryu, Jesus described his self-realisation of oneness with God as 'being born from above'. With this realisation of non-duality with God comes the awareness of our status as the son of God. Ryu holds

---

32. Lee Dong-Joo, 'Religious Pluralism and Theology of Religion,' *Ministry and Theology*, 26 (August 1991), p. 75.

33. Seiichi Yagi, 'Christ and Buddha,' in *Asian Faces of Jesus*, pp. 25-44.

34. Park Young-Ho, *Ryu Young-Mo and His Christian Thought* (Seoul: Munhwa Ilbo, 1995), p. 25.

that Jesus, Gotama, Confucius and Lao Tsu all attained this self-realisation of oneness with the Ultimate Being/God, so there is no possibility of competition and/or conflict among them.

Although reflecting from within the Buddhist context, Aloysius Pieris and C. S. Song present the image of Jesus Christ in a different way. Aloysius Pieris, a Jesuit priest in Sri Lanka, attempts to interpret Jesus Christ in a way that makes sense of him in the Sri Lankan context. Pieris is not interested in the ontological articulation of the identity of Jesus Christ. By pointing out that Jesus and his religion have failed to win large-scale acceptance in Asia,[35] he discloses his concern to relate Jesus Christ in a meaningful way to the people living in the Buddhist society.

Pieris divides the dominant Christologies in Asia into two groups: Christ-against-religions and Christ-of-religions. He criticises the Christ-against-religions discourse as a crypto-colonialist Christ because it still expresses triumphalism over Asian religions. He also comments negatively on the Christ-of-religions discourse (i.e., the universal Christ) because it neglects the connection between religions and the praxis of liberation. However, though he talks about the Christology out of Asia, Pieris does not seem to be interested in presenting his own image of Christ parallel to that of cosmic Christ. His question is how to present Jesus Christ in the Buddhist context where Jesus is regarded as Bodhisattva (the one who is still awaiting the enlightenment), whereas Gotama is accepted as Buddha (the one who attained the enlightenment). Here, we notice that Pieris refers to the way Christ is pictured within the anti-Christian ethos in Sri Lanka, rather than a general Buddhist understanding of Christ. Anyway, given this religious reaction, Pieris seeks a way to facilitate an encounter between Christ and Buddha, avoiding the kerygmatic clash between the Christian confession of Jesus as Christ and the Buddhist understanding of Gotama as Buddha. Pieris asserts that Christ and Buddha meet in their path of human liberation. As the core of Jesus' mission was the realisation of the kingdom of God for the poor and oppressed people, Jesus, with Buddha, can and should be accepted as the mediator of salvation for Asian people. For Pieris, Christology of liberative agape and the liberative knowledge in Buddhism do not compete but complement each other, and therefore can be accepted

---

35. Aloysius Pieris, *An Asian Theology of Liberation* (New York: Orbis, 1988), p. 59.

as legitimate ways of salvation, for both embody the practice of voluntary poverty and the struggle against forced poverty. Regardless of his effort to reconcile Christianity with Buddhism, Pieris is still requested to clarify the relationship between Christ and Buddha. It is worth quoting what Pieris says about Christ:

> But the fact is that "Christ" (like "Son of God" or "Lord") is only a title, a human categorisation by which one particular culture tried to "capture" the ineffable mystery of salvation communicated in the person and teaching of Jesus. What is absolute and unique is not the title, but what all major religions, some in theistic, others in nontheistic terms, have professed for centuries as the mystery of salvation manifesting itself at least in a trinal (if not trinitarian) form.[36]

We cannot fail to note in this statement that Pieris merges the Christian concept of Christ with the Buddhist concept of Buddha. Therefore, we may say that it is rather difficult to draw a clear picture of Christ in Pieris' Christology.

The Christology of C. S. Song, a Taiwanese theologian based in America, has occupied the centre of his theological reflections as evidenced by his recent trilogy on Christology: *Jesus, The Crucified People* (1990), *Jesus and the Reign of God* (1993) and *Jesus in the Power of the Spirit* (1994). In these books, Song has attempted to present the image of Jesus Christ through Asian eyes and explored the significance of Jesus Christ for us today. In his first book, Song talks about the Christological shift from the historical Jesus to the historical Christ. What he means by the historical Christ is that Christ is present in history *here and now* in the sufferings of the people. Song interprets Jesus on the cross as the personification of the collective people who were crucified. The people whom Jesus represented on the cross were those socially, religiously and politically alienated people like women, children, the poor and the sick and so on. Song's second book traces how the life and mission of Jesus as the collective personification of the people manifested concretely in the historical realm. In his struggle to bring the reign of God, the boundary between the historical Jesus and the Christ of faith disappears.[37] Here Song even uses the image of liberator to describe

---

36. Aloysius Pieris, *An Asian theology of Liberation*, p. 62.
37. C.S.Song, *Jesus and the Reign of God*, pp. 3-7.

Jesus whose announcement of the reign of God entails the socio-political vision for a just society. In the last book of his trilogy, Song investigates the significance of Jesus in the multi-cultural and multi-religious context. He tries to illuminate the truth of Jesus in the broader context of the compassionate God's plan of salvation. The theological framework within which Song situates his Christological reflections is the idea that the creator God was present in Asia before the advent of Christianity. Therefore he freely uses the Asian stories, along with the biblical stories, as the legitimate resources for doing Christian theology. He compares the cross with the Lotus, the symbol of Buddhism, but he does not seem to attempt to interpret Jesus Christ through the traditional Buddhist concepts. His main interest is to juxtapose the biblical stories with the Asian stories.

Some Critical Reflections
The theological agenda we detect behind the presentation of Christ as the cosmic Christ and the awakened Christ is to interpret Jesus Christ through traditional religious and cultural concepts. The rationale for this enterprise is the assertion that the Christian way of presenting Jesus Christ to the non-Western (particularly Hindu and Buddhist) people is hardly accepted by them. A detailed examination of religious pluralism (or, more correctly, religious relativism) goes beyond the scope of this paper. But, reflecting from within the Asian multi-religious context, it is difficult to accept these images as the appropriate ways of articulating Christ for the following reasons.

(1) We may say that such interpretation has missiological concern. But we need to remember that in many cases the differences, not the similarities, between Christianity and other religions cause people to convert to Christianity.

(2) Besides the possibility of being criticised as Christian inclusivism, such images of Christ may cause objection rather than foster understanding on the part of the non-Western people. What these theologians do not realise is the fact that, in a religiously plural society, it is also possible for Buddhists to assert that the Spirit of Buddha has been guiding the popes and Western people for thousands of years. In a religiously plural society, each religious tradition must be seen *as it is* and allowed to present its understanding of God, humanity, history and other religious symbols in its own way.

(3) The fundamental question we can pose to these Christian

theologians who attempt to interpret Christ through their pre-existing religious concepts is: why do they need to bother with the Christ when they can stay within their own traditional religions with equivalent concepts?

(4) It is true that Jesus Christ has cosmic and universal dimension. The biblical image of the cosmic Christ serves as the ground to invite all humanity to accept him as their saviour, whereas the cosmic Christ in the Asian religious context as examined above is used to nullify such Christian invitation.

Conclusion and Prospect

The quest for relevant images of Jesus Christ is a very significant enterprise for anyone within the faith community in non-Western Christianity because he is the founder of the religion. As Buddhists endeavour to rediscover the teachings and spirit of Buddha here and now in their concrete historical context, it is natural for Christians to explore the teachings and spirit of Jesus Christ. The various Christological constructs are inevitable because the perception of Jesus Christ is not static or fixed but dynamic in that people see the person and life of Jesus through their own eyes in their own historical and cultural context. Therefore, a *local* understanding of Jesus Christ is inescapable. In this regard, there can be no question that we need to perceive Jesus Christ through our own eyes in our own context, but we should not mould Jesus into an exotic image that is hardly approved by the biblical texts nor facilitates a contextual understanding.

Finally, I must make it clear that the Christological images we have sketched above do not represent the majority of Christians or Christian theologians in the non-Western world. Though these Christologies reflect the struggles of non-Western theologians to articulate Jesus Christ in a contextually meaningful way and are widely known in Western theological circles, they are seldom communicated to the local Christians. In most theological schools in the non-Western world it is the traditional Christological formulae that are taught. At the same time, we need to point out that the indigenous images non-Western Christians have associated with the traditional Christological titles have been largely ignored by most theologians thus far. The investigation of the actual and contextualised images of Jesus Christ on the popular level is the essential challenge for our future Christological enterprise in the non-Western world.

Pannenberg - God breaking into history was amenable to the investigation of history.

Barth - God breaking into history was not available to historical investigation.

10

The Christology of Wolfhart Pannenberg – An Interpretation

Bultmann - pure fideism & individualism

Tim Bradshaw

Pannenberg - Barthian in the sense of God: revelation are integrated but now history was added.

Introduction

Pannenberg broke onto the world theological scene in the early 1960s with his programmatic *Revelation as History*,[1] a set of essays written with other scholars seeking to break out of the German theologies of the word in favour of a theology of history.

Pannenberg there rejected dualism in all its forms. He broke with Barth in his theology of the divine Word breaking into history but not amenable to the insights of critical investigation of history; such a theology was akin to a ghetto, shutting out the rest of creation and history, dependent on an act of blind faith. Likewise Bultmann's programme was criticised for its pure fideism and individualism. History there was funnelled solely into the individual and the now, in Kierkegaardian fashion.

The new theology had to take forward the insights of the past, in particular Barth's recovery of the notion that revelation entails the being of God, that God is sovereign and not some detached deity. But the whole realm of reason, historical reason, had to be integrated into the picture so as to give a unified field of knowledge and avoid the authoritarian claims of ghetto theology.

Pannenberg made this case not simply for apologetic reasons, that is to commend the faith to the cultured despisers of witnesses to revelation. He also made it on theological grounds, because God is the 'all determining reality', including all reason and creation. Therefore to omit these from the theological scheme was to offend against a basic principle and produce a one sided system. Pannenberg wished to produce a more integrated and unified theology, which would honour the creator who is also the redeemer. Faith has to be

---

1. *Revelation as History* (London: Sheed and Ward, 1968).

On theological grounds God is the God of reason & realities and this should not be omitted from the theological scheme → more integrated & unified.

reasonable, while retaining due humility before God who is the sovereign Lord.

In terms of ontology Pannenberg rejected both liberalism and traditionalism in theology, since neither managed to integrated God into history in their theological systems. Liberal theology, he argued, was fundamentally deistic, keeping the divine at a very safe distance from history and reality to allow space for the liberal enterprise after Kantian principles of a basis in the self, the legislative power of human reason. The liberal project therefore splits divine being from being in history. Likewise the classical theology of orthodoxy operated with a dualism of divine and historical, since the divine could not be affected by the human historical. Here Pannenberg joined Moltmann in criticising the Platonist heritage affecting traditional theology: God is defined as the reverse of the human historical, rather than as its basis and sustainer.

Jesus God and Man   *History will be revealed only at its end. The end has proleptically been revealed in the resurrection*

Revelation as History set out a distinctively new programme both philosophically and biblically. Pannenberg insisted that the whole of history was to be seen as the divine self-disclosure, and therefore only to be comprehended at the end of history, when all the puzzles and problems of events would fall into place. The future held the key to the overall meaning of things. God would be disclosed as just and loving at the end of the process of history. But we are not in fact left in the dark, the night in which all cows are black, since the end time event has come in advance, proleptically, with the resurrection of Jesus of Nazareth.

This argument proved to be Pannenberg's tour de force, attracting the interest of conservatives and liberals alike: here was a modern critical German theologian arguing for the historicity of the resurrection rationally rather than fideistically or existentially in non-historical mode. Pannenberg tells his readers that he is conducting an investigation in line with critical historical and hermeneutical method, making no initial assumptions of faith. This is a matter of the one field of knowledge, not of special pleading demanded by faith in the ghetto.

Pannenberg's *Jesus God and Man*[2] developed the argument. In terms of historical debate the data of the New Testament, treated on

---

2. *Jesus God and Man* (trans Wilkins and Priebe, London: SCM 1968).

Noted as a theologian who argued for the resurrection on a rational basis rather than fideistically — using

the same basis as any other texts, prompt the conclusion that the resurrection of Jesus did occur. The appearance narratives are his main basis of support, and the fact of some conflicting traditions is taken as strengthening the probability of facticity, showing that texts had not been doctored in the interests of a single version. Other explanations of the data seem less convincing to Pannenberg than that a resurrection event did happen. He is careful always to point out that if further evidence should arise, then he would need to reconsider his position. In this he represents the extreme opposite to Bultmann, who taught that the resurrection was not about an event in time at all, that seeking historical data is simply a mistake, that even if strong evidence arose it would be irrelevant since the resurrection is language about a leap of faith.[3] Pannenberg eschews such dualism.

Having concluded that the resurrection of Jesus is probable on the data available, he asks the hermeneutical question as to its meaning. Here again his work made an impact because of his creative use of what had seemed embarrassing and difficult material, the apocalyptic tradition in the New Testament. Pannenberg holds that the event must be interpreted in its context of thought for its meaning to be disclosed. Here we note importantly an assumption that events have meanings which can be divulged given the right approach, and this itself needs careful assessment. The thought context of Jesus' time was that of apocalyptic, of end time expectation, an expectation which looked to the end of history for God's vindication and for the resurrection of the dead. *[margin handwritten: then comes meaning]*

Taken in this context of ideas, the resurrection of Jesus, which was more than a mere resuscitation as that of Lazarus, amounts to the end time moment of divine fulfilment and revelation. From this follows the identity of Jesus as having a 'revelational unity of essence' with God. Here again we run into an important assumption, that revelation needs to be defined with the help of Barth as involving the being of the revealer. Hence he develops a link between the resurrection event and divine being through the category of revelation. The resurrection event encapsulates the meaning of the totality of history whose course as a whole reveals the divine being, therefore Jesus is united with God in terms of being. Such is the shape of the argument advanced in *Jesus God and Man*. ✳

---

3. I have found this contrasting viewpoint an excellent topic for seminar discussion!

critical historical method [handwritten]

Chalcedon fails to present a fully human historical figure.

Tim Bradshaw

To focus down further onto more detail, Pannenberg firmly denied the classical christological structure of Logos theology and of incarnation of the pre-existent word. Like other critics of Chalcedonian orthodoxy, he regarded this as failing to present a fully human historical figure. He insisted on beginning from the man Jesus, then seeking to ask how he relates to God whom he regarded as 'Father' in an apparently unique way in 'filial dependence'. Jesus trusts his father totally and at the end of his life throws himself onto this God, the God of the future, for vindication. He goes to Jerusalem in total trust, is judicially killed by those who called him a blasphemer, only to be raised from death by God and so constituted Son of God. Pannenberg adduces Paul for this christological structure: 'the gospel concerning his Son, who was descended from David according to the flesh and designated Son of God in power according to the Spirit of holiness by his resurrection from the dead, Jesus our Lord' (Rom. 1:2-4).

At this point we run into the difficulty of trying to understand Pannenberg's view of history as coming from the future rather than being victim of the past. The new occurs in history because God is God of the open future, the basis of freedom. Pannenberg rejects the interpretation of history which understands things as stemming from the past, since this would rule out novelty. This is a philosophical problem, he argued in his *Basic Questions in Theology*,[4] which raises the question of God for the atheist who otherwise is hard pressed to account for freedom in history and for the surprising and new event. Here we see how Pannenberg's theology and philosophy or metaphysics cohere as two sides of the one coin; his argument for the resurrection, his doctrine of the God of the open future, his understanding of faith as reasonable hypothesis, all exemplify his metaphysic, a metaphysic heavily indebted to Hegel.

Hegel dependency

Perhaps the most difficult aspect of the christology in *Jesus God and Man* is the claim to retroactive constitution of being. Pannenberg argues that the essence of a person is decided at the end of life, what the person becomes is decisive for the meaning of that person. So for example, a person might enjoy a great reputation for a time, only to have this ruined later. Or vice versa, a person might be disregarded or unknown till very late, or even after death. Mozart died in penury

---

4. *Basic Questions in Theology*, vol 2 (London: SCM, 1971) ch 7, for example.

and was buried in a pauper's grave, yet now is one of the world's great figures. This I take to be an example of retroactive validation or even constitution from the end of a life 'backwards'. I think that Pannenberg's metaphysic involves him teaching that meaning constitutes being: hence the meaning of Jesus' life, death and resurrection divulges his meaning and so his being.

The life of Jesus shows the future orientation of things, and the resurrection which vindicated Jesus shows that God meets us from the future in his faithfulness. Indeed God confers our identity on us from the future, even as we walk towards it. The filial dependence of Jesus on the Father, and the Father's vindication of the man Jesus as Son exemplifies the metaphysical structure of reality, a feature of christologies influenced by Hegel and indeed perhaps a danger. But over against the fear that christology may be merely a picture form of a metaphysic, Pannenberg points to the concrete individual person of Jesus, his destiny and fate, which is a unique one.

Trinitarianism

The christological programme developed by Pannenberg contained some trinitarian theology but it was little stressed. H. Burhenn wrote of Pannenberg's doctrine of God concerning 'the paucity of references to the doctrine of the Trinity' and asserted that 'the doctrine of the Trinity cannot function for Pannenberg, as it does for Barth, as a structural principle for theology.'[5] This judgement was very premature and can now be seen to be very mistaken. Even then it was evident that a trinitarian ontology was in fact assumed behind the christology of history, and this has become ever more emphasised by Pannenberg in subsequent works.

His untranslated essays, *Grundfragen Systematischer Theologie* band 2,[6] not to be confused with the translated volumes of *Basic Questions in Theology*, explicate the very trinitarian underpinning of his ontology, later to be central to his three volume *Systematic Theology*.[7] The philosophy of time Pannenberg developed from the outset, that is the orientation of reality from the open future of God,

---

5. 'Pannenberg's Doctrine of God' *Scottish Journal of Theology* 1975 vol.28.6 p 535.

6. *Grundfragen Systematischer Theologie* band 2 (Vandenhoeck und Ruprecht: Gottingen 1980).

7. *Systematic Theology*, Trans. G. Bromiley (Edinburgh: T&T Clark, 1991-1998).

had already suggested a trinitarian dynamic of past, present and future. The Spirit knits together the past with the future in the present; as we walk ahead into God's future for us we bring our past with us and this is not merely lost or wasted but brought into new situations. The trinitarian schema is linked to the three tenses of temporal experience. Again we can see that the experience of Jesus illustrates this as he goes ahead trusting in the Father in the power of the Spirit.

While the Hegelian ethos of this is clear and acknowledged, it is now also important to point out the influence of Heidegger's thought on Pannenberg. Heidegger taught that we run ahead into the future, that our being, Dasein, is a being towards our final future and that is death. As Pannenberg explains, for Heidegger 'the identity of Dasein is supposed to be constituted first of all by the future, in such a manner that Dasein, from the future of its own death, is disclosed as a whole in its finitude.... For Heidegger, the key is this "running forward", this act of anticipating one's own death'.[8] Pannenberg in fact appropriates much of this structure, but christianises it by displacing death as the final point by the God of the future. An important part in the interpretation of Pannenberg's systematic theology now must include taking account of Heidegger as an important influence, particularly on his theological anthropology of anticipation and wholeness for the meaning of our being.

Essays in *Grundfragen Systematischer Theologie* band 2 developed the trinitarian understanding of God especially in terms of an economic Trinity. Pannenberg, who had taught in the USA with leading exponents of Process theology,[9] sought to appropriate its criticism of traditional doctrine while avoiding what he perceived to be its error of producing a victim God who was not sovereign but at the mercy of the process of history. His doctrine was that God indeed was really affected by history, as Process theologians stressed, but that God was not rendered a victim thereby since he remained the free God of the future. God had freely chosen to enter into the process of temporality, while remaining its sovereign lord.[10] This entailed the trinitarian structure of involvement as past, present and future. God sustains the past and future as temporality runs it course.

---

8. Pannenberg, *Metaphysics and the Idea of God* trans Philip Clayton (Edinburgh: T&T Clark, 1990), p. 84.

9. ibid. p. 113ff.

10. *Grundfragen Systematischer Theologie* band 2 p 118, for example.

Pannenberg's trinitarianism arose from his christology and also his metaphysics. The theological conclusion that the resurrection constituted the man Jesus as the Son of God because of the 'revelational unity of essence', means that God is revealed as embracing a distinction in his very being. God is revealed as being Father and Son in the economy of history. The filial dependence of Jesus on the Father throughout his life pointed all the time in this direction, but the resurrection actually demonstrated and enacted it in a way that was also true for God.

Pannenberg establishes the unity between Jesus and God the Father as the basis for the doctrine of the Trinity, but he goes on to stress the distinction between them in terms of Jesus' 'self differentiation' of himself from God. It is the sin of pride in mankind to 'count equality with God a thing to be grasped', and Jesus on the contrary firmly distinguished himself from God, in so doing paradoxically thereby reinforcing his divine identity as the Son. This idea is found in *Jesus God and Man*, but it grows ever stronger in emphasis in Pannenberg's writings. It is basically a version of the idea that one finds one's life by losing it, by giving oneself in total trust into the hands of the other, of God the Father. We read in *Jesus God and Man*: 'The God who reveals himself is essentially person. He shows himself to be such in his revelation as Father in relation to the Son, who as the Son of the Father belongs indissolubly to the divinity of God.'[11] Hegel's influence in developing this notion is acknowledged, and he goes on 'Through this profound thought that the essence of the person is to exist in self-dedication to another person, Hegel understood the unity in the Trinity as the unity of reciprocal self-dedication.'[12] 'Die to live' forms the key principle.

A key question pressing here is whether Pannenberg teaches only an economic Trinity, given his metaphysic of history as reality and divine involvement in and through history to the extent of God being affected by it. Pannenberg's *Systematic Theology* answers this question by upholding a doctrine of the immanent or essential Trinity while insisting that this cannot be separable from the economic Trinity of divine action in the world. 'Even though we must finally distinguish between the immanent Trinity and the economic Trinity, because God in his essence is the same as he is in his revelation, and is to be

---

11. *Jesus God and Man*, p. 182.
12. ibid.

Trinity – economic / immanent Trinity distinct but inseparable, –

economic Trinity is not one way only since God is affected by the world process.

viewed as no less distinct from his revelation than identical with it, nevertheless the unity of the trinitarian God cannot be seen in detachment from his revelation and his related work in the world in the economy of salvation.'[13] Pannenberg, as Rahner, regards the distinction between the immanent and economic Trinities as real but also not to be over stressed.

It is the same trinitarian God *in se* who is at work *ad extra* and not another. Moreover, for Pannenberg the economy is not the one-way street of classical doctrine since God is genuinely affected by the world process, even 'bearing the pain of the negative' into himself on its behalf. 'The mediation of the Son and Spirit cannot be extraneous to the monarchy of the Father'.[14] On the other hand, 'The Father acts in the world only through the Son and the Spirit. The Father remains transcendent'.[15] The transcendent God is present to the world, and the eternal self identity of God goes hand in hand with the debatability of God in history until the final eschaton finally vindicates his reality.

Talk of the future orientation of history and of the God of the future, so stressed in Pannenberg's earlier writings, seems less emphasised in the final systematics where the divine eternity gains more and more focus. This is not, I believe, a covert contradiction in his position. Rather, he has always worked with an ontology of what I have called a theology of the 'future perfect tense'.[16] This phrase seeks to express the often puzzling way Pannenberg seems to want to have his cake and eat it with his notion of future consummation deciding reality. Pannenberg argues, for example, that Jesus' deity is given by the resurrection and this retroactively feeds back through his life and work to constitute his life divine; he 'always will have been' this person. The reality somehow was genuinely developed in history, while yet being secured in God's purposes. In his *Systematic Theology* he says 'By his resurrection from the dead Jesus was instituted into the dignity of divine sonship. But the Son of God was also at the side of God from all eternity. The idea of his pre-existence does not contradict the fact that his divine sonship will be revealed only eschatologically or that it is already manifest in a historical

---

13. *Systematic Theology* vol 1 p. 327.
14. ibid.
15. ibid. p. 328
16. In my *Trinity and Ontology* (Edwin Mellen Press, 1991).

event which like the resurrection of Jesus anticipates the eschato-logical consummation. The fact that all will be eschatologically manifest in the hidden world of God, in heaven, is already present, is in keeping with a common rule of apocalyptic presentation.'[17]

It must be said that such quotations show a shift towards a reappropriation of the notion of pre-existence, which Pannenberg had attacked quite vigorously in *Jesus God and Man* earlier, but then admitted to rehabilitation. But the shape of the reasoning remains fairly consistent, that is a genuinely human Jesus of Nazareth whose life culminates in the resurrection which determines his unique identity as the divine Son, and it was to have been so in the eternity of God. It is this last note of divine eternity which is quite new in relation to earlier works, but Pannenberg does not wish to return to the Neoplatonic view of eternity which drew his fire, and that of Moltmann, from his younger days.

Pannenberg develops his trinitarianism to the extent of holding that creation reflects and is based upon the divine Trinity as the life of God which in itself gives space for the other. Hence the activity of creation is a making of space for the created partner to exist and be free in relation to God. 'Only the doctrine of the Trinity', he says at the end of his first volume of Systematics,

permits us so to unite God's transcendence as Father and his immanence in and with his creatures through Son and Spirit that the permanent distinction between God and creature is upheld. The same holds good for an understanding of God's omnipotence. The power of God over his creation as the transcendent Father finds completion only through the work of the Son and Spirit because only thus is it freed from the one-sided antithesis of the one who determines and that which is determined, and God's identity in his will for creation is led to its goal. The same holds good also for an understanding of God's eternity. The incarnation of the Son sets aside the antithesis of eternity and time as the present of the Father and his kingdom is present to us through the Son. This present not only contains all the past within it, as the idea of Christ's descent into Hades shows, but it also invades our present in such a way that this becomes the past and needs to be made present and glorified by the work of the Spirit.[18]

---

17. *Systematic Theology*, vol. 1, p. 265.
18. ibid. p. 446.

God is eternal but has chosen to be with his creation; this is a symbiotic relationship with the world.

Tim Bradshaw

Pannenberg has developed a doctrine of eternity to include the simultaneity of things after the analogy of a melody, the experience of listening to which involves duration but yet a simultaneous grasp of the whole tune and rhythm. This analogy, used by Augustine and Plotinus, can apply to the trinitarian life of God. This God is the creator who therefore produces duration and difference in his creation, somehow mirroring divine being. Pannenberg has significantly advanced his theological ontology by this proposal for understanding divine eternity, and it may well enable him to fend off criticism that his system is purely historicism in dogmatic dress since now he is claiming that God is eternal and always would have been so irrespective of the created order. But God has created the world and chosen to be intimately associated with it; therefore his eternal trinitarian life is symbiotically linked to the world's destiny.

The Identity of Jesus

Logos theology retrieved
Where does this leave Pannenberg's fully mature christology? He began his career by rejecting Logos christology and the notion of pre-existence of the divine word assuming humanity, arguing instead that Jesus was a man whose identity was realised or given by the divine act of the resurrection as Son of the Father in the sense of a unity of divine essence. In what way, we may ask, is Jesus more than a man inspired by, and utterly faithful to, God on this account of things? Pannenberg insists that ontologically the resurrection has implemented the very being of Jesus as Son in relation to the Father. This is a unique identity, and because it is rooted in God therefore it was always going to have been actualised in this way; it is not simply a contingent accident or human achievement; the being of God in and through the process of history has the primary initiative.

> If the Father is from all eternity the One he is shown historically to be in relation to Jesus his Son, and through him, then we cannot think of the Father apart from the Son. This means on the one hand that the risen Lord is exalted to eternal fellowship with the Father. His relationship to the eternal Father as the Son, however, means that the Son was linked to the Father before the beginning of the earthly existence of Jesus. The relation reaches back also to the time

Pannenberg recovers the Logos theology of pre-existence but differently then Patristic : Chalcedon — more from an historical perspective

before his earthly birth. If the relation to the historical person of Jesus of Nazareth in eternity characterises the identity of God as Father, then we must speak of a preexistence of the Son, who was to be historically manifested in Jesus of Nazareth.[19]

Here we see clearly how Pannenberg has reclaimed a Logos theology and a notion of pre-existence, although in a form different from the patristic version, certainly the Alexandrian and Chalcedonian version. Pannenberg carries back into the being of God the relationship of Jesus and the Father, and again works with his theological 'future perfect' tool: it would always have been so because it was so in history. 'Theologically the eternal relation of the Father to the Son may not be detached from the incarnation of the Son in the historical existence and work of Jesus'.[20]

Pannenberg brings in his emphasis on the 'self-distinction' of Jesus from God, considering not equality with God a thing to be grasped, to further define what he means by the Logos background to the man Jesus. The Logos is of cosmological significance; 'As the generative principle of differentiation, he establishes and permeates the distinctive existence of all creatures....We humans, then, participate in a special way in the Logos, to whom all things owe their existence or life...Without this premise the incarnation of the Logos would be alien to our nature.'[21] Creation is by the trinitarian God of unity and differentiation whose activity mirrors this mode of being. Human beings are conscious of differentiating things and finding unity between what is differentiated; 'behind such an understanding is the theological premise of self-distinction from the Father that constitutes the sonship of Jesus.... From the standpoint of our relation to the Logos, the appearance of Jesus Christ may be understood as the completion of creation.'[22] Logos seems to represent the principle of self differentiation and unity, precisely the meaning of the resurrection for Jesus and the Father.

---

19. *Systematic Theology*, vol. 2, pp. 367-68.
20. ibid. p. 368.
21. ibid. p. 292.
22. ibid. p. 293.

Tim Bradshaw

Jesus the man and the divine Word

Clearly we are invited to press Pannenberg further at this point. Who is Jesus, who is the Logos? How do the two realities relate? If we take the classic christological debate prior to Chalcedon as a catalyst for this, we can point to the issue of *theotokos* which so exercised the Alexandrians. The fact of Mary being 'God bearer' was so vital to them because it was a way of clarifying the identity of the person of Jesus Christ: who was born of Mary? The only acceptable answer for them was 'the divine word'. The Alexandrians had a crystal clear definition for the subject or person of Christ: he was the divine Logos who assumed human nature.

When their Antiochene opponents begged to differ over the term 'God bearer', they were asked to clarify this issue of identity, who then was born to Mary? The answer 'the baby human being Jesus, who was constantly empowered by the divine word',[23] was the fatally wrong note to sound. That gave a human identity or person as the subject of Jesus Christ. This seemed to leave open the possibility for the interpretation of Jesus as prophetic figure associated closely with the divine word, but not the word himself. So, for example, we might read in the opening verses of Jeremiah: 'Now the word of the Lord came to me saying, Before I formed you in the womb I knew you, and before you were born I consecrated you; I appointed you a prophet to the nations'.[24] However closely the prophet was empowered and inspired by the word, and although this might have been the case from before his conception and birth, so avoiding the charge of adoptionism, such a figure was not the word but a human being indwelt by the word.

Pannenberg does not seem to be taking the Alexandrian line of approach, in fact if anything the Antiochene, and he uses the language of indwelling, for example in asserting 'that no personal union is conceivable without an indwelling of the Son of God in the human reality of Jesus or the sharing of Jesus as man in the divine attributes of the Son of God.'[25] His emphasis on the self-distinction of the man Jesus from the deity of the Father complicates things in this regard.

---

23. see e.g. the pithy description of Nestorius' christology in Stuart G. Hall *Doctrine and Practice in the Early Church* (London: SPCK, 1991) p 220.

24. Jeremiah 1:4-5.

25. *Systematic Theology*, vol. 2, p. 387.

Only in the Son's distinction from the Father can there be participation; also, The Christology of Wolfart Pannenberg -
the man Jesus in self-humbling exalts the divine identity

Does Jesus the man differentiate himself from the Logos and from the Father? Or does the fact that the Logos also, in trinitarian life, distinguishes himself from the Father in a union and differentiation find the Logos with Jesus in co-self differentiation vis-a-vis the Father?

The divinity of Jesus, epistemologically and also ontologically, belongs to this radical self-distinction from deity which is precisely divine: the self humbling of the man Jesus is the exaltation of him to a divine identity.[26] Only in distinction from the deity of the Father can we speak of a participation in it, says Pannenberg; 'The human nature of Jesus Christ shares in the deity of the Logos, but only through the mediation of self-distinction from God.'[27] The theme of self-distinction, self-subordination, waxes stronger and stronger in Pannenberg's final theology, so that we envisage 'the self distinction of Jesus from the Father and his deity in the twofold sense of self-distinction as creature and as Son of the Father' in the trinitarian life of God. The two seem to coincide and belong at the very heart of the identity of Jesus as man and as eternal Son.

Jesus the man and the eternal background
Another useful comparison to draw might be with the christology of D.M. Baillie and his theology of grace as the dynamic to interpret the claim that God was in Christ.[28] Baillie like Pannenberg sought a start to christology away from the traditional doctrine of the assumption of humanity by the divine Logos, and a start with Jesus the man. This man, however, perfectly lived out the life of grace, the very life of God mediated to human beings who are never fully open to this life. Jesus was unique in his total transparency to this divine life, so we can say of his life that it was fully human while fully divine, that God was in Christ.

The questions arising in particular were not dissimilar to those exercising the Alexandrians about their opponents, notably whether this is a doctrine of an inspired man rather than one of incarnation. Baillie asks the question himself 'would any man who lived a perfect life be therefore and thereby God incarnate?' He answers immediately, 'But such a questioner would indeed be a Pelagian, showing by his

---

26. Barth's dialectic of the royal man and priestly Son seem echoed here.
27. *Systematic Theology*, vol. 2, p. 388.
28. D.M. Baillie, *God Was in Christ* (London: Faber & Faber, 1948).

very question that he regarded the human side of the achievement as the prevenient, the conditioning, the determinative.'[29] Baillie forbids us asking the question because Jesus the man is conditioned so totally by the divine life that it makes no sense to ask about this person as if detachable from God.

But the questions persist. As Baillie says:

> the divine is always prevenient. And so from the human life of Jesus on earth we are, paradoxically but inevitably, led back to its divine origin and eternal background in heaven, on which it all depended. "When the fullness of time was come, God sent forth his Son", and He who was "born of a woman, born under the law", lived as He did because He was the Son of God. In that sense it is impossible to do justice to the truth of the Incarnation without speaking of it as the coming into history of the eternally pre-existent Son of God.[30]

Here we seem to have to been led back to the eternal life of God and indeed a trinitarian ground for the doctrine, in a fashion not dissimilar to that of Pannenberg whose 'open future' corresponds to Baillie's 'prevenient grace' christologically. Baillie's next sentence reads 'This does not mean, it need hardly be said, anything like a conscious continuity of life and memory between Jesus of Nazareth and the pre-existent Son. Nor are we to think of the human personality of Jesus of Nazareth as having had any heavenly or eternal pre-existence.'[31] Pannenberg's emphasis on the self differentiation of Jesus from deity would likewise fit this assertion.

Could Baillie's description of the heavenly background to the earthly life of Jesus be satisfied by a doctrine of election rather than necessitating a doctrine of the Trinity? Given that God's grace indwelt the man Jesus from the very first, would this indicate a man chosen from the foundation of the world for the particular role of being totally open to divine grace, whereas the rest of us are open only in the most fragmentary fashion? That could be an eternal background whereby Jesus the man is also the Son of God, living out divine life in human history, like us in every possible way, yet without sin – because of grace.

This is a plausible interpretation of Baillie's christology, and one

---

29. ibid. p. 131.
30. ibid, p. 150.
31. ibid.

wonders how Pannenberg might address this issue of an eternal election of the man Jesus resting on the will of the Father, over against a trinitarian doctrinal background. As might have been expected, he does indeed discuss the point in his *Systematic Theology*, but in relation the theology of Karl Barth.[32] Pannenberg points out that Barth used the doctrine of election to connect the eternal deity of the Son with the historical existence of the man Jesus. The divine Son was the object of one act of election, so as to be destined as Son of Man, the pre-existent God-man Jesus Christ, who is the eternal basis of the divine election.

Barth in effect 'doubled' the doctrine of election to include the divine Son and the man Jesus, but Pannenberg regards the attempt as failure. His reason is significant: he says that the action of divine election is part and parcel of the freedom of God's relation to the world 'so that its content cannot be constitutive for the eternal identity of his divine essence. If it were, the world itself would be the correlate of this essence. Hence we must derive the link to the incarnation from the eternal relation of the Son to the Father, and by the detour of the doctrine of predestination.'[33] This is interesting in view of Pannenberg's great stress on divine freedom as the content of meaning of the 'God of the open future' in his earlier theological writings. His mature position now wishes to ground itself increasingly on a relational trinitarian base, but not a neo-platonic one, rather one which relates the Father to the man Jesus whose identity is most truly that of the eternal Son, as a matter of being not simply as a matter of choice or grace.

Meaning as Being?

So far we have found Pannenberg hard to pin down in terms of getting an answer to our question about the identity of Jesus and this is to a large extent because of Pannenberg's distinctive ontology of meaning as the constitutive factor for being, in my opinion. If we ask about the identity of Jesus we need to look at the whole life of Jesus, his ministry and destiny, in order to gain an understanding of his meaning and unique oneness with God, a oneness which includes a distinction.

While we have seen that Pannenberg has adjusted his criticism of

---

32. *Systematic Theology*, vol. 2, p. 368, fn. 127, for Pannenberg's account and assessment of Barth's doctrine of election.
33. ibid.

[handwritten margin note at top: Pannenberg still rejects the notion of the Logos assuming human nature at birth.]

Logos theology so as to develop a rather different version of the doctrine, he still rejects the notion of the assumption of human nature by the Logos at a moment of conception: 'If we limit our understanding of the incarnation to the conception and birth of Jesus, then we cannot think of the union of the eternal Son with this human life as mediated by the relation of Jesus to the Father'.[34] This led theology into problems it could not solve, either from an Alexandrian or an Antiochene approach, since the latter assumed the full man Jesus to be independent, the latter could not present Jesus as having a free creaturely individuality. Pannenberg regards these traditional positions as trapped in a dilemma which 'is insuperable as long as we think the event of the incarnation was complete with the birth of Jesus.'[35] Instead of this, and along with the grain of his ontology, he teaches 'The statement about the incarnation of the eternal Son in Jesus of Nazareth relates, however, to the whole of his history and not just to its commencement.'

Pannenberg's anthropology entails this as the case for all of us, that our identity is more than our ego or self consciousness which is the assumption of modernity. Who we really are is a decision lying ahead of us; we await our final personhood as given in the future, and ultimately given by God to whom we 'run ahead'. The Heideggerian ontology of Dasein is helpful to recall here: our 'being in the world', rather than merely a subjective sliver of consciousness detached from nature and the world around us. Jesus' essence or being is defined by the resurrection ontologically and given to us epistemologically – although these are not finally separable, if I am correct in holding that Pannenberg's basic category is that of meaning.

The meaning of Jesus' whole life constituted his being as the Son, as in relation to the Father, a relationship which has an eternal background going beyond merely an electing choice of God. The 'person' of Jesus is not therefore to be interpreted solely as an acting agent or subject. Pannenberg's christology is historically objective rather than psychologically subjective – we are reminded of Baillie's rejection of any continuation of life or memory between the eternal background and the human Jesus. 'The process of this history is the concrete form of the human reality of Jesus. Only here does he have

---

34. *Systematic Theology*, vol. 2, p. 384.
35. ibid.

identity as a person. In this history he is the Son of the Father...'[36]

The hypostasis of Jesus is defined in terms of the meaning of the life of Jesus in its historical and theological context, his life history defines his personhood – as this particular person, the Son of the Father. Pannenberg carries back this Sonship into eternity, hence making the history of the man Jesus a manifestation or incarnation of the Son. Richard Bauckham was correct to remark that Pannenberg's understanding is 'a highly original and important attempt to show how the enhypostasia, instead of depriving Jesus of human particularity, could mean something intelligible precisely in terms of the actual historical particularity of Jesus.'[37] This appreciates Pannenberg's project well. In terms of the hypostatic union, the identity of the Son incorporates or includes that of the man Jesus in his relation to the Father, enhypostatically.

Pannenberg says:

> The person of Jesus Christ is identical with the eternal Son. But this does not mean that the human reality of Jesus lacks personality. Precisely in his human history Jesus has his personal identity solely in being the Son of his heavenly Father. This fact integrates all the features of his earthly existence into a unity. The man Jesus has no other identity than this, though he cannot have been aware of it from the very outset. It is enough that his human life was lived to and from his heavenly Father. The history of Jesus led him deeper and deeper into this identity of his person as the Son of the Father. Hence his human existence never had its personal identity in itself but always only in the relation to the Father, and therefore in his being the Son of this Father. Herein he was both truly man and true God.[38]

Here we note again the process nature of personhood and its eccentricity, a notion developed by Pannenberg from his early writings. Perhaps what he is seeking to articulate is that the person of the Son is greater than merely the human consciousness or ego of Jesus, that the meaning and being of Jesus is only gradually understood by Jesus himself through his life and ministry, and that his final act of entrusting himself into the hands of his Father coincides with the trinitarian being of the Son in eternal relationship to the Father.

---

36. ibid. p. 386.
37. *Churchman*, vol. 99, no. 2, 1985, p. 163.
38. *Systematic Theology*, vol. 2, p. 389.

I trust that some of the ideas developed by Pannenberg will prove sufficiently fertile to stimulate some useful discussion and debate. I have not indulged in much critical appraisal, as I think that perhaps the main initial task is to seek to grasp what is being said sympathetically before launching into criticism, notably about time and eternity, knowing and being, which are obvious points needing scrutiny.

11

The Future of Jesus Christ

Richard Bauckham

1. The strange absence of the Parousia from Christology

My title is a phrase used by (among others[1]) Jürgen Moltmann in his *Theology of Hope* (see the title of chapter III). In a striking definition of eschatology, Moltmann wrote that, 'Christian eschatology does not speak of the future as such.... Christian eschatology speaks of Jesus Christ and *his* future.'[2] This is a statement about eschatology rather than Christology, but, since for Moltmann not only must eschatology be christological but also Christology must be eschatological, it is not surprising to find a substantial treatment of the parousia in his book on Christology, *The Way of Jesus Christ.*[3] But Moltmann is very unusual in this. The parousia is ignored or barely mentioned in most books on Christology.[4] Surprisingly, perhaps, this is true despite the strong sense of the eschatological nature of Jesus' preaching of the kingdom and his resurrection which much Christology in the twentieth century has recovered. It is the risen Christ, not the coming Christ, who dominates the eschatological perspective of modern Christology. If we suppose that the neglect of the parousia in Christology results from the persistent influence of traditional divisions between theological topics and turn to studies of eschatology for reflection on the parousia, the picture

---

1. E.g. S. H. Travis, *Christian Hope and the Future of Man* (Leicester, 1980), ch. 5.

2. J. Moltmann, *Theology of Hope* (tr. J. W. Leitch; London, 1967), p. 17.

3. J. Moltmann, *The Way of Jesus Christ* (tr. M. Kohl; London, 1990), ch. 7.

4. One exception is the now forgotten but excellent essay by H. Frick, 'The Hidden Glory of Christ and its Coming Manifestation', in G. K. A. Bell and A. Deissmann, *Mysterium Christi* (London, 1930), pp. 245-73.

is not much improved. With notable exceptions (I think especially of G. C. Berkouwer[5] and Wolfhart Pannenberg[6]) treatments of eschatology tend to treat the parousia simply as emblematic of the end of history and give it little attention in itself, concentrating instead on such end-time topics as resurrection and judgement. A properly christological interest in the parousia, that is, a consideration of the parousia with respect to what it says about Jesus Christ, is as rare in eschatology as it is in Christology.

I doubt that there is a single explanation for this strange absence of the parousia from Christology. The reasons may be, in part at least, as follows. Classical Christology focused in a rather static manner on the constitution of the God-man as established by the act of incarnation. This required one to think backwards to the pre-existence of the Logos but not forwards to the future of Jesus Christ. Insofar as Christology in the modern period has continued the concerns of classical Christology, even if in new forms such as kenoticism, the issue has been how to conceive of incarnation in a way that similarly has focused on pre-existence and incarnation as such (How could God become human? How can divinity and humanity be united in the one Christ?). It is significant that in such discussions, which bring to Christology a particularly modern sense of the thoroughly human nature of Jesus' human experience, it is the humanity of Jesus in his earthly and mortal life that is at stake, not the humanity of the risen, exalted and coming Christ. Kenoticism, indeed, makes the latter peculiarly difficult to conceive, a problem sometimes rightly alleged in criticism of kenotic theories. But even when the need to understand the incarnation in a way that does justice to the differences between the pre-Easter Jesus and the post-Easter Jesus has been recognized, the interest has been merely in the contrast between these two states: humiliation and exaltation. The state of exaltation itself is perceived statically, with the result that the parousia raises no questions not already raised by exaltation as such.

---

5. G. C. Berkouwer, *The Return of Christ* (tr. J. Van Oosterom; Grand Rapids, 1972), especially ch. 5.

6. W. Pannenberg, *Systematic Theology,* vol. 3 (tr. G. W. Bromiley; Grand Rapids, Edinburgh, 1998), pp. 608-30.

Looking more broadly at the context of Christology in the modern period, there are two very relevant features, both concerned with history. One is the rise of the modern understanding of history in the sense of the scientific study of the past, which has put the question of the historical Jesus and relationship of the historical Jesus to the Christ of faith in the dominant position in much modern Christology. This is a further reinforcement of the tendency for Christology to look backwards at the expense of looking forwards.

The other factor is the rise of the modern understanding of history in the sense of the modern idea of historical progress, to which Christian theological thought about history and eschatology has often more or less assimilated itself. Here the attention certainly turned towards the future in the sense of Enlightenment optimism about the historical future that arises out of the present. But this has encouraged the reduction of the parousia to a symbol of the utopian goal towards which human history, under the influence of the gospel and the Spirit, is evolving. What is here found problematic in and therefore removed from the traditional understanding of the parousia is twofold: both the traditional reference to the future coming of the human individual Jesus of Nazareth and also the positing of a discontinuity between the course of history and the end which God gives to the world in the parousia. In a modern progressivist understanding, the goal of history is wholly continuous with the steadily increasing advance of the kingdom of God within history, and is related to Jesus only in the sense that this utopian goal is envisaged as a fully Christlike human society. Therefore, instead of the biblical parousia images of Jesus coming from heaven, which suggest a transcendent rupture of the course of history, in which the human figure of Jesus is central, the Pauline images of the body of Christ and being 'in Christ' are sometimes considered more helpful and taken to depict, not only the influence of the Spirit of Christ in the church now, but also the progressive course of history towards some kind of christification of the world. Christ here becomes, in effect, some kind of principle or form of relationship to God, exemplified in the historical Jesus and propagated through his historical influence in the church, but entirely unrelated to the 'post-existent' Christ, as Geoffrey Lampe labels the biblical picture of the risen, ascended and coming Christ.[7]

Lampe's own reductionist Christology dispenses with both the really 'pre-existent' and the really 'post-existent' Christ, arguing that all that matters in the traditional view of 'post-existence' can be preserved by speaking of the presence and activity of the Spirit of God who was in Jesus. Lampe helpfully illustrates how a thoroughgoing reconception of Christianity in terms of the historical progressivism of the modern age eliminates not only the future of Jesus Christ but also the presence of Jesus Christ, not only the parousia but also the resurrection and the ascension, as ways of speaking of the real relationship between the eternally living human person Jesus Christ and this world. This is in reality a new kind of docetism: a dissolution of the human Jesus himself into divine immanence in history.

The modern theological tendency to dispense with the parousia thus seems to me to have much to do with an inability to conceive of the human individual Jesus in an active role in relation to this world and its future and also to the enormous influence of the Enlightenment doctrine of immanent historical progress towards utopia. These issues seem to me to go much deeper than the pseudo-scientific arguments with which Bultmann, in oft-quoted remarks, dismissed the parousia as belonging to a pre-scientific worldview and as in any case disproved by the failure of the early church's expectation of the parousia in the near future. It has become clear that, in the following attempt to understand the parousia as an aspect of Christology, two important aspects of our task will be to elucidate the sense in which Jesus as a human individual can play the role the biblical image of the parousia assigns him and to define the sense in which the parousia represents something qualitatively different from the merely continuous development of present.

2. The future of narrative Christology

In the trinitarian structure of the creeds of the ancient church, such as the two which are still in use, the Apostles' and the Niceno-

---

7. G. W. H. Lampe, *God as Spirit* (Oxford, 1977), esp. ch. 6.

Constantinopolitan, the second credal article always takes the form of the story of Jesus. The christological reflection on Jesus' relation to God, which is characteristic of the Eastern creeds and appears as expressing Nicene orthodoxy in the Niceno-Constantinopolitan Creed, is placed within this narrative of Jesus and serves to interpret it. Moreover, the narrative looks to the future of Jesus as well as recounting his past. According to the Apostles' Creed, 'he will come again to judge the living and the dead', to which the Niceno-Constantinopolitan Creed adds that 'his kingdom will have no end'.

Thus implicitly, in the form of its creeds, the early church recognized that the identity of Jesus is a narrative identity, an identity which can only be adequately rendered by telling the story in which his identity takes place. The conceptual tools with which the Fathers could develop Christology did not easily lend themselves to expressing such a narrative understanding of identity. The Fathers give the impression that Christological definition is in principle separable from the narrative, even though it is derived from the narrative and is in turn intended to enable an appropriate reading of the narrative. We can perhaps go further in asserting that the story of Jesus is integral to his identity.

However, recent examples of narrative Christology[8] seem to give no more place to the parousia than other forms of Christology. Of course, the parousia cannot be narrated in the same way as the past history of Jesus. The narratives of it in, for example, 1 Thessalonians 4 and Revelation 19 are not historiography, as the Gospel accounts of the crucifixion, for example, are. This is for two reasons: the parousia is not only a still future event, but also the event which will end history and is therefore intrinsically transcendent of history. For both reasons it lacks the contingent and concrete actuality of narrated history (even the theologically interpreted history in the Gospels) and can be narrated only in symbols that convey its essential meaning. Its images depict only what, in the purpose of God, must be so, nothing of what, through the contingencies of history, may or may not be so.

---

8. E.g., most recently, M. L. Cook, *Christology as Narrative Quest* (Collegeville, MN, 1997).

Nevertheless, the parousia is the end of the story which must be in some sense anticipated and articulated for the sake of the meaning of the rest of the story. The story the Gospels tell is, by their own testimony, an unfinished story, open not only to the history of the church as its continuation but also to this projected conclusion, the parousia, which the Gospels are able to narrate in the form of prophecies by Jesus. (Rarely noticed is the fact that the last words attributed to Jesus in the Fourth Gospel, according to the best text of 21:23, are the words 'until I come' – a fact the more remarkable in that this Gospel's eschatology is usually thought to be overwhelmingly realised.) The parousia is the narrative prospection of Jesus' identity, as the Gospel histories are its narrative retrospection.

It is by no means unusual for narratives to include projects, expectations and anticipations which reach forward beyond the time frame of the narrative itself, but in this case, the story of Jesus, there is a unique aspect to its prospection. The parousia concludes not only the story of Jesus but also the story of the whole world. Though the rest of Jesus' story is implicitly related to the whole world, only the parousia makes clear its unique character as a story which will finally include the whole history of the world in its own conclusion. This is why the parousia is essential to Jesus' identity. It defines him as the one human being whose story will finally prove to be identical with the story of the whole world. In New Testament terminology, it defines his identity as that of the Messiah. Apart from the parousia he could not be called Christ in the New Testament meaning of the word.

3. Now and then
In the context of most christological work, this sub-heading would naturally be understood to refer to the 'then' of the pre-Easter Jesus and the 'now' of the exalted Christ in the present. I want to ask if there is not as important a qualitative difference between the 'now' of the exalted Christ and the future 'then' of the coming Christ. To put the question differently: is the parousia adequately understood as the completion of historical process, the outcome of some kind of incremental process of immanent divine activity

in the world, such as theological versions of modern progressivism have so often assumed, or does it represent something really new, something quite different from what will have happened hitherto in the history of the world, an event in which Jesus himself relates in some important sense differently to the world? This is a critical question not only with regard to liberal theologies assimilated to modern secular progressivism, but also in respect of the tendency in Karl Barth and others to reduce the parousia to an unveiling of what is already true, a revelation of what has already been accomplished in the past history of Jesus, new only in the sense that this is now made unequivocally known to all.[9]

This latter view could be supported by appeal to the way the New Testament can speak of the parousia as the 'unveiling' (or revelation: *apokalupsis)*[10] of Christ or his 'appearance' *(epiphaneia).*[11] Corresponding verbs are also used.[12] But in that case we must also notice that the New Testament also, and most often, refers to the parousia by the use of the verb 'to come' *(erchomai)* and by the word *parousia* itself,[13] which in this context must mean not merely 'presence,' but 'arrival'. In many of the texts what will be 'seen' at the parousia is precisely Jesus 'coming' from heaven.[14] In these usages we have, in fact, three forms of contrast between now and then: the Jesus who is now not seen will appear or be seen; the Jesus who is now hidden will be revealed; the Jesus who is now absent will come.

In the last case, we should not be troubled by the implication that Jesus is presently absent, as though this were in contradiction with the various ways in which the New Testament understands

---

9. For a brief account of Karl Barth's understanding of the parousia, see J. Thompson, *Christ in Perspective* (Edinburgh, 1978), ch. 10: and for criticism, see Moltmann, *The Way of Jesus Christ,* p. 318.

10. 1 Cor. 1:7; 2 Thess. 1:7; 1 Pet. 4:13.

11. 2 Thess. 2:8; 1 Tim. 6:14; 2 Tim. 4:1, 8; Tit. 2:13.

12. E.g. *apokalupto:* Luke 7:30; 2 Thess. 1:7; 1 Pet. 1:13; *phaneroo:* Col. 3:4; 1 Pet. 5:4; 1 John 2:2, 3:2; *opthesomai:* Heb. 9:28.

13. Matt. 24:3, 27, 37, 39; 1 Cor. 15:23; 1 Thess. 2:19, 3:13, 4:15, 5:23, 2 Thess. 2:1, 8; James 5:7, 8; 2 Pet. 1:16, 3:4; 1 John 2:28.

14. E.g. Matt. 16:28, 24:30, 26:64; Mark 13:26, 14:62; Luke 21:27; Rev. 1:7.

him to be present with his people now, including Jesus' promise, at the end of Matthew's Gospel, to be with his disciples until the end of the age. Presence can take many different forms and is therefore compatible with forms of absence.[15] When I speak to someone on the telephone I am in one sense present to them by means of my voice conveyed by the telephone line, while also being in another sense absent. To collapse the parousia into Christ's presence with us already is to evade the essential question of the form and purpose of his presence to his people and to the world in each case. From the way the New Testament texts speak of Jesus' coming at the end it is clear that it is a coming to do things that he has not done hitherto: to save (in the sense of bringing believers into their final destiny in resurrection), to eliminate the powers of evil from the world, and, most often in the texts, to judge the living and the dead.[16]

While the language of coming makes it especially clear that the parousia brings not just more of the same, but something new, we should not miss the fact that the language of hiddenness and manifestation or revelation also makes this point in its own way. What is hidden now is Jesus' heavenly glory, his lordship over the whole world which his sitting on God's heavenly throne at God's right hand portrays, and also his fellowship with his people in which their true nature as his people is hidden. This present hiddenness of Jesus' rule explains why, for example, in the book of Revelation the beast's power can appear godlike and invincible, triumphant over the Christians whom he puts to death. The real truth of things from God's perspective – for example, that the martyrs, by their witness to the truth even to the point of death, are the real victors – breaks through to those who have eyes to see, but it is only at the parousia that it finally prevails as the truth which all must acknowledge. This revelation is more than the unveiling of what is already true, though it is that, because the

---

15. See the helpful discussion of presence as a christological category in G. O'Collins, *Christology* (Oxford, 1995), ch. 14, which, however, lacks any discussion of the parousia!

16. The phrase 'to judge the living and the dead' is stereotyped: Acts 10:42; 1 Pet. 4:5. Cf. also Acts 17:32; 2 Cor. 5:10; James 5:9; Rev. 19:11.

unveiling itself makes a difference: no longer can anyone pretend or be deceived, those who wield power by deceit can do so no longer, all illusions and delusions must perish before the truth of God and all who insist on clinging to them must perish also. It is in this sense that Jesus, though seated on the throne of the universe, has not yet brought all things into subjection to God. The revelation of his lordship will also be its final implementation.

From this point of view, the parousia is the event which concludes history by making the final truth of all things manifest to all. This is why the language of 'revealing' and 'appearing' is used in the texts not only of Jesus, whose true relationship to the world is made evident to all, but also of all that his judgement of every person who has ever lived will bring to light (1 Cor. 4:5). There is nothing hidden that will not be uncovered (Matt. 10:26). The full and final truth of each person's life will be made known, not least to that person. Similarly, the language of 'revealing' and 'appearing' is used of the final destiny of those who believe in Jesus, 'a salvation ready to be revealed in the last time' (1 Pet. 1:5[17]). The parousia is that revelation of all that is now hidden, the disclosure of the full and final truth of all who have lived and all that has happened, that determines the form in which this present creation can be taken, as new creation, into eternity. Thus in the parousia, both as coming and as unveiling, something happens which, in relation to the world as it is now, will be both new and conclusive. As the New Testament understands it, the parousia cannot be taken as a symbol merely of the outcome of history that history itself will provide.

4. Jesus' human identity in universal relatedness

In this section and the next, I shall consider the parousia in relation to Jesus' human identity and to his divine identity respectively. This is not intended as some kind of Nestorian division of the one Christ, but simply as a matter of two perspectives on the one Jesus Christ. Jesus, as I understand Christology, is God's human identity. He is both God's *truly human* identity and *truly God's* human

---

17. Cf. Rom. 8:19; Col. 3:4; 1 John 3:2.

identity. Since this is a narrative identity, it should be possible to look at the parousia as the end of his story from both of these perspectives.

Christology involves the assertion of Jesus' universal relatedness. In the history of Christology a variety of concepts have been used to express this: representativeness, substitution, incorporation and participation, universal humanity, and others. All these concepts are attempts to express the fundamental conviction that this one human individual Jesus is of decisive significance for all other human persons, whether they are yet aware of it or not. Other human individuals, of course, have exercised very extensive historical influence, and in some cases, such as the unknown people who first discovered how to make fire or who invented the wheel, it might be said that they have made a difference to the lives of virtually all subsequent human beings. But the Christian claim about Jesus asserts something more than an historical impact of this kind. The claim is that in some way Jesus is intrinsically – in his very identity – related to each and every other human being.

How can this be said of a human individual? Some of the christological concepts I mentioned in fact attempt to conceptualize Jesus' universal relatedness by denying him human individuality. The attempt is made to view his humanity as some kind of supra-individuality in which others are included. Or his humanity is in effect dissolved in the universal presence of God. Unless we are prepared to deny individuality to all humans in the resurrection, a position surely contradictory of the very notion of resurrection, such views must be considered docetic. They fail to preserve the true humanity of Jesus, human (as the Fathers said) in every respect as we are, and no less truly human in his risen and exalted humanity than in his earthly and mortal humanity. In not maintaining the true humanity of the risen and coming Jesus, such interpretations contradict the New Testament principle that our eternal destiny is to be like him.

I suggest that a more satisfactory approach is by means of the only way in which human individuals can transcend their individuality without losing it: that is, in relationships. Human individuality is also relationality. There are individuals only in relationships – with other humans, with God, and with the non-human creation. Such relationships are integral to the narratives in which human identity is found. We are who we are in our relationships with others and in the story of our relationships with others.

In Jesus' case – and focusing for the purpose of our argument now only on his relationships with other humans – his human individuality is unique in its *universal* relatedness. He is the one human being who is intrinsically related to each and every other. How does this universal relatedness take place narratively? It is not constituted solely by his incarnation as human, but by the particular course of his human story. We can say that in his earthly life and death Jesus practised loving identification with others. In his ministry he identified in love with people of all sorts and conditions, excluding no one, and finally in going to the cross he identified himself with the human condition of all people in its worst extremities: its sinfulness, suffering, abandonment and death. Only because Jesus died in loving identification with all could his resurrection be on behalf of all, opening up for all the way to life with God beyond death. Thus in his life, death and resurrection, the exalted Christ has established his identity as one of open identification with others, open in principle and potential to all who will identify with him in faith. Until the parousia his identification with all remains open to all. This means that, insofar as his human identity is constituted by his universal relatedness, it is open to all that takes place in relation to him. His narrative identity cannot be complete until every human story with which he has identified himself has turned out as it will have done at the end. The parousia as the completion of his own identity, as revelatory of the final truth of his loving identification with all, will be also the completion of the identity of all others. Their identity, the truth of their whole lives brought to light at the end, will be defined either by his loving identification with them or by their refusal to let it be so defined. For those who have sought their own identity in his identification with them, his parousia will be the revelation at once of who he finally is and of who they themselves finally are: 'your life is hidden in Christ with God. When Christ who is your life is revealed, then you also will be revealed with him in glory' (Col. 3:3-4; cf. 1 John 3:2).

Thus Jesus' identity at the end is inclusive of others, but not in a way that dissolves his properly human individuality. As the one who has identified in love with all other humans in their own stories, his story finally includes also theirs. Since his loving identification with them is prevenient but not pre-emptive, that is, it is open to all but actualized only in the living of their own lives, his own identity as the one human whose identity is found in the story of his relatedness to all others remains to that extent open until his parousia.

We may perhaps take a little further this principle that Jesus' own identity is open to the future because it includes his relationships to all things (and not only to all people). We should be more cautious than many of us have been in speaking of the finality of Christ with reference to the Gospel story of his life, death and resurrection. His story will not be complete until his parousia. I would say that Jesus in his history, Jesus of Nazareth crucified and risen, is definitive for our knowledge of who God is, of who we are in relation to God, of who Jesus is in relation to God and to us and to all things. It is definitive, in the sense that anything else must be consistent with this, but not final, in the sense that there is nothing else to be known. Since Jesus' identity is in universal relatedness, Christian understanding and experience are not to be focused on Jesus to the exclusion of all else, but on Jesus in his relatedness to everything else. We shall know Jesus better as we see everything we can know or experience in its relatedness to him, just as we shall know and experience everything more truly as we see it in its relatedness to Jesus. To put the issue in relation to our theological work, neither the Bible nor Jesus in himself contains all the data of theology; rather Jesus in his relatedness to all human knowledge and experience constitutes the potentially inexhaustible data of Christian theology and by the same token requires the necessary provisionality of its conclusions. Only the parousia will reveal all things in their final truth as they appear in their relationships to Jesus and only the parousia will reveal Jesus himself in the final truth of his identity in universal relatedness.

5. Jesus' divine identity in universal lordship

The meaning of incarnation – what it really means that Jesus is God's human identity – appears most clearly in the way the New Testament tells and interprets the story of Jesus in two very remarkable ways. First, Jesus' loving identification as one human being with others, taken to the depths of degradation and abandonment on the cross, is *God's* loving identification with all people. Secondly, God's universal sovereignty over his whole creation, God's uniquely divine relationship to the world, is exercised by the *human* Jesus, exalted to God's heavenly throne. It may not be too much to say that all of New Testament theology consists in the understanding of each of these two new theological truths and of the relationship between them.

In biblical thought it is intrinsic to God's identity, what distinguishes him as the only true God from all other reality which is not God, that he is the sole Creator of all things and the sole Lord over all things. But even God's identity for us is, biblically speaking, a narrative identity yet to be completed. Since his ultimate sovereignty coexists now with much in the world that opposes his will and contradicts the destiny he intends for his creation – failure and evil, suffering and death – God's rule remains to be achieved, in the sense of implemented in the overcoming of all evil and the redemption of the world from nothingness. God's identity as the one true God of all is at stake in the achievement of his eschatological kingdom. He will prove himself God in the overcoming of all evil and in the acknowledgement of his deity by all creation. If it is in Jesus that God's sovereignty comes to universal effect and universal acknowledgement, which is what the New Testament writers intended when they depicted his enthronement and parousia, then Jesus' own story belongs to the narrative identity of God himself.

This is why a great deal of what is said about the parousia in the New Testament echoes, with verbal allusions, Old Testament prophetic expectations of God's demonstration of his deity in a conclusive act of judgement and salvation. Many of these Old Testament texts are those which speak of God's 'coming' to implement his rule in judgement and/or salvation: hence the frequency with which the New Testament speaks of the parousia as Jesus' coming. Most of these Old Testament texts speak of God's 'coming'; and even more of them speak in some way of God's action, not through the agency of a messianic or other non-divine figure, but simply as God's own action.[18] (Daniel's vision of the humanlike figure coming on the clouds of heaven is the most notable exception.[19]) Jesus' future coming as Saviour and Judge of all is God's eschatological coming to his creation to establish his kingdom. It brings to completion God's own narrative identity for us. It does so already in the sense that to believe in God truly as God we must expect it and look forward to it.

6. Jesus Christ the same yesterday, today and forever

The title of this section may not, in its original context in Hebrews 13, mean what I here take it to mean: the commentators disagree. But it does express succinctly what I assume is uncontroversial: that Jesus in his earthly history, in present heavenly session, and in his future coming is in each case the same Jesus Christ. His narrative identity is a narrative *identity*. Narrative identities of course frequently contain surprises and puzzles which put someone's identity in doubt. Yet narratives must convince their readers that their characters remain credibly the same persons. Acting, as we say, 'out of character' requires the kind of explanation which we also always seek in real life, even if

18. Hos. 6:3* (James 5:7); Mic. 1:3* (?1 Thess. 4:16); Zech. 14:5b* (1Thess. 3:13; 2 Thess. 1:7); Isa. 2:10, 19, 21 (2 Thess. 1:9); Isa. 40:5 (?1 Pet. 4:13); Isa. 40:10* (Rev. 22:12); Isa. 59:20 (Rom. 11:26); Isa. 63:1-6 (Rev. 19: 13, 15); Isa. 66:15-16* (2 Thess. 1:7-8); cf. 1 Enoch 1:9* (Jude 14-15). (* indicates those OT texts which include the word 'come'.) Note also the OT phrase 'the day of YHWH' appearing as 'the day of the Lord Jesus Christ' (1 Cor. 5:5), 'the day of the Lord Jesus' (1 Cor. 1:8; 2 Cor. 1:14), 'the day of Christ Jesus' (Phil. 1:6), 'the day of Christ' (Phil. 1:10; 2:16); and 'the day of the Lord' (1 Thess. 5:2; 2 Thess. 2:2).

19. Dan. 7:13* (Matt. 24:30, 26:64; Mark 13:26, 14:62; Luke 21:27; Rev. 1:7. Note also Zech. 12:10, 12 (Matt. 24:30; Rev. 1:7).

unsuccessfully, when people we know surprise us. Even in people's inconsistencies we seek some degree of consistency. Random and arbitrary inconsistencies threaten our perception of personal identity. Yet in Jesus' case we expect more: absolute moral consistency, complete self-constancy in adherence to the purpose of God which he embodies and enacts. Without such self-constancy his identity could not be God's human identity.

Therefore we must seek Jesus' self-identity in the three phases of his identity which we have considered, i.e. his self-humiliation in loving self-identification with all, his exaltation in hidden sovereignty over all, and his future coming in manifest sovereignty over all. One way in which the New Testament texts maintain his self-identity is by insisting that the risen, ascended and coming Christ is the same Jesus who was crucified. In the resurrection appearances Jesus shows the marks of his crucifixion to identify himself. In Revelation 5, it is the slaughtered lamb who is enthroned in heaven and receives the acclamation of his sovereignty from all creation. It is the one they have pierced whom all the tribes of the earth will see at his coming on the clouds (Rev. 1:7), preceded by 'the sign of the Son of man,' most likely the cross as his sign of identity (Matt. 24:30). Even the rider on the white horse who comes to judge and to make war wears a robe dipped in blood (Rev. 19:13).

This means that Jesus' loving self-identification with all, which reached its furthest point in his death abandoned and under condemnation, is not, as it were, laid aside in his exaltation, but is established as the permanent identity of the one who rules all things from God's throne, as the permanent character of God's universal sovereignty. If the crucified Jesus rules for God, then God's rule is radical grace.

What of the parousia? This understanding of Jesus' self-identity is most easily understandable in what we might call the optimistic eschatology of the Christ-hymn in Philippians 2 and of the similar scene of cosmic acclamation in Revelation 5. There God's rule comes to be universally acknowledged when it is seen to be exercised by the crucified Jesus. But we know that in their context in the New Testament such passages offer only one perspective.

More commonly the Christ who comes in glory comes to judge and his judgement includes condemnation. Is this the same Jesus as the crucified one who bore the condemnation of sinners in his love for them? Is this the faithful friend, the one who laid down his life for his friends, now become the judge who metes out retributive justice? Is the slaughtered lamb turned slaughterer? It is important to see that the parousia poses this issue very sharply. Essentially it is the same question about God's love and God's judgement that we should have to ask even if Jesus were not depicted as the end-time judge. But since he is, we cannot divide God's activity into his love in Christ and his wrath outside of Christ. It is the crucified Christ who comes in judgement, and certainly not to avenge his blood on his murderers, but as the one who forgave his murderers as he hung dying. Should we perhaps turn our questions around: what kind of justice can it be that the crucified Jesus comes to provide? In any case, the parousia brings us face to face with one of the most difficult issues in New Testament theology and discourages too ready and easy an answer.

I leave the question open here, but my final, short section has a kind of relevance to it.

7. Jesus' story as the story of the whole world

In the penultimate verse of the Bible, Jesus says – his last words within Scripture – 'Behold I am coming soon' – and the prophet John answers, on behalf of all his readers: 'Amen. Come, Lord Jesus!' (Rev. 22:20). This eager prayer for the parousia sums up much of the attitude to the parousia expressed throughout the New Testament. Modern Christians not uncommonly have difficulty understanding why the parousia should be so desirable. It is, of course, because the parousia brings an end to all evil, suffering and death, the final redemption of ourselves and all creation that we know to be God's purpose in Christ. To love or to long for his appearing, as 2 Timothy 6:8 puts it, is fundamentally a response to the theodicy problem, especially by those who suffer the evils and injustices of this world, whether on their own account or on behalf of others. The Christian form of the theodicy problem is: why does God delay the parousia? Why does God not intervene at once to deliver his creation from the evil that ravages it? Why did the twentieth century, which George Steiner memorably calls the most bestial in human history, have to happen? Why must children be burned alive in Auschwitz and buried alive in Cambodia and still the Lord does not come to halt the carnage for ever and wipe away every tear from every eye?

Yet, although it is not for us to know the times and the seasons, we are not left wholly uncomprehending of the delay. God in his longsuffering mercy keeps open the opportunities for repentance; he extends the time of his grace. And therefore the patience he requires of those who wait for the parousia, that courageous holding out for God in testing circumstances, is a kind of trust in his grace, an alignment with his gracious longsuffering. Thus, with regard to the parousia, we are pulled two ways, even as we seek to share God's concern for the world. The parousia does not solve for us the agonizing problem of world history. We cannot really tell its story and reach a satisfying conclusion, as the modern myths of historical progress have all tried to do and failed. We can only tell Jesus' story as the story that will turn out to be also the world's story. So what we know of the end of the world's story is that it lies in the hands of the one who has lovingly identified himself with both the guilt of the perpetrators of history and the fate of the victims of history.

Persons' Index

Index

Subject Index

★ ★ ★ YOUR ★ ★ ★
PERSONAL
TRAINER